# EDGAR

## King of the English 959-75

PETER REX

TEMPUS

*For*
*Edmund, Henry, Sebastian, Oliver, Maximus and Ferdinand,*
*My grandsons*

This edition first published 2007

Tempus Publishing Limited
The Mill, Brimscombe Port,
Stroud, Gloucestershire, GL5 2QG
www.tempus-publishing.com

British Library Cataloguing in Publication Data.
A catalogue record for this book is available from the British Library.

ISBN-13 978 0 7524 4124 5
ISBN-10 0 7524 4124 8

Typesetting and origination by Tempus Publishing Limited
Printed in Great Britain

of the English 959-75

# About the Author

Peter Rex is a retired history teacher. He was Head of History at Princethorpe College for twenty years. His other books include *Harold II: The Doomed Saxon King*, *Hereward: The Last Englishman* and *The English Resistance: The Underground War Against the Normans*. He lives in Ely.

# Contents

# Preface

No 'Biography' of King Edgar the Peaceable (as he is usually referred to) has been attempted hitherto, largely because the usual sources available to historians are unusually scanty for his period, the second and third quarters of the tenth century. The *Anglo-Saxon Chronicles*, so useful for other periods, concentrate on the king's religious policy almost to the exclusion of all else. Most of what can be learned about this king's reign, of his life before he became King of the English, and of his marriages has to be looked for in the writings of those monks who were concerned to produce 'lives' of the saintly churchmen, Dunstan, Aethelwold and Oswald. These works are hagiography, designed to promote the claims to sanctity of their subjects, and so inherently unreliable. Much of what they say must be used only with great care. References to King Edgar in the later, Anglo-Norman writers are even less reliable and, indeed, downright slanderous.

Something of the nature of the king's government can be recovered from the study of the law codes of his reign, although scholars have reduced the known number of these to two. The charters issued by his immediate predecessors and by the king himself, where these can be shown to be authentic, provide useful information about his dealings with property owners and the composition of his council and household.

A biography in the accepted modern sense is clearly impossible, since the sources say little about his personal life or activities. What has been attempted in this work, therefore, is to recover something of the nature of the kingdom and kingship of King Edgar and some account of his life and times.

The book and its author owe a great debt to the work of scholars whose writings about the tenth century have been ransacked for information. Those scholars are in no way responsible for the views expressed, which are entirely the responsibility of the author.

I would like to thank in particular the librarian of St John's College, Cambridge, for his permission to use the resources of the college library.

I thank also my son, Dr Richard Rex, for his assistance with the computer programme used in producing the text.

I am indebted most of all to my wife, Christina, for her support and forbearance while I have been researching and writing this book, and especially for her invaluable and most enlightening criticism of the text which has saved me from innumerable blunders and irrelevancies which marred my original draft. She has also been of the greatest assistance in the production of maps and tables which accompany this work and for taking many of the photographs which illustrate it.

# Introduction

Edgar, younger son of Edmund (King of England 941–946), was born in 943, two years after his father had come to the throne. He became King of the Mercians and Northumbrians in 957 and then King of all England in 959, at the age of sixteen, after the death of his predecessor King Eadwig the 'All Fair'. He then reigned for the next sixteen years, dying in 975 at the age, if the chroniclers are to be believed, of 32. According to the *Chronicle of Chronicles*, usually known as 'Florence of Worcester', he was known as '*Rex Pacificus*'. The source of his use of this adjective might be a charter of Edgar's, dated 968, in which he is '*Anglorum rex Pacificus*'. Usually translated as 'the Peaceable', this more appropriately means 'Peacemaker'. The name is quite apposite because for the whole of the period embracing Edgar's reign, from the expulsion and death of Erik Bloodaxe (the last Viking 'King' of York) in 954 to the accession of Aethelred II in 979, a quarter of a century, England, and indeed all Britain, was free from foreign invasion and from internal strife.

Just exactly why this was so is one of the many aspects of Edgar's reign in need of explanation. The conventional accounts of his reign, which simply accept this peacefulness as a fact and conclude that Edgar was simply very fortunate, are in no way adequate. That he was a 'peacemaker' rather than the lucky beneficiary of a peaceful interlude in the blood-stained history of the tenth century entails an interpretation of the reign of Edgar which puts the emphasis on the king as an active and energetic ruler who promoted peace at home and abroad by positive means. What these means were needs to be fully analysed.

In order to do this it is necessary to tease out of the available sources every last scrap of evidence and to give some weight to what is not, as well as what is, said. This is because the sources for Edgar's lifetime and reign are all too limited. For much of the tenth century the source, the *Anglo-Saxon*

*Chronicle*, which for other periods is a comparatively rich and invaluable text, fails. Those responsible for writing the tenth-century continuation of what should more accurately be termed the *Anglo-Saxon Chronicles*, in the plural, seem to lose interest in their work or to be singularly ill-informed about events. They seem content to make only short and uninformative entries from the accession of King Aethelstan in 924 or 925 to the murder of King Edward 'the Martyr' in 978. This is the case especially when the text is compared to the fuller accounts of the reigns of Alfred the Great and Edward the Elder. Facts about the reigns in the middle decades of the tenth century have to be eked out by using everything that can be gleaned elsewhere.

The surviving charters from these five decades have been subjected to detailed analysis by scholars, making much valuable information available. Even charters which, in the form in which they have survived, are either forgeries or have been heavily interpolated or altered, can sometimes provide valuable clues. Thus a charter which is not regarded as genuine may nonetheless have appended to it a genuine witness list. The charters, more technically known as 'diplomas', allow scholars an insight into the composition and membership of the king's council (the Witenagemot or 'Witan'). They can provide information about a king's whereabouts on a given day in a known year and help to identify the location of royal estates. They can reveal the composition of a king's 'household' and allow historians to track the rise and fall in office or favour of individual great men, the ealdormen and thegns, the bishops and abbots.

The study of the coins issued by these kings can indicate how a particular king wished to be seen by his people, just as charters can reveal his royal style and titles. In many cases the only way in which an ordinary thegn or ceorl or citizen of a borough might become aware of what sort of man the king was would be through the image and superscription on his coinage.

For Edgar in particular, much can be learned from the biographies of the saintly men, Dunstan, Aethelwold and Oswald, who served him as bishops and abbots in the churches and monasteries he did so much to encourage and revive after the vicissitudes of the ninth century. Close study of the policy adopted by Edgar towards the Church, a policy adopted as much for social and political as for purely religious or devotional reasons, provides an insight into his character and the means by which he tightened his grip on the English state. Monastic bishops, largely introduced by Edgar, supported by the abbots of newly revived or re-founded monasteries, proved to be the pillars of Edgar's reign, though it would seem that he died too soon to be able to ensure that his successors, who came to the throne so young, had learned statecraft from him.

This has led some to conclude that from the very beginning of his reign, perhaps even when only King of the Mercians and the Northumbrians, he was 'heavily influenced, if not controlled, by a political faction committed to a particular development of socio-ecclesiastical policy'.[1] That is no doubt an over-simplification; a great deal depended on the nature of the king's upbringing and how his character developed. It should be noted, however, that his reign was distinguished by the absence of any major conflict, which cannot have been due to anything done by his ecclesiastical advisers.

Much about the reign can be deduced from ecclesiastical sources, though the *Vitae* or lives of the saints are hagiography, dedicated to demonstrating their subjects' wisdom and sanctity, rather than biography as it is understood today.

Something of value can sometimes be derived from the accounts of the tenth century written by monastic historians in the Anglo-Norman period, especially if they copy into their text information derived from earlier sources. However, the information they provide is subject to the undeclared bias of these writers who had their own reasons for writing about tenth-century kings. One of the most valuable sources, because it is derived from texts which have now been lost, is the *Chronicle of Chronicles* of 'Florence' of Worcester (currently attributed to another Worcester monk called John). The author certainly makes use of earlier sources, no doubt found in the library at Worcester, such as the *World Chronicle* of Marianus Scotus. He also appears to have included his own Latin translation of a text of the *Anglo-Saxon Chronicles* similar in many ways to the Worcester text (D). Of the other Anglo-Norman writers, the work of Eadmer of Canterbury is useful, as is that of the editor or compiler of the *History of the Church of York*, known as Simeon of Durham. There is also the *Liber Eliensis*, and of course the invaluable work of William of Malmesbury.

Edgar was not, as one might have expected, brought up at the court of his father Edmund, nor anywhere else in Wessex. That was reserved for his elder brother, Eadwig, who was presumably intended to be his father's heir. Instead, Edgar was sent to be fostered in the household, one might almost say at the court, of the mighty Ealdorman Aethelstan Half-King of East Anglia, and was, as the Danes would have said, 'Aethelstan's Fostri'. The ealdorman's sons were therefore Edgar's foster-brothers, and are to be found high in his service after 957. It would seem that this circumstance made Edgar acceptable to the Mercians, East Anglians and Northumbrians in 957, certainly more so than Eadwig who proved to be a sore disappointment to the magnates north of the Thames. The family of the half-king was thus responsible for Edgar's early education.

What exactly that education was is not recorded, but there are a number of clues which might indicate something of the nature of it. Alfred the Great, Edgar's great grandfather, had pursued a vigorous policy directed at improving the standard of learning and literacy in ninth-century England. He certainly, as Bishop Asser states,[2] committed his son Aethelweard, as well as Edward and Aelfthryth, 'to the diligent care of masters at schools of learning'. The bishop says that Aethelweard was taught together with other young nobles and some children who were not noble, and that at the school, books 'in both the Latin and Saxon languages' were read constantly and that the children learnt to write. They did this before they were old enough or strong enough for the 'manly pursuits of hunting and similar occupations suitable for the nobility' and they became studious and skilful 'in the liberal arts'. That is possibly a reference to the arts of music and drawing.

Alfred employed many Mercians for this purpose of promoting education, like Plegmund, who was Archbishop of Canterbury, and the learned priests Athelstan and Werwulf, the king's chaplains, who belonged to a Mercian family. Plegmund was to consecrate five bishops of the West Saxons in Edward the Elder's reign and a sixth, Oda of Ramsbury, the later Archbishop of Canterbury. Alfred's policy extended beyond children to the ealdormen and reeves in his service who were, as Asser puts it, commanded to acquire 'wisdom', by which he meant that, under pain of dismissal from office, the king's men had to learn to read, so that 'though illiterate from their cradles, [they] began to devote themselves to the acquisition of learning'. If unable to learn by reason of age or slow wits, they had their sons taught to do so instead, or some other close relative.

The king's purpose, it is thought, was that they should be able to study at least his translation of the *Dialogues*, and the *Regula Pastoralis* or *Pastoral Care*, of Pope Gregory the Great. He may also have expected them to be able to read messages sent by him, or at least have them read to them. Alfred refers to the use of a 'written message and seal' as though it were quite usual to use such methods. The king's most trusted men also sent messages in writing accompanied by a seal, but it is not certain that these were sealed writs such as were in use in the eleventh century. More likely, the letter was sent by messenger and he was given a seal, a ring, or some other unmistakeable token, to authenticate the letter.

A letter from Alfred to his bishops, in the preface to his translation, proposes a programme of education and asks them to arrange instruction in reading English for 'all free young men' with the means and opportunity. His translation frequently makes the Pope address 'rulers' rather than 'bishops' as in the Latin, so that the work becomes a means of instructing men how a leader should conduct himself, and his duties and responsibilities. He also published a *Domboc* or book of laws, containing all that he thought worth preserving of his predecessor kings' laws with his own additions. All this so that his ealdormen and reeves, and his son Edward, should be educated in rulership. It seems likely that Edward in turn saw that his sons, Aethelstan, Edmund and Eadred, were taught, and that Edmund saw that his own sons, Eadwig and Edgar, were also educated. They too perhaps studied the *Domboc* and the *Pastoral Care* and other works by Alfred.

So Edgar was sent to be fostered and educated in the household of Aethelstan Half-King, and would also have been instructed in all the skills required of a noble youth, particularly one who was *aetheling* or throne-right-worthy. That meant horsemanship and possibly seamanship, as well as all the skills required of a fighting man, the use of sword, shield and spear. When old enough, the youth was sent, probably to Abingdon, to have his education completed by Abbot Aethelwold (not yet Bishop of Winchester). It was perhaps this man's influence, as well as that of Ealdorman Aethelstan, which made Edgar the man and king he became. Aethelwold's teaching would have brought to Edgar's attention the merits of Dunstan, and would have stressed the importance of reviving Benedictine monasticism in England with the need to remove secular clerks (forerunners of the canons of the eleventh century) from cathedral churches (the minsters) and the other surviving religious houses which were still, not quite accurately, known as monasteries.

Aethelwold's purpose was to revive the real Benedictine monasticism, under which monks lived a communal life as members of a community bound together by oaths of poverty, chastity and obedience. This was in contrast to the lifestyle of the secular clerks who, although in a sense living a collegiate life centred on a cathedral minster or other religious house, were apt to be married and own property, without any superior other than a titular head clerk whom they were by no means sworn to obey.

Aethelstan Half-King must also have had religious inclinations. He retired from the world in his last years, to Glastonbury, where he ended his days. His son, Ealdorman Aethelwine, was also a strong supporter of monasticism; he was instrumental in the founding of Ramsey Abbey, and defended the monks from the depredations of Ealdorman Aelfhere of Mercia during the reaction against the reform movement in Mercia after Edgar's death. He was known as *Dei amicus* or God's friend.

Born in 943, 'in the purple', so to speak, after his father Edmund had become king, Edgar was old enough by 950 to have had some understanding of the military and political situation in England under his uncle, King Eadred (946–955). In 948 Eadred had ravaged Northumbria 'with much slaughter', as a punishment for those Northumbrians who had broken the oaths they had sworn at Tanshelf in 947 by accepting Erik Bloodaxe as their king. That policy had had the desired effect as the Northumbrians promptly drove out Erik, who was slain shortly afterwards, and paid tribute to Eadred in compensation.

Edgar would have had before him that example of forceful kingship, just as he would have known of the punishment meted out to Thetford in Norfolk after the murder there of Abbot Eadhelm. He could only have watched from the sidelines at the court of his brother Eadwig while he drove Abbot Dunstan into exile and confiscated the property of his own grandmother, the Queen Dowager. What he thought when Eadwig proceeded to make an unsuitable marriage, allegedly within the forbidden degrees of kinship, only to have the marriage annulled by Archbishop Oda in 957, is unknown. What is known is that Edgar directly benefited from this when the northern nobility decided to throw off Eadwig's direct authority over Mercia and Northumbria and made Edgar 'King of the Mercians and the Northumbrians'.

Edgar was then able to recall Dunstan from exile, presumably on the advice of his new advisers, and make him a bishop, in turn of both Worcester and London. There is no very obvious explanation for the northern démarche, but it must have had something to do with the manoeuvring at Eadwig's court between rival factions which had led to Dunstan's exile. It does look as though the ranks of the Witan were divided by this issue and probably over the king's marriage.

The story, related in the *Vita Dunstani*, about Eadwig's scandalous behaviour at his coronation (he left the banquet and was found 'enjoying himself' in the company of two women), provides no real background to these events, and the tale might well have grown more scandalous in the telling. Whatever actually happened, the story is perhaps evidence that the king's marriage was unacceptable to an influential section of the Witan, and its annulment suggests that Eadwig's queen and her mother were themselves part of a cabal which used the incident at the coronation as an excuse to exile Dunstan.

Unfortunately, the monks responsible for writing up the *Chronicles* were more interested in the impact of events on the Church than in explaining the politics of the time. They record various deaths, mainly clerical, between 959 and 963 and then devote their attention to the king's monastic policy. When secular affairs are mentioned no details are provided. It is certain, from hints in other sources, that much more was going on, but none of it impinges on the consciousness of the writers. There is, for instance, no word about Edgar's lawmaking or administrative measures. They merely record that Edgar 'bettered the peace of the people more than any king before him' and that 'kings and earls bowed eagerly to him and were ruled by him as he would', but not a word about how he did it. They say that 'without fighting, he conquered all that he himself wished'.

They add to the mystery by complaining that this king, who was such a champion of the monks, 'loved alien customs and heathen practices' (a possible reference to his toleration of Danelaw customs) and brought them 'too much into this land' by 'inviting in foreigners and attracting harmful people to the land'. Some specific details would have been useful. It does fit rather uncomfortably beside other statements that are made about Edgar, for instance that 'he honoured the name of the Lord and meditated on God's laws often and long' and was 'lifted up by the love of God'. Exactly what lies behind these contrasting views cannot now be discerned. The passage, in the Peterborough (E) text of the *Chronicles*, is entered under 959 but is obviously an evaluation of his reign written some time later and inserted in what was thought to be a suitable place.

Some account of the events leading up to the reign of King Edgar is necessary if the nature and course of his reign is to be understood. Just as the reign of Alfred the Great had seen the kingdom of Wessex first halt and then, having consolidated the ground won, drive back the Viking invaders, so it also saw him expel them from the heartland of Wessex. After the death of King Alfred, his son Edward (known as 'the Elder' in order to distinguish him from Edward 'the Martyr', King Edgar's son, and Edward 'the Confessor') gradually, over a period of two decades, recovered English territory south of the Humber lost to the Danes earlier in the ninth century and incorporated it into the West Saxon realm. This process is often called 'the re-conquest of the Danelaw' – wrongly, since West Saxon kings had never ruled these lands previously. He was aided in this by his sister Aethelflaed, 'the Lady of the Mercians', and her husband, Ealdorman Aethelred of Mercia.

At the height of his power, Edward was recognised as in some sense overlord of the Scots, Northumbrians and Strathclyde Britons, although those peoples probably saw the matter in a different light from that found at the West Saxon Court. This recognition might well have reflected what was actually a stand-off arrangement or peace treaty, with face-saving gestures made to appease Edward and avoid an extension of the war against the Danes.

Edward's son Aethelstan found it necessary to carry the war into Scotland. This pre-emptive strike was possibly intended to prevent exactly the sort of coalition of his enemies which was to materialise in 937 and result in his overwhelming victory over them at the Battle of Brunanburh, the fame of which was to echo down the decades of the rest of the century, to the ultimate benefit of Edgar. Aethelstan's triumph did not, however, end the conflict, and both of his successors, Edmund and Eadred, had in turn to impose their domination over Scotland and Northumbria by force in the teeth of strong resistance, especially from the Norse kingdom of York.

Some account of the methods by which all this was achieved, and of the process, which reached its apogee under King Edgar, by which the kingdom of the Angles and Saxons became the kingdom of England, is the subject of Chapter One. Other chapters will deal with the nature of the state so achieved, describe the progress of Edgar's religious policy and the reasons for it, and consider the contributions to all these developments of the various magnates and the families to which they belonged, and the careers of Aethelwold, Dunstan and Oswald. Something will be said about the development of law-making and the machinery of government, both local and national, which owed so much to Edgar and his predecessors.

Edgar's own contribution can be assessed and described, and an account given of the 'mystery' of his allegedly long-delayed coronation. Finally, some attempt will be made to explain in greater detail exactly how it was that Edgar earned for himself the sobriquet of *Rex Pacificus*, the Peacemaker King. There has been a great deal of scholarly research into tenth-century England in recent decades and it is now possible to present Edgar in a very positive light. It can be suggested that the peacefulness of his reign was the result of a vigorous and dynamic policy carried out by the king and his Witan, which can be deciphered by close examination of the significant clues indicating that the surface calm presented by traditional accounts of his reign conceals a great deal of positive political and legislative action and structural organisation by an innovative and creative personality.

# I

# The Foundation of England

In the year 900, when Edward the Elder 'took the kingdom' (*feng to rice*), the boundary between Wessex and western Mercia on the one hand and the Viking-held area later to be known as the Danelaw (*danelagh*) on the other lay approximately along the Roman road called Watling Street. To the north and east were Viking York and Danish East Anglia, areas ruled by jarls and holds in command of individual war-bands or armies, nominally controlled by kings, in York or East Anglia. Farther north lay English-held Bernicia, 'St Cuthbert's Land', and the territory of the House of Bamburgh. All this had, by 954, fallen to the West Saxon kings, who could then rightly style themselves Kings of the English – *Reges Anglorum*. In the process of recovering English control over these areas they had, in fact, created the kingdom of England. They also, with widely varying degrees of success, laid claim to the overlordship of Wales, the North-West and even Scotland.[1]

The process by which this had been accomplished was begun by Alfred the Great, especially by his emphasis on the building and manning of fortified enclosures called 'burhs'. These were manned by relays of men according to a scheme which defined the number of hides of land (units of assessment for the levying of taxation) required to provide for 'the necessary defence of strongholds against enemies'[2] and calculated the number of men required to defend a given length of wall. The burhs were used rather as motte and bailey castles were used by the Normans; the burh, like the castle after it, dominated the countryside around it for miles. So successful were they that the mere building of a burh could bring about the submission of Viking armies. A line of burhs could hold back the Danes from areas reoccupied by the English.[3]

In 900 the territory of Aethelred, Lord of the Mercians, lay south of the Humber on the east and the Mersey on the west. The western border ran along Offa's Dyke and then as far as the Thames valley, its southern border.

It included London. Watling Street divided his lands from the Danes. By the end of Edward's reign every Danish colony south of the Humber (and previously part of Mercia) had been annexed by Wessex.[4] Edward, acting in conjunction with Aethelred and Aethelflaed, launched a two-pronged attack, using burhs to hold and defend, and then control, the land they had won.[5]

The rapid expansion of the kingdom of Wessex (roughly all of England south of the Thames but excluding Cornwall) followed Edward's victory at Tettenhall, Staffordshire, in 910. This annihilated a raiding army but left Northumbria weak, a target for the ambitions of the Dublin Norse who set about founding a kingdom at York for themselves, which they achieved by 918. There had been close and persistent connections between York and Dublin which continued during the first half of the tenth century through the descendants of the Viking chiefs and brothers Ingwar and Halfdene. That was why it was so important for Aethelred and Aethelflaed to re-fortify Chester and control the Cheshire plain and the Mersey. Edward had inherited Alfred's naval force and could now interrupt communications between Dublin and York. After Ealdorman Aethelred's death in 911, his wife Aethelflaed assumed control of the government of Mercia and took command of the struggle in her sector; however, she had to concede control of the Thames valley from Oxford to London, including the latter city itself, to her brother Edward. To the east, his attack on Essex in 912 ensured that his control of London became permanent. A threat from the direction of the Severn valley was repelled by the Mercians, which ended any possible threat to Wessex and allowed Edward to resume his advance.

## THE ANNEXATION OF THE DANELAW

The building of burhs continued, especially by Aethelflaed, who built a new one every year to secure the defence of western Mercia. All Danish counter-attacks were defeated and Derby was taken and annexed to Mercia, until by 918 only four boroughs remained in Danish hands: Leicester, Stamford, Nottingham and Lincoln. East Anglia had submitted to Edward, swearing to keep the peace, and the army of Cambridge made a separate bargain. Then Leicester surrendered to Aethelflaed without a fight. Unfortunately, the Lady of the Mercians died before she could exploit the surrender, and it may be that the opportunity to secure a peaceful annexation of Northumbria died with her, because Edward had to spend time strengthening his hold on Mercia.

Edward had to halt his advance in order to secure his control over Mercia, as a faction of Mercian magnates wanted Aethelflaed's daughter Aelfwynn to succeed her. Edward simply seized the girl and took her deep into Wessex, which ensured Mercian allegiance. Edward's assumption of power over Mercia so overawed the Welsh kings that they accepted him as overlord of western Wales, which effectively meant that they paid tribute to him in the hope that he would leave them alone. That left him free to resume his attack on the Danes,[6] who now found themselves between a rock and a hard place and submitted to the West Saxon king. Edward the Elder had advanced against them from the south while the Norse kings of York were endeavouring to expand their authority south of the Humber. Perhaps the Danes submitted to Edward because they preferred the marginally more civilised West Saxon king to the blood-stained Norsemen. This submission enabled Edward to advance to the Trent and into the Peak District, to Bakewell, in 920, whereupon, according to the *Anglo-Saxon Chronicles*, the whole of the North of England submitted to him.

It is likely that the various powers in the area saw the matter very differently, and the whole affair looks suspiciously like a stand-off. Each of the northern rulers had his own reasons for wanting peace. Ealdred of Bamburgh was isolated, surrounded by Scots, Norsemen and Strathclyde Britons, and preferred to accept the protection of a strong 'King of the English'; the Lords of Strathclyde secured the recognition of their seizure of Northumbrian territory; the Scots secured temporary relief from the threat represented by the Norse under Raegnald; and Raegnald himself secured recognition, for the time being at any rate, of his kingship in York. Later writers, in the Anglo-Norman era, saw this as foreshadowing the claims to feudal overlordship secured by the Norman kings. The *Chronicles* presented this, in the light of the later claims of Kings Aethelstan and Edgar, as showing that Edward had supreme power over all lesser rulers within reach of his formidable armies.

But the agreement actually reached looks more like a peace treaty or mutual non-aggression pact. No charters record Edward's kingly titles during his years of greatness, so there is no way of knowing whether Aethelstan, his successor, was the first to claim such titles as *Basileus* or overlordship of all Britain. Edward in his early years had been *Rex Anglo-Saxonum* and then *Rex Anglorum*, King of the English.[7] There was no further opportunity for campaigning in the North and Edward had reached the climax of his reign. He died at Farndon on the Dee on 17 July 924, while on his way to deal with a rebellion by the men of Chester in league with the Welsh.

The first military task had been accomplished by Edward the Elder, to secure the safety of Wessex and to pass from defence to offence, conquering land beyond the Thames, making use of his father's invention, the burhs. His effort had ended in the 'voluntary' submission of the Danes in 917, but only on condition that they were allowed to retain their lands and their customs. Edward fully incorporated Mercia into Wessex by 918, becoming 'King of the English', and by crossing the Mersey in 919 he cut off the Norse from their source of strength in Dublin. That was why he had attained the prestige needed for other rulers to take him 'as father and lord': Constantine of Scotland, Raegnald of York, Ealdred High Reeve of Bamburgh, Donald of Strathclyde and the Princes of West Wales, at Bakewell in Derbyshire in 924.[8]


## OVERLORDSHIP

It is noteworthy that the phrase 'take him for father and lord' marks an agreement by an inferior king to an alliance with his superior.[9] The first step towards the shadowy suzerainty over Scotland and Bernicia seems to have been taken by Aethelflaed by securing an alliance with Constantine, Ealdred and the Yorkshire Danes who were 'under her direction' (Aethelflaed's, that is).[10] Alfred the Great in his time had been the first king to be acknowledged by all the kings of Wales as their overlord, setting the pattern for Anglo-Welsh – even Anglo-Celtic – relationships. But Edward's campaigns had, in a sense, been somewhat counterproductive, in that they drove the Scots into the arms of a York-Dublin alliance which bore fruit in Aethelstan's reign.[11]

Although the extension of the power of the West Saxon kings, first over Mercia, then over the southern Danelaw, and finally over Northumbria, can be so described as to look like 'remorseless progress to a pre-conceived end' and thus the fulfilment of a deliberate policy, traceable to 'visions' of a united England, it most certainly was not. It was as much the result of accident as design, and depended to a great degree on the character and ability of individual kings. But they did from time to time receive the submission of Welsh and Scottish rulers, which tended to increase both their pretensions and their prestige so that they strengthened the institutions of their government.[12]

This is not to deny that there was a political development, not just from a kingdom called 'Wessex' to one called 'England' but a series of stages which can be labelled, after Wessex, 'the kingdom of the West Saxons and other southern peoples' on to 'the kingdom of the Anglo-Saxons' and thence to 'the kingdom of the English', and finally to the kingdom of England. In this process it may even be that the claim to be 'King of the Anglo-Saxons' was a much more politically overt statement than to claim to be 'King of the English', signalling his lordship over both peoples. After 927 the kingdom of the Anglo-Saxons developed, first under Aethelstan and then under Edmund and Eadred, into something new, larger and more grandiose. As the poem on the agreement at Eamont was to put it, *'Ista perfecta Saxonia'* – 'this England is now made whole'.[13]

The contrast under Aethelstan, therefore, due perhaps to the absence of charters in the latter part of Edward's reign, was very marked. He appears to assume a status for the King of England which was not abandoned until 1066. But Edward had been in no position to impose or dictate terms on anybody. Even the phrase 'accepted as father and lord' was speculative interpretation by the chronicler who wrote it. The northern kings were a collection of past and present enemies and allies, some of whom had fought one another quite recently, so that Edward appears as a neutral figure who could preside over the making of a peace treaty. Despite a dispute over the succession, his son Aethelstan was accepted as king in both Mercia and Wessex before the end of the year and he was crowned at Kingston upon Thames on 4 September 925.[14] Thus began the conversion of the West Saxon kingship into an English monarchy, a process that began in 899 and ended in 975.

This was to create a kingdom in which all petty rulers, whether English or Danish, accepted one man alone as the undisputed rightful king. The next stage in this process was to take half a century. Two problems were involved. The subject peoples were all too likely to break out in rebellion, and the English had in their midst an alien race which could not be removed and had to be accepted, the Danes. Their presence made their fellow countrymen in Scandinavia very restless and ambitious and their fleets infested the seas around Britain. In addition, the Norsemen based in Dublin supported the claims of their royal house to the Kingdom of York.

In Wessex there was a tradition that Aethelstan had been robed, when still a child, by Alfred himself, in a scarlet cloak, jewelled belt and a 'Saxon' sword, which suggests that efforts were made to present Aethelstan as an aetheling and therefore throne-worthy. But he had been brought up by Aethelred and Aethelflaed, the rulers of Mercia, rather than by his own father, King Edward, so that he was probably the first West Saxon king to be familiar to the Mercian aristocracy. They seem to have recognised him as King of Mercia quite independently of his assumption of the throne in Wessex. This gave him an advantage that his father had lacked because it also made him acceptable to the Northumbrians.

## AETHELSTAN AND BRUNANBURH

One indication of Aethelstan's acceptability to the Scandinavians is that the Norse king Sihtric of York offered an alliance which Aethelstan promptly accepted and sealed by marrying off his sister to him. The alliance did not last long as Sihtric died before summer 927. Good came of it, however, because it gave Aethelstan the excuse he needed to take control of York, destroying its fortifications and distributing Sihtric's treasure to win support.[15] Then, at Eamont Bridge near Penrith, his success at York was marked by the submission on 27 July of the kings of Scotland and Strathclyde, Hywel Dda of Dyfed and the English Lord of Bamburgh, when they all undertook to suppress 'idolatry' (a reference to the practices of the pagan Norsemen). The river at Eamont marked the boundary of Aethelstan's power, some eighty miles beyond the frontier of Edward the Elder's kingdom. Lancashire and Westmorland were now part of the English kingdom.[16]

Aethelstan had come to the throne with a high reputation as a soldier and his opponents were wary of him from the start. He was the first English king to set foot in York for sixty years, though his control was recent and superficial.[17] He faced the risk that collaboration between the Dublin Norse raiders and Norse kings at York would one day establish a Scandinavian bloc from the Mersey to the Humber.

Over the next few years he extended his authority over the western kings also, possibly by force or perhaps by its mere display. He brought the Welsh princes to a meeting at Hereford where he secured promises of the tribute they had paid his father, and, more usefully, set the River Wye as the boundary between the Welsh and the English. A document known as *Dunsaete* which dates from this period seems to be the record of an agreement by those dwelling on opposite sides of the river to appoint twelve 'lawmen', six from each side, to agree on the manner of settling disagreements between them.

The Welsh princes, Hywel Dda of Dyfed, Idwal of Gwynedd and Morgan of Morgannwg (Glamorgan), visited Aethelstan's court repeatedly between 931 and 937, as did Owain of Gwent and Teowdor of Brycheiniog.[18]

Aethelstan then moved on to deal with the Cornish Britons (there is an implication that they were in revolt), by refortifying Exeter and driving the Britons further west, compelling them to accept the River Tamar as the boundary with Wessex. Aethelstan seems to have set out to define his borders more precisely.

His settlement in the North seems to have held for some six years, but in 934 Aethelstan was again perhaps pursuing his policy of defining his borders, possibly in response to breach of the settlement in the North by the Scots. His invasion was a demonstration in force. He made his arrangements at a great court held in Winchester at Pentecost on 28 May where he was attended by a great crowd of thegns, twelve of his ealdormen (five with Danish names), the magnates of the House of Bamburgh, Ealdred, Uhtred and Oswulf, and four Welsh princes including Hywel Dda. He then advanced north by way of Nottingham. The gifts he made to churches visited en route mark his progress through Beverley, Ripon and Chester-le-Street. The intention behind such gifts was to win over the support of the local magnates.

He also seems to have taken the opportunity to consolidate his control over Lancashire as he bought the region of Amounderness from its pagan Norse occupants and gave it to the Archbishop of York, his most powerful lieutenant in Yorkshire. He also took control of the York mint, where his coinage now advertised his commitment to Christianity. From there, having made gifts to St Cuthbert, presenting himself as the champion of the saint, he advanced into Scotland.[19]

The Scots, intimidated by this demonstration of military might, offered no resistance, preferring to retreat before the advancing English army which ravaged the countryside as far as Fordoun, Kincardineshire, while the English fleet sailed along the coast as far as Caithness. So Aethelstan demonstrated that the collapse of the Norse kingdom of York had brought the heart of Scotland within striking distance of the English king's power. But he failed to detach Constantine from his allies.[20]

The consequences were reaped three years later when it became clear to the northern rulers that only united action by his enemies stood any chance of containing Aethelstan. Olaf Guthfrithsson of Dublin married the daughter of Constantine of Scotland, a sure sign of an alliance, and they struck in 937, making a joint invasion deep into English territory, anticipating a welcome in Deira (southern Northumbria). There is no indication of resistance. Aethelstan appears to have deliberately waited, possibly until the invaders began to turn back or until all his forces were ready. The battle at Brunanburh that ensued united Mercians and West Saxons in a common cause and a common memory of their achievement which tended to blur memories of previous wars. It is not known where this battle was fought but the favoured location is Bromborough in Cheshire, because that area looks the most likely strategically. A Scots army coming down through Strathclyde into Lancashire could easily rendezvous there with Norsemen from Dublin.

It was not perhaps quite as decisive in practice as Alfred's great victory at Eddington, but it consolidated the work he had begun and laid the foundations for the peace that prevailed under Edgar. To Aelfric of Eynsham at the end of the century, Aethelstan became the central figure in a triumvirate of great kings of which Alfred was the first and Edgar the third. 'Aethelstan fought with Olaf, destroyed his army, drove him to flight and then reigned peacefully'.[21]

So it was a decisive victory, celebrated in verse in the *Anglo-Saxon Chronicle* as the climax, if not yet the end, of an era, when the previous political system, from 886 to 937, perished and several independent kingdoms with it. But the disputed succession when Aethelstan died, and the invasions which marred the peace of the next two reigns, showed how much the kingdom still depended on the personality of its king.

One effect of Brunanburh was that Aethelstan now attracted the attention of continental rulers, and another was a distinct triumphalist tone adopted by Aethelstan's charter makers. The royal style and titles now adopted claimed for Aethelstan authority over the whole of Britain, as his charters and even his coins testify: 'King of the English and Ruler of All Britain' they boast, 'King of the English raised to the throne of the kingdom of Britain by the right hand of the Almighty', and even *'Imperator Orbis Britanniae'* – 'Emperor of the World of Britain'.

His prestige was high, and the rulers of Francia and Germany sought alliances cemented by the marriages of his sisters: Eadgifu to Charles the Simple, Edith to the Emperor Otto I, and Eadhild to Duke Hugh Capet. Eadgifu's son Louis d'Outremer was fostered at Aethelstan's court, as were Alan of Brittany and Hakon, son of Harald Fairhair of Norway. Other ways in which Aethelstan's continental impact can be demonstrated include the exchange of embassies with foreign rulers and the exchange of suitably magnificent gifts.

Yet at home, despite his Britain-wide prestige and imperial claims, Aethelstan did not venture far outside the hereditary limits of Wessex. He is found, as charters show, in Devon, Somerset and Dorset, in Hampshire, Wiltshire and Berkshire, or in Sussex, Surrey and Kent. The meetings of king and council are found north of the Thames, in peacetime that is, only in places like York, Tamworth, Northampton and Buckingham, and to the east at Colchester and London. But his authority was such that he could compel the attendance of great magnates from the Danish areas: Aethelstan 'Half-King' came from his East Anglian ealdormanry, and many nobles with Danish names, some styled *dux*, recorded in charters,[22] were the successors of those who had led the Danish armies in eastern England and the Danelaw.

In the later years of his reign he held together his composite realm, made up of Wessex, Mercia and Northumbria, and dominated the Britons of Cornwall and the Anglo-Scandinavians of the Danelaw as well as the Englishmen living around York. The invasion of 937 had shaken this realm but had not broken it. His 'united kingdom' was secure when he died, but might well have been 'an artificial product of statecraft'.[23]

When Aethelstan died on 27 October 939, he was succeeded, since he had no heir of his own, by his brother Edmund, who had proved himself at the battle of Brunanburh. He was to prove a warlike and politically astute ruler. Unfortunately his reign was to be cut short by an untimely death.

## VIKING RESURGENCE

The Vikings, down but as yet by no means out, seized the opportunity presented by the change of king to renew their assault. The unity of Aethelstan's fragile composite realm all but collapsed. Olaf Guthfrithsson of Dublin reoccupied York without opposition early in 940 and raided into the Midlands, where he was repulsed at Northampton but took Tamworth by storm and laid waste the countryside. Edmund confronted him near Leicester but there was no battle. The Archbishops of Canterbury (Oda) and York (Wulfstan) mediated between the two armies and arranged a peace; Olaf was allowed control of the whole region from Watling Street to the Northumbrian border, though Simeon of Durham[24] says that Stamford was not included so that the Viking had only four out of the Five Boroughs won by Edward the Elder. Edmund had been obliged to abandon the area to

Norse rule although it had been under the sway of the King of the English for twenty years.

This ignominious surrender was the first significant setback since Edward the Elder had begun his advance. There are hints of treachery and betrayal if the story in Roger of Wendover[25] is correct. He claimed that Olaf owed his success to a 'count' (that is an ealdorman or jarl) called Orm, whose daughter, Ealdgyth, married Olaf, but adds no details. There was a *dux* called Orm who witnessed Aethelstan's charters. What these events do show is the weakness which affected a new king at the start of his reign until he had secured control over all of the magnates. Any oaths of allegiance given to the previous king became void at his death and the new king had to secure their renewal. That left a window of opportunity for invasion and betrayal.

Olaf managed to extend his authority in 941 into English Northumbria, north of the River Tees, but then, unaccountably, upped and died. His successor, another Olaf, the son of Sihtric, proved to be no match for King Edmund, who had used the time to secure his authority over Wessex and Mercia. He seized control of the region between Watling Street and the Humber in 942, which suggests that the lords of that area had little real liking for renewed Viking rule, and drove Olaf Sihtricsson out of Northumbria in 943. The control of the Viking kingdom of York fell prey for some time to disputes between rival Viking factions. Some Northumbrians chose Raegnald, brother of Olaf Guthfrithsson, while others supported Sihtricsson. They both visited Edmund's Court and were even baptised there, a sign that this was part of the negotiations for peace. When Olaf Sihtricsson managed to reassert control of York, Edmund expelled both Viking leaders and retained control of York for the rest of his reign.

It does look as though English rule was not yet fully accepted in Northumbria, but the quarrels among the Viking leaders meant that they were no threat to the rest of England, and those south of the Humber seem to have looked upon Edmund as their deliverer from Viking rule. A poem from that time records Edmund's recovery of the Five Boroughs and Danish Mercia and claims that the Danes living there had been held by the Norse by force until Edmund 'redeemed' them.[26] The Danes who had benefited from Aethelstan's rule now saw themselves as subjects of the King of England, and antagonism between Danes and Norsemen underlies much of the history of this period.

## THE FALL OF ERIK BLOODAXE

Edmund was able to reassert his authority by ravaging Cumberland and Strathclyde but this seems to have been only a demonstration in force. He promptly placed the area under the control of Malcolm, King of Scots, on the usual condition that he became Edmund's 'co-worker by land and sea', a coded reference to a mutual pact of non-aggression.[27] Edmund had launched a major strike, involving the use of Welsh auxiliary troops, but the cession of Strathclyde to Malcolm was a politically astute move, neutralising any ambitions he might have had to attack Bernicia. It was not a permanent settlement. Strathclyde is found back in the hands of its British rulers a few years later.

The real significance is that it shows that Edmund had realised the need to set a realistic limit to his kingdom at its northern end, and foreshadows the equally astute cession of Lothian to the King of Scots by King Edgar. But that was to be Edmund's last move. He was murdered while defending his steward when at Pucklechurch in Gloucestershire, stabbed by a returned criminal called Leofa on 26 May 946. His sons, Eadwig and Edgar (the latter born after Edmund had become king), were still far too young to succeed him and the crown went to his brother Eadred, known as 'Weak-in-the-feet'.

He was to spend most of his reign, like Edmund, dealing with northern rebellion. Unlike Edmund, Eadred at first met no opposition. He was consecrated king at Kingston, as his first charter states. At Tanshelf on the River Aire near Pontefract, in 947, Archbishop Wulfstan and the northern magnates swore fealty and gave security (which probably means hostages). Then the notorious Viking Erik Bloodaxe came on the scene, probably the most famous Viking of his age. He was a son of Harald Fairhair and had been driven out of Norway by his brother Hakon, Aethelstan's foster-son.

Erik descended on Northumbria where he was welcomed by the Norsemen. King Eadred responded immediately, invading Northumbria, advancing as far as Ripon (where he burnt down the minster) and meeting no resistance until he reached Castleford on the Aire. There, on turning south, he met an army from York which defeated his rearguard. Despite this he was able to dictate terms to the Northumbrians and compel them to abandon Erik. Presumably Eadred had secured control of York. Nonetheless, the men of York welcomed the return from Dublin of Olaf Sihtricsson who ruled at York until 952, when Erik Bloodaxe drove him out and ruled for

two years as King of the English and the Irish. The exact chronology of
these events is still uncertain; accounts in the various texts of the *Chronicle*
conflict and cannot be satisfactorily reconciled. Further north the situation
remained even more obscure.

The turning point came when Eadred decided to arrest Archbishop
Wulfstan of York 'because he had often been accused to the king' (of
treachery presumably, though the exact charge is not recorded). It does
look as though Eadred was unable to rely on Wulfstan's loyalty. He was kept
prisoner until shortly before Eadred's death,[28] so he must have been able
to clear himself. He probably still had enough support in York to find the
necessary oath-helpers. It seems that the Archbishop and his supporters had
been Eadred's real opponents in York and that Wulfstan had been arrested as
soon as Erik Bloodaxe fell.

Although released, Wulfstan was not allowed to return to York and was
put in charge of the See of Dorchester. He was the last Northumbrian-born
Archbishop of York until after the Norman Conquest. Later archbishops
could be of Danish blood, but came from East Anglia and were loyal to the
West Saxon dynasty. One result was that Northumbria became remarkably
united and Englishmen and men of Viking descent lived together in
tolerable harmony.[29] Eadred appointed Oskytel as Archbishop, a sign that
his authority had been established and a landmark in the formation of a
united England, now under one king and one royal family. Eadred's charters
show him claiming to be conqueror of the North.

The men of York, the 'Eoforwicings', now realised that they had chosen
badly in opting for Erik Bloodaxe and had little choice but to drive him
out and to accept Eadred as king. Yet for a century it had sometimes looked
as though a large part of England would become part of a united kingdom
based on Dublin, though hindsight suggests that it would not have proved
stable. English military supremacy at York had decided matters in favour of
the West Saxon dynasty, and it was now possible to speak of England rather
than of Wessex, Mercia and Northumbria.[30]

Eadred then apparently engineered the expulsion of Erik by the
Northumbrians and 'succeeded to the kingdom of Northumbria'. Exactly
how and why Erik's rule came to an abrupt end in 954 remains obscure.
Norse accounts are confused attempts to reconstruct a lost history and the
*Chronicles* give no explanation at all. After his flight from York, Erik is said
to have been killed by Maccus, son of Olaf (but which Olaf?), at Stainmore
in the Pennines and to have been betrayed to him by Oswulf of Bamburgh,

the High Reeve.[31] A battle at Stainmore, in the nature of a last stand, sounds plausible. The Scandinavian north remembered the kingship of Erik for centuries, though the traditions are contradicted by English sources. Erik's fall is recorded by Simeon of Durham:

> The Kings of Northumbria came to an end... afterwards that country was ruled by earls. The last king was Erik whom the Northumbrians made king in violation of the faith they had sworn to King Eadred. Wherefore that king, in wrath, gave command that all Northumbria should be laid waste. Thereupon the Northumbrians expelled Erik their king, who was killed by Maccus son of Anlaf (Olaf), and appeased King Eadred with oaths and gifts. The country was then entrusted to Earl Oswulf (of Bamburgh).[32]

This was an event of immense significance. A leader with the ability to call on the support of all landless Scandinavians had failed to establish himself in an English kingdom. The North seemed to have grown tired of the constant disruption caused by the intrusion of Viking adventurers as the first Viking Age drew to a close. They now began to prefer the relative peace and freedom from interference that they enjoyed under an overlord from south of the Humber. Eadred himself could not perhaps have known the extent of his achievement; in his will he left a sizeable sum to be spent, if need be, on buying peace from a heathen army.[33]

Edward the Elder and his sons had now firmly established their West Saxon dynasty as Kings of the English, and survived the crises which had threatened the unity of their kingdom. That kingdom now extended from the Channel to the Firth of Forth and included West Saxons, East Anglians, Mercians, Northumbrians and Danes.[34] Eadred died after a long illness (he had never been a well man) on 23 November 955, leaving no heir. That he had been ill for so long does suggest the possibility that much of the decision-making during his reign had been the responsibility of his magnates, men like the great Aethelstan Half-King of East Anglia. Eadred's heirs were therefore his nephews, Eadwig and Edgar. No rebellion marred the actual accession of Eadwig.

2

# The Kingdom of the English

The realm created in the first half of the tenth century by a succession of able kings was a formidable military and administrative machine which was to be inherited and perfected by Edgar. Unfortunately, the premature murder of his successor, Edward the Martyr, meant that with Edgar the line of able kings came to an end and his work was, to some extent, undone by the inability of Aethelred II 'the Unraede' to cope with renewed Danish invasions led by Swein Forkbeard and his son Cnut. Even so, much of Edgar's work lived on to be successfully utilised by Cnut.

The improvement in military organisation and tactics had begun with Alfred the Great, and it was his achievement to stem the tide of Scandinavian advance by both military and administrative means. He cemented the dependency of Mercia on Wessex and set a pattern of conquest and treaty which was followed by his son Edward and his successors.[1] Alfred had divided the army, known as the *fyrd*, into two divisions. One half could fight while the other returned home to maintain food production, and they served in the field turn and turn about, serving for a fighting season of six months in three-monthly relays.

Alfred's second major innovation was to create the nucleus of a defensive fleet. It avoided pitched sea battles and was used to rush assistance to beaches where a Viking landing had taken place within a couple of hours of the alarm being raised. The ships were based at coastal burhs which could resist invasion and send for assistance.[2]

In 910 Edward the Elder raised a fleet of one hundred vessels, but used it to act as a decoy to the Viking raiding army, to persuade it that most of his reinforcements were in the ships, which sailed along the Kent coast in an easterly direction. The Vikings took the chance to raid further into Mercia and were caught by Edward with an army raised from both Wessex and Mercia which put them to flight with heavy losses.[3] There is no indication that Edward sought to defeat the Vikings at sea. That might be because it became unnecessary as the Viking fleets seem to have fought among themselves. During 912 to 913, an Irish fleet from Dublin was defeated and a rival Norse fleet was attacked off the Isle of Man by the reinforcements for a third fleet from Brittany which had been repulsed when it attacked Wessex.[4]

Of his immediate successors, only Aethelstan made use of naval forces, using a fleet to accompany his raiding land army in the invasion of Scotland in 933–934. The army advanced as far as Dunnottar near Aberdeen and the fleet was ordered to sail along the Scottish coast as far as Caithness. Again there is no evidence of real naval warfare. It seems to have been a response to the presence of pirate fleets led by Anlaf Quran and Anlaf Guthfrithsson. The fleet was used to deter seaborne intervention, particularly perhaps from the Earls of Orkney.

The existence of this naval force did not prevent the invasion by the same Norse leaders from Dublin in 937 that led to Brunanburh. Aethelstan's only other naval foray came in 939 when he sent an English force to the Continent in support of his foster-son Louis d'Outremer. His ships' crews ravaged parts of the coast opposite England but took no real part in the war. These fleets seem to have been raised as occasion demanded, as there is no evidence until Edgar's reign of a permanent navy.[5]

Alfred the Great had developed the system of 'burhs', forts consisting principally of ramparts and a ditch surmounted by a stout palisade. Use was also made of existing stone walls, especially where a burh was established on the site of a former Roman town, as at Winchester. Many were fortified towns, others were just military camps. They were constructed in strategic locations throughout Wessex in Alfred's own reign, and then extended, principally under Edward the Elder and his sister Aethelflaed, wife of Ealdorman Aethelred, 'the Lady of the Mercians'. As existing boroughs were recaptured or surrendered, they had advanced into Danish-held areas. Often the mere fact that a burh had been built was enough to bring about the surrender of a Danish-held borough and its dependent territory.


## DEFENCE AND CONSOLIDATION

The essence of the burh was that it could be efficiently manned by men whose maintenance was provided by a given number of hides of land.

Analysis of the document known as the *Burghal Hidage*[6] has revealed the basis of the system. It lists the burhs of Alfred's kingdom with a small number of additions north of the Thames, about thirty-three in all. The manning system worked as follows: an acre's breadth of wall (0.405 hectares) required the support of sixteen hides, so that on the assumption that one hide provided one man, then one rod, pole or perch (approximately five metres) of the wall would be manned by four men, twenty poles of wall (100 metres) required eighty men with eighty hides for its maintenance and a furlong of 220 yards (about 200 metres) would need 160 hides and be manned by 160 men.

These ratios have been confirmed by comparing this system with the known or estimated sizes of a number of burhs for which information is available or has been recovered by archaeology. Winchester was rated or assessed in the *Burghal Hidage* at 2,400 hides and would thus need defences 3,300 yards long (2,970 metres). The Roman wall at Winchester is 3,280 yards long (2,952 metres), remarkably close to the length calculated from the text of the *Burghal Hidage*. Similarly, Wareham had ramparts of 2,280 yards (2,052 metres) and the text demands 2,200 yards (1,980 metres). Other burhs also fit quite well, such as Lewes, Malvern and Wallingford, as do the very small burhs, mere forts, at Southampton (150 hides for maintaining a wall of one furlong), Lyng (100 hides) and Lydford (a mere forty hides). The number of hides, at one man from one hide, does seem to reflect the number of men needed for defence. Other shires whose assessments are recorded also fit the pattern, but many shires cannot be made to fit so easily because their assessment in hides was changed by the time it was recorded.[7] The overall result, for Wessex, was that by the end of Alfred's reign the burhs surrounded the kingdom and no village was more than twenty miles from a burh – a normal day's ride for a horseman.

It may seem an obvious point, but it should be remembered that at this time, when the Danelaw had not yet been re-absorbed into the Kingdom of the English, government was all about war and taxation. Kings had to be able to impose obligations on their peoples and raise money for their armed forces. The burghal system depended on resources raised from individual hides, but the assessments given in the *Burghal Hidage* must have been broken down into levies on the units smaller than a shire, known as hundreds later in the tenth century. That hundredal system was to be developed further for other purposes.

Many of the institutions of local government and administration developed out of stratagems adopted by tenth-century kings and their advisers, especially concerning the functions of shires, hundreds, boroughs and vills, which became units of assessment, of administration and of justice. The development of burhs stimulated the growth of towns; even the word 'borough' derives from 'burh'. This framework became the backbone of English local government throughout the Middle Ages and beyond, and parts of it still survive in the form of county councils and county courts. As a result of the actions of several kings, from Edward the Elder onwards, all of England south of the River Tees was divided into shires as units of administration, and into smaller units called hundreds or wapentakes for tax purposes and the maintenance of peace and order. However, they are not mentioned by name until the reign of Edgar, nor even by implication before that of his father Edmund. Many of the shires which are found in existence after Edward the Elder's reign are centred on, and derive their name from, a burh constructed by Edward or his sister Aethelflaed, and have all the hallmarks of artificial creations since they ignore all previous regional boundaries. They are the result of the establishment of West Saxon supremacy between 900 and 955.[8] Examples of such shires are Warwickshire, Staffordshire and Derbyshire.

As for the burhs themselves, within fifteen years of Edward the Elder's death at least fifteen of them had become centres of local trade – in effect, fortified markets. Coins were now struck by moneyers settled at previously defensible places such as Chester or Hereford or new ones like Tamworth, Hertford or Maldon. People settled in them for security or at the king's command, and there are signs of deliberate town planning with a grid layout of streets and houses as at Oxford or Wallingford.

As a result of the successful prosecution of the war against the Danes under Edward the Elder, the Kings of the West Saxons had become first Kings of the Anglo-Saxons, then Kings of the English and so, by extension, Kings of England. They had extended their power initially over Mercia, then into the southern Danelaw; finally, under Aethelstan and his successors, they extended it over Northumbria. Thus it has been well claimed that they imposed at least a semblance of political unity on peoples who still remained conscious of their respective customs and separate past.[9] From time to time Welsh and Scottish rulers made some sort of formal submission which at least increased the prestige and pretensions of the English kings, though there is precious little evidence of any real increase in political power in these kingdoms.

The increase in prestige increased the kings' control over their own subjects and allowed them to strengthen various institutions of government, a process which extended itself into the reign of Edgar. They were brought into closer contact with the continental powers, not least because as Aethelstan's prestige and power increased his sisters suddenly became very attractive as wives for continental princes. Edward the Elder's daughter Eadgifu had already, in her father's lifetime, been married to Charles the Simple, then ruling most of France and claiming successfully to rule Lotharingia. Hugh Capet, Count of Paris, proposed marriage alliance in 926, after Aethelstan's accession, because he needed to secure good relations with the protector of the Carolingian claimant, Louis d'Outremer.

Hugh sent Adelolf, Count of Boulogne, with an embassy which was received by Aethelstan and his Witan at Abingdon.[10] Rich gifts were presented to flatter the English king and win him over; perfumes and gems, horses, an onyx vase and a jewelled diadem, and of course sacred relics. Aethelstan was to be a great collector of relics. He was given the Sword of Constantine, the Emperor, which had a nail from the True Cross in the hilt, the Lance of Charlemagne, which was said to have been that which pierced the body of Christ while on the Cross, fragments of the True Cross and of the Crown of Thorns, set in crystal, and the Standard of St Maurice.

There were sound reasons for proposing an alliance, as Louis was unlikely to regain his throne without Hugh's aid. Counter-gifts were sent of comparable magnificence and Count Hugh married Aethelstan's sister Eadhild.[11] The marriage brought Aethelstan into contact with Henry the Fowler of Germany, who was engaged in a similar task to that of Aethelstan and his father. Henry was endeavouring to reunite the fragments of Carolingian Germany and seeking to detach Lotharingia from France. The presence of Louis d'Outremer at Aethelstan's court was one motive. The other was the English king's possession of a fleet which might be used to support a Lotharingian revolt.

## AETHELSTAN AND THE CONTINENTAL POWERS

Overtures to Aethelstan for an alliance came in 928 and a bride was sought for Henry's son Otto (the Great, founder of the Ottonian dynasty). The tale was that Aethelstan sent two of his remaining sisters so that Otto could take his pick, and he chose Edith. The other sister was then said to have been married off to some unidentified prince; Conrad the Peaceable of Burgundy is one possibility. Thus through these marriages Aethelstan's brothers Edmund and Eadred became brothers-in-law to several European rulers and Edmund's sons Eadwig and Edgar had European relatives. Edith's was perhaps the most important of these marriages, though she was never Empress. She died in 946, sixteen years before Otto became Emperor; her son, Liudolf, was Duke of Swabia, and died in 957 just as Edgar became king in Mercia.

But the marriage created a pattern of Anglo-German contact which influenced English history in Edgar's reign, affecting English Church history and the advent of monastic reform. The English royal family kept in contact with its continental relatives. Aethelweard the Chronicler, who was of collateral royal descent, wrote his celebrated chronicle for Edith's granddaughter Matilda, Abbess of Essen.

In 936, Louis d'Outremer was recalled to France as a result of a proposal made at Aethelstan's court, held at York, and he was sent back escorted by Oda, Bishop of Ramsbury (and later Archbishop of Canterbury) who completed the negotiations for his return. Louis was crowned in June. The situation anticipated by Henry the Fowler materialised and there was war in Lotharingia. Aethelstan sent his fleet to Louis's aid, but it did little good. In any case, Aethelstan died before the campaign was completed and his successor, Edmund, was unable to continue because of Norse attacks on England. It was, however, another first: an English fleet had been sent to help a continental ally. That Aethelstan was able to act in this way, and send his fleet abroad, indicates the degree of control he exercised over his newly united kingdom and it was no surprise that he was able to destroy the northern alliance that came against him in 937.

Because of Aethelstan's continental contacts it has been argued that there was much Frankish (that is, Carolingian) influence on English government in the tenth century, as there had been at the beginning of the ninth when Aethelwulf, son of King Ecgbert married Judith, daughter of Charles the Bald.[12] Frankish government provided, in some sense, a model for the government of a large area and the English learned something of the theory and practice of kingship from its contacts with the Frankish monarchy.[13]

Following from that it can then be suggested that the period from Alfred to Edgar was a 'Carolingian' phase composed of military success, unifying legislation, and the development of nationwide local institutions. It is even suggested that Carolingian 'capitularies' (the written ordinances of the Frankish kings), a collection of which reached England in the early tenth century, provided the stimulus for legislative development revealed by the surviving law codes of the tenth-century kings. So they not only caught up with continental developments in law but outstripped them.[14] There were other areas in which Carolingian influence was to make itself felt, notably in charter production, in the use of Carolingian minuscule script and in the development of king-making rites, the orders of service for a coronation.

Aethelstan also intervened on the Continent outside his system of alliances. Vikings had invaded Brittany at about the same time that Edward the Elder was completing his conquest of the southern Danelaw. King Edward had been made a member of the Confraternity of the Canons of Dol, and therefore many Bretons, fleeing the Norsemen, came to England. Among them was Mathedoi, Count of Poher, husband of the daughter of Alan the Great, the last ruler of all Brittany. Their son, Alan of the Twisted Beard, was baptised, if not actually born, in England and was Aethelstan's godson. In 936, with English help, Alan of the Twisted Beard re-established himself at Nantes and Vannes, his family's hereditary lands, which brought Aethelstan up against the Scandinavian invaders of Northern France. He had helped Alan against the Vikings of the Loire valley.

Before King Aethelstan's death, Count Alan's new opponents, the Normans, had begun occupying ports opposite England, seizing the Cotentin and the Avranchin in 933. The king had also had contacts with Scandinavia itself, especially with Harald Fairhair, contacts which might explain why Erik Bloodaxe came to England later in the century. Aethelstan and Harald Fairhair of Norway found a common enemy in the Viking fleets roving the North Sea and an embassy arrived from Harald, which also met Aethelstan at his great Witan at York. There Aethelstan was given an ornate warship with purple sails, and gilded shields, stern and prow.[15] It was perhaps after that that Harald's son Hakon was fostered by Aethelstan, since he was known in Norway as Aethelstan's fostri. It seems likely he was with King Aethelstan for some time and that he then returned home after his father had created his kingdom of Norway.

All these diplomatic, and warlike, manoeuvres contributed to the impression that Aethelstan was master in his kingdom. He claimed, in his royal titles as expressed in charters and on his coins, to be lord over all Britain, although his real authority still lay in southern England. The list of places where he held Witans, derived from study of his charters, shows that he rarely travelled far outside the hereditary West Saxon kingdom except perhaps on campaign.

## UNITING THE KINGDOM

Nonetheless, Aethelstan's reign, like that of his father, marked a real advance towards the formation of a united kingdom of England. Despite that, his successors, who were his brothers because, perhaps by choice, he remained unmarried and without an heir of the body, were unable to hold the unity of the kingdom and both had to fight to reinstate it. But fight for it they did, and successfully. Eadred, as a charter of his records, ended his days calling himself 'King of the Angulsexana and Overlord of Northumbria, governor of the Pagans and Defender of the Britons'.[16] He could do this because at last the Danes of Northumbria had become unwilling any longer to accept the incursion of Viking adventurers like Raegnald and Erik Bloodaxe and now preferred the peaceful rule of a southern king who could bring both law and order and trade.

It was a united country that Eadred passed to Edmund's elder son Eadwig who, despite the fact that no Viking attacks came in his short four-year reign, was unable to preserve internal unity and was compelled by resistance from the magnates, though without the overt use of force, to concede real control of northern and eastern England (Mercia, East Anglia and Northumbria) to his younger brother Edgar. On Eadwig's death, Edgar automatically became King of the English with political control, no doubt in the early years exercised through his Witan, over the whole country, a control that he held almost effortlessly for sixteen years, growing from strength to strength. He was to reduce Scandinavian influence until it re-asserted itself under Cnut.

All of Edgar's tenth-century predecessors had, with the exception of Eadwig, carried out a slow but sure territorial expansion that had enhanced the prestige of the kingship, produced greater political stability and, in the case of Aethelstan, even initiated a foreign policy with an interest in continental affairs and a European reputation. Royal patronage of the Church had continued throughout the period, with an uncontested right to appoint bishops, and the sacred character of the monarchy had been enhanced by coronations involving anointing and crowning by the Archbishops. New regnal titles had been devised and are found frequently used in charters, not just *Rex Anglorum* ('King of the English'), but titles like *Basileus*, meaning 'High King'.

Kings had widened the area covered by their written law, and from the time of Edmund an oath of fealty had been required of all free men, binding them to their king as a man was bound to his lord: personal allegiance to the king.[17] It is probable too that these kings were literate, as Edward the Elder certainly was and as the ealdormen of King Alfred and their sons, who lived on to serve Edward, also were. It seems reasonable to assume that Aethelstan, who possessed books and gave them as gifts to Churches, was literate. He had been brought up in the household of Aethelflaed, who had also been educated at her father's command. As written legislation developed during the century it is logical to suggest that those involved in government, from the king himself down through his ealdormen and *ministri* (thegns), as well as the bishops and chaplains who inhabited the court and saw to it that royal charters were produced, could all read and write. In his turn, Edgar had been brought up in the household of Aethelstan Half-King, ealdorman of East Anglia from 932, with his education completed at the hands of Abbot Aethelwold, so he too can confidently be said to have been literate.

The use of written instruments in government had revived under Alfred the Great, and as a result, law codes were preserved in writing and royal instructions were issued in written form. (It might be premature to refer to these as 'writs', though, despite the evidence that they were possibly sealed and accompanied by an actual seal as evidence of authenticity.) Royal charters from Aethelstan's reign onwards were produced under conditions that suggest the development of a writing office, a secretariat devoted to the production of charters. It would be premature to call this a chancery or postulate the appointment of an official in charge of it called a Chancellor.

Royal messages had to be authenticated, because to disobey a genuine royal command given in this way was to disobey the king himself. To make a system of written orders, written law codes and charters required the existence of a writing office, and it has been demonstrated conclusively[18] that the charters (no written royal orders have survived from this period) were produced by a writing office and not, as in former times, by the clerical recipients themselves. The origins of this office can be traced back certainly to the reign of Aethelstan.

Some charters show signs of having been produced in specific ecclesiastical centres, themselves used as centres for the activity of the royal court, such as Winchester and Sherborne, and it has been persuasively argued that there was a small group of royal clerks available at court recruited from the scriptoria, or writing centres, of the monasteries or Episcopal sees. This was necessary because the king's household and his court were peripatetic. Medieval kings were constantly on the move, not least because they had to move from one royal estate to another to consume the stores of provisions held there for them, the product of the right to be supplied with a set number of days and nights of provisions called the 'feorm'. The study of charters has revealed that on many occasions several of them were produced from one location, suggesting that they were issued at meetings of the Witan (the royal council or Witenagemot) attended by archbishops and bishops, ealdormen and Danish earls, king's thegns (*ministri* in Latin) and members of his household. On occasion even subject kings and princes from Wales, Strathclyde, Scotland or the Western Isles might attend, and foreign embassies be received.

All this required, as Alfred the Great is thought to have realised, a supply of literate, educated royal servants. It has even been suggested that the writing office might in fact have already been in use in Alfred's day and that he was imitating the forms of Carolingian government, such as the *Hof Kapelle* of Charlemagne with its chancery and royal messengers, the *missi dominici*.[19]

Below the royal court there operated the highest group in the population, subject only to the authority of the king himself, who presided at tribunals, gave their opinion, and enjoyed established rights of all kinds: the ealdormen, bishops (and, under Edgar, abbots), king's thegns and his reeves. Kings found ways of fostering the image, and reality, of a united kingdom by employing all these officials in a nationwide administrative system.

Military supremacy, especially over York, had been decided in favour of the West Saxon dynasty as the use of the word 'England' to describe their kingdom emerged over the second half of the tenth century. Kings found that they still had to respect local custom and law-making, hence the emergence of the convention that there were three areas of law in England: West Saxon Law, Mercian Law and Dane Law. So law-making and administration was left in the hands of the local aristocracy, whether English or Danish, notably in the region of the Five Boroughs (Lincoln, Leicester, Stamford, Nottingham and Derby), where local autonomy was recognised by Edgar in the 960s.

Further north, power was left in the hands of the House of Bamburgh, and at York a Dane, Oslac, was earl, with his power constrained by the appointment of Archbishops of York who, though of Scandinavian origin, came from south of the Humber.[20] Those northern earls, as they gradually became known (rather than ealdormen), probably exercised power from the old palace complex at York, gave the region leadership in war, lordship and secular patronage, and had their own household troop or genge, to be known in the eleventh century as housecarls. The archbishops, too, played

their part in the administration of justice, and even the merchants of York had
a degree of self-government. Elsewhere, the territorial aristocracy was led
by magnates called holds (previously the title of a subordinate commander
of raiding armies), equivalent in power and rank to the northern English
high reeves.

Strangely, royal interest in the maintenance and diffusion of the *Anglo-
Saxon Chronicles* was allowed to lapse, and the entries for most of the
mid-tenth century are sparse except when the reform of the monasteries
under Edgar was concerned. Even then, most of what is known derives
from the saints' lives rather than the *Chronicles*.

So the roots of Edgar's reign and of his power lay in the making of the
Kingdom of England by his predecessors, Edward the Elder and his three
sons, Aethelstan, Edmund and Eadred. Edgar's reign was to see the return of
more settled conditions, especially south of the Thames.

At one time, historians might have sought an explanation in terms of the
effect on society of the ownership of the means of production – which in
the tenth century, as for most of the Middle Ages, meant the ownership of
land – or else in terms of a class struggle. Others might have tried to explain
the events of the tenth century in terms of a struggle for racial domination
between men of Saxon, Anglian, Danish or even Norse origin.

A combined view would see it as the wresting of the means of production
(land) from the hands of Viking exploiters, which restored it to the control
of English kings and ealdormen. Then Edgar would be seen as transferring
control over large parts of that means of production into the hands of monks.
The significant point here is that the Church as an institution did not die,
and although abbots and bishops always have heirs, their ecclesiastical estates
did not render heriot[21] to the king as lord as lay land-holders did. But it is
by no means certain that men in the tenth century would have viewed the
situation in that way.

The class struggle interpretation would require historians to see a source
of possible conflict between laymen, as a class, and the monks, hence the
rather lazy label applied to events after Edgar's death as an 'anti-monastic
reaction'. None of these facile interpretations really serves to explain the
success of Edgar's reign. That is to be found in Edgar's own ability and
character, so different from that of his predecessor, Eadwig, or that of his
successors Edward the Martyr and Aethelred the Unready.

Aethelstan's reign had seen the creation of an ideology, an ideas system,
for British politics and government. This is visible in official documents,

especially charters, reflected in the somewhat overblown and inflated style and titles attributed to him. Edmund in his turn had inherited a single realm, a political unit, created by his predecessor, though he had to fight to hold on to it. His success in war meant that he governed all England, and, as master of all that Aethelstan had acquired, was lord of what has been termed a 'Pan-British Imperium' or overlordship of Britain. This means that he had the power to exact tribute from 'vassal' kings (as they would have been termed in continental Europe) and to require their obsequious attendance at meetings of his court. It did not mean that he had an 'empire' for which he made laws and governed directly.[22] Edmund could be called *Curagulus multarum gentium* and *favente superne numine basileus Anglorum caeterarumque gentium in circuitu persistentium*, that is 'guardian of many peoples' and 'by divine favour High King of the English people and of peoples dwelling round about'.

It is a fact that Aethelstan had conquered Strathclyde, which he then granted on favourable terms to Malcolm MacDomnaill, and that by the end of his reign all the kingdoms of Wales were under English overlordship (though by the eleventh century much of this dominance had been lost and Cnut made no attempt to recover it). In 942, Idwal of Gwynedd, who had presumably either rebelled or refused tribute, was killed during an English incursion; as a result, Gwynedd was occupied by Hywel Dda of Deheubarth, a true Anglophile.

Aethelstan had begun the practice of governing through great councils of state, enlarged Witenagemots, which brought together magnates from all parts of his dominions, creating opportunities for them to find common ground and promoting cultural assimilation. His reign thereby saw fifteen years of legislative activity. By 927 he had seen to it that there was no other king in England and ensured at least nominal overlordship of Scotland and Wales. His army operated further north than Edward the Elder had ever done but his campaigns were, in a sense, counter-productive in that they provoked a Norse-Scottish alliance.

All the evidence suggests that Aethelstan had become aware of the changed nature of English kingship, which perhaps explains the quasi-imperial pretensions displayed in his charters. Even his coins claimed that he was *Rex totius Britanniae*, King of the whole of Britain. Although those charters which make use of the word *Imperator*, emperor, are now regarded as forgeries and so cannot be used, as hitherto, to substantiate theories of an Anglo-Saxon Empire, they are evidence that forgers, looking back to his reign, perceived him as an imperial figure, impressed by his success and his continental reputation. He legislated for the use of a single currency throughout England, licensed to be minted in boroughs, and excluded the use of foreign coins. To his reign belongs the first use on coins of a crowned head of the monarch.

There does seem to have been an 'imperial' dimension to the concept of English kingship, as evidenced by the use of the style *basileus*, often used by Greek emperors in addressing foreign rulers. It was perhaps used in the sense that the King of the English was an independent monarch with no overlord as well as ruler of several peoples, Angles, Saxons, Danes and Norsemen, and overlord of Scots and Britons. Overlordship is a dominant theme of his charters, as it is of later kings – overlordship of a domain called either Britannia or Albion. Later writers saw him as first King of England, who transmitted his overlordship of Celtic peoples to his successors.[23]

Aethelstan's rule had been repeatedly challenged, as was that of his successors, Edmund and Eadred. It is Edgar who really deserves the accolade of being the first unchallenged King of England. It was from his reign onwards that English kings ruled a realm that included Northumbria as a matter of course. Aethelstan had used three powerful instruments of royal propaganda, charters, coinage and legislation; Edgar was to make excellent use of all three, and to add to them the tremendous coup of a magnificent quasi-imperial coronation against the backdrop of Roman Bath, followed by an equally elaborate demonstration of his overlordship at Chester. Well could he boast that he was 'monarch of the whole of England and of the kings of the seas and islands round about it'.[24] England truly was in Edgar's day the preponderant element in what was eventually to become the United Kingdom. In his reign, also, the Church came to play its full part in the administrative and psychological unification of England.

# 3

# Edgar and his Circle
# Rise to Power

Edgar's reign cannot be described in terms of a long series of events and incidents, as can be done for some of his predecessors and successors such as Aethelstan or Aethelred, simply because such material is not available. He apparently fought no wars and so they cannot be described by the writers of the *Anglo-Saxon Chronicles*, who turned instead to his religious activities. Even their account of those has to be filled out by reference to other sources.

Instead, an account of his reign, divided into its secular and ecclesiastical components, depends upon the interpretation of such sources as codes of law, both those of Edgar and those of his predecessors and successors, the content of charters, especially their witness lists, the many references to him in the lives of the saintly men who played such a striking role in his affairs, and the later Anglo-Norman chroniclers. Both of the latter sources of information need to be treated with circumspection since their authors all had their own agenda. All sorts of information can be integrated and focused on Edgar to demonstrate the ways in which he was part of a long-standing tradition, deriving from his great-grandfather Alfred, and the ways in which he differed in character and achievements from the other kings of his dynasty.

Some explanation has to be found for the fact that his reign was a sea of comparative calm amid an ocean of warfare, and why he was able to deter the attacks which were to overwhelm his son Aethelred. Some part of this may lie in the unknown and so far irrecoverable history of the relations between English kings and Scandinavia. Edgar certainly deterred attacks from Scots and Welshmen, from the Norsemen of Dublin and the petty kings of the Isles and from the Viking fleets roaming the North Sea and the Channel. But that is not the whole story. His reign was also remarkable for the lack of opposition to his rule from within. There were no rebellions of any consequence, no alliances of northern magnates with roving Viking intruders, and his ealdormen and nobles acquiesced without recorded demur in the revival of Benedictine monasticism and the transfer of large quantities of landed property to the hands of monastic communities.

In 955 and as the elder aetheling, probably aged about fifteen, Eadwig was recognised in preference to Edgar, then only about twelve, in succession to King Eadred. Yet, within two years, by sheer irresponsibility, Eadwig had lost the support of over half of his magnates, probably the more powerful half, and the major part, geographically speaking, of his kingdom. In 955 the West Saxons and the Mercians each separately chose Eadwig for king. The Northumbrians appear to have accepted the decision of the southerners. Then, some time between May and December 957, the Mercians, supported by the Northumbrians, renounced their allegiance and chose Edgar, now rising fifteen, as their king.

It does not seem to have been a separatist movement, nor a rejection of the Anglo-Saxon system of government. Eadwig was still recognised as 'King of the English', but Edgar was now 'King of the Mercians and Northumbrians'. Three of those appointed to positions of authority by Eadwig remained in office under Edgar: Aethelwold, ealdorman of East Anglia (the successor of his father the half-king), Byrhtnoth, ealdorman of Essex, and Aelfhere, ealdorman of Mercia. The fourth, Aelfheah of Hampshire, supported Eadwig. He was to remain in office, even under Edgar, until his death in 971 or 972. Despite the criticisms made of him, Eadwig does seem to have chosen, or accepted, good servants.

## EADWIG, LORD OF MISRULE

Eadwig, known according to Aethelweard the Chronicler as 'All-Fair' (*Pankalus*) for his beauty, is known mainly through the writings of monks devoted to the saintly trio, Dunstan, Aethelwold and Oswald, who were either disliked or ignored by Eadwig. The monastic writers, therefore, give him a very bad reputation. One writer, for example, says that Eadwig could rule neither himself nor others, and they all seem pleased that he died young. Yet his reign marks the beginning of a period of twenty-five years during which England remained free of the threat of invasion until the Danes began raiding again in 980.

Writers in the following generations attributed this peace to the good government and wisdom of his successor, King Edgar. Yet the four secular pillars of Edgar's reign, Aelfhere, Byrhtnoth, Aethelwold and Aelfheah, all came to power under Eadwig. Edgar, as King of Mercia and Northumbria, also benefited from the support, until his retirement and death in 960, of Aethelstan Half-King. But Eadwig should have benefited from the absence of Viking raids during his short reign and therefore from his not having to raise heavy taxes.[1] It is possible that the loyalty Edgar commanded as king in the North actually explains why no Viking attack took place; no one in the North made any move to invite them back.

Eadwig's problems, in part at least, seem to stem from his indifference to the movement for monastic reform and he might even have been opposed to it. Yet he was not an enemy of the Church in general. He began his reign rich in land, inheriting the royal demesne, as his gifts of land recorded in some sixty charters demonstrate. He might have been trying to buy support. He gave lands to Oda, Archbishop of Canterbury, and to the priests of Brampton in Oxfordshire.[2] Southwell Minster was founded on land provided by Eadwig, and though his reign was short his gifts are numerous enough to suggest that he and his council were not actually hostile to monasticism as an institution. Perhaps he opposed Benedictine reform because of its associations with Dunstan, whom he came to regard as his enemy and sent into exile.

Dunstan came into conflict with Eadwig from the very start. It was he who reproved the errant young king when Eadwig absented himself from the coronation banquet for a period of dalliance with a certain noblewoman, Aethelgifu, and her daughter, Aelfgifu, who were endeavouring to entice him into marriage. He did subsequently marry the daughter. (Such a marriage would have been seen by the supporters of Edgar as a threat to his chances of succeeding to the throne.) The tale of this affair lost nothing in the telling and the details were obviously exaggerated soon afterwards. They were enlarged upon even more in the Anglo-Norman period. Whatever the truth, the king's absence was noticed by the assembled nobles and by Archbishop Oda. Dunstan and Cynsige, Bishop of Lichfield, were sent to find him. He was discovered, his crown thrown aside into a corner of the room, *in flagrante* with the two ladies. There was a heated confrontation and the two clerics dragged him back to the feast. By Christian standards, his conduct had been poor, as a coronation was a real attempt to secure God's blessing on a king and his kingdom.

Men in the tenth century genuinely believed in the power of God's grace and saw a real connection between the hallowing of a king and the prosperity of his country. So Eadwig's behaviour had shocked those present, caused real fear for the future and quite possibly turned many men's thoughts towards Edgar. The elder of the two ladies, Aethelgifu, 'the cynges wifes moder' as she later became for a time, never forgave Dunstan for frustrating her designs; it is said that she had actually hoped to marry Eadwig herself, and through her influence over the young man, Dunstan was exiled and lost his property. His exile was to have unexpected benefits for English monasticism.

The later versions of this story add grotesque and unhistorical detail such as the subsequent branding and barbarous death of Aethelgifu, and the whiff of scandal in the earliest version is contradicted by the fact that the king actually married her daughter. Archbishop Oda was subsequently said to have annulled the marriage on the grounds of consanguinity between the couple,[3] which suggests that either Aelfgifu or her mother could have been of collateral royal descent. Aelfgifu was apparently a third cousin once removed (descended from Aethelred, King of Wessex), and so within the forbidden degrees of marriage. The relationship would certainly have been known before the marriage took place and the annulment therefore looks like a calculated political gesture, since, had the will to do so been there, a dispensation could have been granted. Then Eadwig died on 1 October 959, and Aelfgifu subsequently became a nun at New Minster, Winchester, where the *Liber Vitae* records her as the wife of King Eadwig and one of the 'illustrious women, choosing this holy place for the love of God'.[4] Churchmen of high rank did not shrink from attending court when both women were present.

The statement about the annulment comes from only one source and that rather too late to be entirely authoritative. The essential point seems to be that Dunstan had managed to insult the king, the woman whom he married, and her mother, and so got himself exiled. Eadwig also deprived his grandmother, Edward the Elder's widow Eadgifu (mother of Edmund and Eadred), of her estates.[5] She was a witness to many of her sons' charters, but none of Eadwig's. She was perhaps an advocate for Edgar's claims rather than those of Eadwig. In the tenth century the rule of primogeniture did not apply. It looks also as though Eadwig might have ignored the terms of Eadred's will and buried him at Winchester, contrary to his wishes. The clerks at the Minster in Winchester, who were unable to gain full possession

of estates left to them by Eadred, together with Dunstan and the Queen
Dowager Eadgifu, were the main objects of Eadwig's spite.

Whatever the truth behind all this, and one must suspect a great deal
of political in-fighting, Eadwig had fallen out with several of his most
influential magnates. Dunstan's biographer attributes Eadwig's failure to his
having chosen young advisers 'as thoughtless as himself', which suggests a
preference for the advice of West Saxons amongst whom he had grown up
rather than the Ealdorman Aelfhere of Mercia and the sons of Aethelstan
Half-King. He was accused of 'losing the shrewd and wise who disapproved
of his folly and eagerly annexing ignorant men of his own kin'.

One result of that seems to have been the decision of Aethelstan Half-
King to retire to a monastery, Glastonbury, where he died before 960.[6] He
thus stepped down from his position just as Edgar became old enough
to rule. Eadwig gave as the reason for the exiling of Dunstan that he was
guilty of maladministration of the 'treasure' in Eadred's reign and that he
had refused to account for what he had spent. In Dunstan's absence his
supporters became increasingly critical of Eadwig's rule. He was seen as
dissolute and impatient and disliked for promoting men who were perhaps,
like Aelfgifu and her mother, descendants of King Aethelred of Wessex who
died in 871.[7]

Eadwig might have been trying to break free of the control exercised
by the established magnates who had served and supported his father and
his uncle. The scale of his gifts of land suggests a response to the loss of
confidence in his rule and an attempt to buy support. The lands he used
were not appropriated from the Church to any great extent, nor did
he dissipate royal resources. Much of the land he gave away came from
confiscation of the estates of those who had done well under Edmund and
Eadred. The scandal at his coronation might have had something more
serious behind it, and Dunstan was most surely involved in whatever went
wrong. The habit of political obedience remained strong for a time and no
others joined Dunstan in exile. These tensions then brought about the split
of 957, possibly made all the more likely by Eadwig's protection given to
married clerks at Glastonbury and Malmesbury. That cannot have pleased
those who were pressing for monastic reform, but otherwise the underlying
reasons for Eadwig's unpopularity remain unknown.

Two parties had emerged by 957, one headed by Eadwig's grandmother
Eadgifu, hoping for Edgar's eventual succession, and the other by Aethelgifu
and her daughter, both perhaps seeking control over the fifteen-year-old

king. Eadwig's father Edmund had been a successful king, and Edmund's wife, also called Aelfgifu, was a benefactress of Shaftesbury where a cult of her sanctity had developed. There was no obvious reason why Eadwig should have been the target of slanderous accusations. He and Aethelgifu's daughter were not yet married and their behaviour might have been open to misinterpretation; some commentators have hinted at grandmotherly jealousy and others at a clerical conspiracy, but there is no evidence to support either view.

## A DIVIDED REALM

The result, in 957, was what most authorities label as a rebellion, although the *Chronicles* do not seem to support such a view. One says, '955… Eadwig succeeded to the kingdom of Wessex and his brother Edgar succeeded to the kingdom of Mercia',[8] another that Eadwig succeeded to 'the kingdom' in 956 and that 'the aetheling Edgar succeeded to the kingdom of Mercia' in 957.[9] The other versions ignore Edgar's elevation altogether until after Eadwig's death. Only the *Vita Dunstani* sees it as a northern rebellion and tells the story as one of civil war, though that could be partisan spin. There is no record of any actual conflict. It might be that the two sides took the same view as that recorded on another occasion, in 1051, when Edward the Confessor fell out with Earl Godwin of Wessex. They also almost came to open war; however:

> Then some of them considered it would be very unwise if they joined battle, because there was in those two companies most of the finest that was in England and considered that they would be leaving the land open to our enemies.[10]

In fact the two sides seem to have separated amicably, accepting a political settlement between evenly matched parties. It is the case that York had only come under West Saxon rule three years earlier and that it was only forty years since Edward the Elder had annexed Mercia. In 957 therefore, the royal patrimony, Wessex, went to Eadwig, the elder brother, and the more recent acquisitions to Edgar, the younger brother, just as each in turn was old enough to rule without a regent. As the account in the *Life of Dunstan* admits, the jurisdiction of the two kings was neatly divided at the Thames

'by the decision of the wise men': that is, the Witan of both regions and
'the witness of the whole people'. The bishops and ealdormen north of the
Thames supported Edgar and those to the south supported Eadwig, who
retained the title of 'King of the English'. Edgar was accepted as 'King of the
Mercians and the Northumbrians'. So there was a purely territorial division
between the two courts.

One possible explanation that has been advanced is that such a division
might have been contemplated while Eadred still lived, with the intention
of having it implemented after his death, but that the conditions had not
yet been finalised when he died earlier than expected and while Edgar
was still too young. If so then perhaps the Mercian magnates decided,
unilaterally, to implement the arrangement as soon as Edgar was thought
old enough to reign.[11] Eadwig had never established enough support north
of the Thames. He died young and his uncle Eadred had died relatively so
after long illness. Even Edgar was to die at 32. There might well have been
some sort of hereditary weakness. Edgar reigned in Mercia and over the
Northumbrians, East Anglians and Britons[12] for two years, issuing his own
charters and holding the major part of the whole kingdom of England in
terms of area. He did not issue his own coinage. It might have been part of
the arrangement that Eadwig would retain control of the coinage, just as
Edward the Elder had done while Aethelred and Aethelflaed ruled Mercia.
Edgar was certainly the junior partner.[13]

When Eadwig died, however, Edgar was accepted as king south of the
Thames, and there was little change in the personnel of the government
but momentous change in ecclesiastical affairs. Edgar and his Witan were to
keep England secure from foreign invasion for the next twenty years while
maintaining internal order. Some have rated Edgar lower than Alfred the
Great and Aethelstan simply because he did not, as they did, have to defend
England against barbarians or deal with a barbarian state such as York within
Britain itself. Yet it is a sign of the strength of his rule that his reign is so
singularly devoid of recorded incident. The first event to make a strong
impression on contemporaries, apart from the restoration of Benedictine
monasticism, was his allegedly deferred coronation of 973.

Edgar's rule had begun in 957 when for three years he reigned as King
'of the Mercians and of the Northumbrians'. Little is known of the nature
of his rule, possibly because having come to the throne as the figurehead
of a faction of magnates, and being only a youth of fourteen, he was still
thoroughly under the tutorship of his foster-father Aethelstan Half-King,

ealdorman of East Anglia. The latter, together with his brothers, Aethelwold in the South-East and Eadric in Wessex, had controlled over half the country during the reigns of Edmund and Eadred.

## AETHELSTAN HALF-KING

This man was the country's leading ealdorman, controlling the whole of the eastern Danelaw between 943 and 957, having lived to see his protégé Edgar elevated to the Kingship of Mercia. In that year he went into retirement at Glastonbury (and was buried there when he died some time before 960), leaving his brother Aethelwold, Edgar's foster-brother, as his successor. The other leading figure was Aelfhere, ealdorman of English Mercia.

The family of Aethelstan Half-King was, like most tenth-century ealdormen, descended from a cadet branch of the royal family. Aethelstan himself, at the height of his power, governed the whole of the eastern Danelaw, an area the size of Normandy, and owned vast estates outside his own ealdormanry. As the most influential adviser of Edmund, who had succeeded to the throne in his teens, the ealdorman was, for a short while, virtually regent of the kingdom. He was a son of the Mercian ealdorman Aethelfrith, who controlled south-east Mercia, one of those selected by Alfred to replace the Mercian nobles who had defected to the Danes. His brothers, Aethelwold and Eadric, were also ealdormen. The careers of these three brothers help to explain the choice of Aethelstan to be Ealdorman of East Anglia, as the areas they controlled did not fall vacant at the right moment for him to be given an ealdormanry in Mercia itself. He was appointed by Edward the Elder to succeed the East Anglian Alfred shortly after 932.

East Anglia was the largest and wealthiest province acquired by the monarchy; it included Norfolk and Suffolk, Cambridgeshire and Huntingdonshire and the fenland of 'Holland' in Lincolnshire, as well as the eight hundreds of Oundle which included what became the Soke of Peterborough. But the ealdorman's real authority extended beyond this to take in the whole of the eastern Danelaw from the Thames to the Welland. It was his achievement to ensure that the eastern Danelaw remained loyal to its new kings. There were no revolts, there was no collaboration with the Danes, no subversive encouragement for the Norsemen. The most striking event was the punishment of Thetford, by ravaging, in 952, for complicity in the assassination of Abbot Eadhelm of St Augustine's in Canterbury.[14]

It was probably Aethelstan who brought administration in the East into line with that of Wessex, overseeing the introduction of assessment in hides for example, and, significantly, allowing the Danes under his government a great deal of autonomy, an example followed by his foster-son Edgar when he became king. While Aethelstan held the eastern region, Edmund and Eadred were able to recover control of the North between 942 and 946, and he should perhaps be allowed some of the credit for the planning and execution of their campaigns, especially during the reign of the sickly Eadred. He was a friend of the Church, helping in the consolidation of the conversion of the Danes and the rebuilding of the diocesan framework.[15]

His wife, Aelfwyn, came from a Huntingdonshire family whose household was probably somewhere in the Brunneswald, the wooded lands along the fen edge. It was, as the *Ramsey Chronicle* confirms, Aelfwyn who fostered Edgar, rather than his step-mother Aethelflaed. Aelfwyn's youngest son Aethelwine was probably three or four years older than Edgar and they would have been brought up together. It was almost certainly in this household that Edgar came to accept the need for monastic reform; his foster-brother Aethelwine was the principal lay patron of the movement after the king himself.

It has been suggested that it was in this household too that Edgar came under the influence of Dunstan and Abbot Aethelwold. The charters issued between 942 and 955 may have been under Aethelstan's influence, and it is suggested that they were the work of a scribe from Glastonbury supervised by Dunstan.[16]

The fostering of Edgar by Aethelstan Half-King was to have repercussions during his reign that helped shape the course of English history. Edmund had been influenced by his mother, Eadgifu, and by the half-king, and they must have determined much of his policy. Nor did things change much under Eadred, who was a chronic invalid. Aethelstan remained high in the witness lists under Eadred and after 949 is found at the very top, apparently controlling south-east and central Mercia as well as his other territories. His total possessions in estates were vast, unmatched by any other tenth-century magnate.

It is from the witness lists appended to most charters that historians can find out which magnates were most often at court and which were the most influential. Such lists begin with the name of the king, who is followed in the list of attestations firstly by archbishops and bishops (and from Edgar's reign onwards, abbots). Then come the ealdormen, and any Danish earls, in order of precedence, and they are followed by the king's thegns and miscellaneous clerics. Study of this material shows that men who had started out quite a long way down the list, among the thegns, rise up the list over the years if they prosper in the king's service, while others appear lower down. Some may even rise to become ealdormen. Similarly, priests of the household may become bishops or abbots. Among the ealdormen, also, various individuals may move further up, or down, the lists as they move into or out of the king's favour. So the varying composition of the Witan can be traced in the lists.

As the records show, Eadred's death on 23 November 955 led to a change of fortunes. The reign of his nephew Eadwig was to bring the banishment of Dunstan, the seizure of the queen mother's estates and significant changes in the Witan. New ealdormen were created, and most significantly, Eadwig's kinsman Aelfhere was given central Mercia on 12 February 956, at Aethelstan's expense. Those who were later to be prominent among the supporters of reformed monasticism were out of favour. The half-king's influence waned and by 956 he had decided to retire. His son Aethelwold stepped forward as his father's understudy in East Anglia, and possibly also in Essex, as the ealdorman Byrhtferth ceased to appear in the witness lists at this time. When his father went to be a monk at Glastonbury, Aethelwold succeeded him as ealdorman in East Anglia. Other changes included the appointment of Byrhtnoth to Essex and Aelfhere's brother Aelfheah to western Wessex.

Although his changes secured Eadwig some support in Wessex, the king failed utterly to win any backing north of the Thames, and Edgar broke away in 957 supported by the local bishops and ealdormen to become 'King of the Mercians and Northumbrians'. Aethelwold transferred his allegiance to Edgar and, according to a late and often reliable account, was given overlordship of York and southern Northumbria.[17]

Edgar would have been too young to dominate his council, but he was able to bring to court his other three foster-brothers, Aelfwold, Aethelsige, and Aethelwine. Such young noblemen seem to have begun acting as witnesses with the title 'thegn' at seventeen or eighteen and to have been capable of rising to the rank of ealdorman in their twenties. Most died in their forties, a few surviving into the fifties or sixties (Churchmen and women survived longer).

The brothers dominate the witness lists. Aelfwold had a career lasting until 990, but remained only of thegnly rank under Edgar. Aethelsige rose to be a high court official, *camerarius* or keeper of the king's secrets, until 963. He was active in the administration of East Anglia until about 987 and was a benefactor of Ramsey. Aethelwine succeeded Aethelwold as ealdorman in 962. He was close to Edgar, possibly because he was nearest in age. After 970 he was one of the four most senior ealdormen, along with Aelfhere of Mercia (with whom he was entrusted with the publication of Edgar's last law code), Byrhtnoth of Essex and Oslac of Northumbria.

Thanks to the records at Ramsey and Ely, much more is known about Aethelwine than any other ealdorman. His activities, typical of the work of such men, are recorded in detail: presiding over his shire and over groups of hundreds, sitting in court accompanied by a royal reeve, or a diocesan bishop, attending moots at Cambridge or Ely. He had his own residence in the form of a hall at Upwood near Ramsey, and held land all over East Anglia. Florence of Worcester was to term him *Amicus Dei* or God's friend, probably a translation of some vernacular phrase referring to his leadership of the cause of monastic reform.

## THE MERCIAN EALDORMAN, AELFHERE

This family was not the only powerful group. There is also the family of Aelfhere of Mercia, and his connection. His family rivalled that of Aethelwine of East Anglia. Like the family of Aethelstan Half-King, Aelfhere had acquired power under King Edmund. The origins of the family are obscure, but they claimed to be kin to the Mercian kings. Aelfhere was son to Ealdorman Ealhelm of Mercia (940–941) and he had seen the loss and recovery of the Five Boroughs and the struggle for York. When the kingdom divided in 957 and his brother Aelfheah remained with Eadwig in Wessex, Aelfhere supported Edgar in Mercia, as Aethelstan did in East Anglia. Aelfhere was an ealdorman by 959 and before that probably acted as steward of the household to the young king.

So Aelfhere attained eminence as a lay supporter of Edgar, and, when Aethelstan retired, took his place at the king's side. The *Vita Oswaldi* calls him *Princeps Merciorum Gentis* or prince of the Mercian people, in recognition of his great influence in Mercia, but in the Leases of Bishop Oswald of Worcester he signs simply as ealdorman of Mercia. He witnesses as leading ealdorman early in Edgar's reign after 959 and his brother Aelfwine signs at the head of the *ministri* or king's thegns. Aelfhere ruled first north-west

Mercia after 965 and then the south-west after 970, taking control of central Wessex on the death of Aelfheah in 971 or 972. He might well have objected to the creation of Oswaldslow (the triple hundred or ship soke granted to the bishop by King Edgar),[18] which he was unable to prevent despite his consent being required for Bishop Oswald's leasehold grants. He and his family favoured Glastonbury and Abingdon but gave nothing to Oswald's foundations.

Aelfhere was at the height of his power in the last years of Edgar, one of the elite along with Aethelwine, Byrhtnoth and Oslac. As he became 'the blast of the mad wind which came from the western territories',[19] he had obviously objected to the way things were going and the supremacy of the party of monastic reform.[20]

The web of relationships extended far and wide. Aelfhere's nephew Aelfwine was kin to Ealdorman Byrhtnoth, either by blood or marriage, and Byrhtnoth himself married the daughter of Aelfgar his predecessor as ealdorman of Essex. The chronicler Aethelweard claimed kinship to Aelfheah, brother of Aelfhere.

Byrhtnoth was ealdorman of Essex, often termed earl in later sources, and an important lord in his own right. He is known to have been prominent at Cambridge in the case of a dispute over the ownership of Fen Ditton and associated with Aethelwine in disputes over Ely's estates, such as that at Bluntisham.[21] He regularly presided at shire courts in Cambridgeshire and Huntingdonshire and was to make substantial grants to Ely in Aethelred II's reign. Appointed by Eadwig, he remained in office under Edgar. His wife was called Aelflaed, and in her will she leaves two estates to ealdorman Aethelmaer, son of Aethelweard the Chronicler. Perhaps he too was a relative.[22] Other connections could be established through fostering. Edgar was fostered by Aethelstan Half-King and his wife, and as king he raised five of their brothers and sons to the rank of ealdorman.

The two families of Aelfhere and Aethelstan dominated the councils of King Edgar and it could be that their rivalry enabled him to retain control of the Witan, playing one off against the other. The withdrawal of the northern peoples from the control of King Eadwig in 957 was the last time a Mercian council 'elected' a king, something which had not been done since the election of Aethelstan in 924. They gave Edgar control of all royal prerogatives in Mercia. Even when Eadwig settled a lawsuit at Sunbury in Middlesex, the Mercians referred it to Edgar and his council, who upheld it. Charters of Edgar refer to old Mercian regions such as the Magonsaeta

(Herefordshire and south Shropshire) and the Wreoconsaeta (The Wrekin, Shropshire).

It looks as though the Mercians wanted Edgar to preserve their customary law, something he was also to do for the Danes. This was not separatism but a bid to establish exactly what position the Danes held in the newly united kingdom. It has been maintained that when there was talk of Edgar and empire, that something more like a confederacy than an autocracy was intended; the ancient idea of the king as leader of allied peoples based on the defence of common interests, rather than a regime based on conquest and domination. That goes some way to explaining the peace of Edgar's reign. It coincides exactly with Aelfhere's rise and his acquisition of all the lands of Aethelred, Lord of the Mercians. If that is so, then politics rather than religion would lie behind the so-called 'anti-monastic reaction' led by Aelfhere after Edgar's death. [23]

Little is known of Edgar's rule in the North other than a record of gifts in a number of charters and the decision to recall Dunstan from exile and make him a bishop. [24] Land in Flint and Cheshire was granted to the *familia*, in this case an ecclesiastical household or community, of the Mercian saint Werburh at Chester. Aelfheah and Aethelstan both received grants, in Huntingdonshire and Essex respectively. Aethelstan is titled *Comes*, an elevated version of 'ealdorman' in Latin, and two thegns, Eahlstan and Eanulf, were given land in Herefordshire and Oxfordshire. Finally 'bishop' Oscytel received a grant in Sutton, Nottinghamshire; this was the Archbishop of York. He had been granted land at Southwell and elsewhere in Nottinghamshire by Eadwig in 956 but that had not prevented him from accepting Edgar as king in Northumbria. [25]

Then Eadwig died, somewhat unexpectedly, in 959, and Edgar became king over Wessex and the whole of England without the slightest difficulty. There were no great changes in government; the two Witans combined without causing any disruption and Eadwig's ealdormen and thegns transferred allegiance to Edgar. The only casualty was Bishop Brihthelm, Eadwig's choice as Archbishop of Canterbury to replace Aelfsige, Bishop of Winchester, who had been chosen to replace Oda, who died in 958.

Aelfsige, unfortunately for him, froze to death in the Alps on his way to Rome for his pallium. Then Brihthelm was chosen by Eadwig and unceremoniously dismissed by Edgar (who preferred Dunstan) before he had been consecrated and before he had the chance to visit Rome for his pallium. He had been Eadwig's Bishop of London and had hastily moved into Wessex, taking his episcopal seat to Wells in Somerset, when the division took place in 957. Edgar appears to have taken offence, perhaps because Brihthelm chose to support Eadwig rather than remain at his post in London.

## THE RISE OF DUNSTAN

The exact sequence of events in the career of Dunstan at this time is confused. He was lucky to be recalled by Edgar and made a bishop by a *sapientium conventu*, a Mercian Witan at 'Brandanford' (possibly Bransford, Worcestershire, which is named Bradnesford in Domesday Book).[26] Sources differ about whether he first became Bishop of Worcester and then of London, before being elevated in 960 to Canterbury, or whether, which would fit some of the facts better, he was given London and then Worcester, since the latter see appears to have fallen vacant after Brihthelm's desertion made a vacancy at London. The answer might be that he was at first merely consecrated bishop, without being assigned to a see, as the rank would have given him additional authority and status at the Mercian court. He would have served as auxiliary or suffragan bishop to Cynewald of Worcester, succeeding to that see as well as that of London,[27] before Edgar chose him for Archbishop, then promptly left to visit Rome himself in 960, where he met Pope John XII.[28] (Cynewald witnesses one charter of 958 with bishop Dunstan but not any of the four other charters of that year, and might well have died or been too ill.)[29] London fell vacant before Worcester, so Dunstan would have become bishop of the diocese after Cynewald's death as well as being Bishop of London. He became bishop of that see when it was clear that Byrhthelm had moved his see to Wells and left London vacant.

Edgar had now succeeded to the kingdom of the English, that is 'as well of the West Saxons as of the Mercians and of the Northumbrians', at the age of sixteen, quite old enough by the standards of the time to rule in his own name. The *Anglo-Saxon Chronicles* then relate, with a few scanty references to other matters, an account of his reign which focuses almost entirely on his intervention in ecclesiastical affairs. Yet surprisingly, the Peterborough version, E, records under 959 what is actually an encomium[30] on his reign better suited to the year of his death, 975. Version A, the *Winchester Chronicle*, provides a set of succinct and uninformative entries and then records the great coronation of 973 and his death in 975. Versions B and C, the *Abingdon*

*Chronicles*, and the *Worcester Chronicle* D are almost entirely lacking in useful information. Without the account by Florence of Worcester and the story of the monastic revival in the various saints' lives, little would be known from narrative sources at all.

But that encomium in the *Peterborough* (or *Laud*) *Chronicle* E provides a set of clues that can be followed up in other sources. It states that he 'improved the people's security much more than those kings who were before him within the memory of men', that 'kings and earls readily submitted to him' and that 'without battle he controlled all that he himself wished'. It also records criticism of him, that he 'did too much... one ill-deed' in that he 'loved bad, foreign habits, and brought heathen customs too fast into this land and attracted the alien [stranger] here and introduced a damaging people to this country'. Each of these statements provides a clue to the real nature of his reign.[31]

# 4

# Royal Administration

## FINANCE AND TAXATION

Edgar required that there be a single coinage throughout the kingdom, as Aethelstan had done previously: that is certain.[1] He laid down that 'one coinage shall be current throughout all the king's realm, and no-one shall refuse it'. The same Code also required a single system of measurement (presumably of length) and one standard of weights. They were to be those used in London and Winchester. Matthew Paris[2] says that Edgar issued a new coinage at the end of his reign because the weight of coins had been corrupted.

The system initiated by Edgar for the coinage required that all coins be called in and melted down at regular intervals, on average every six years, so that the metal could be re-minted and new coins issued. This was known as the *renovatio monetae* or renewal of the coinage. The dies were cut in London and distributed to local mints.[3] The number of mints in use rose sharply under Edgar from twenty-seven to sixty, and again under Aethelred II to seventy. A minimum of one mint master or moneyer to one borough was set, but some had more than one. London had eight, and boroughs with more than one moneyer account for more than half the total output of coins. Every coin had to bear the name of the moneyer and the place where it was minted. All this is evidence of the extension of the king's authority, while the growth in the volume of coins minted testifies to the increased demand following the growth of trade as well as the increasing need to pay royal dues and taxes.[4]

The system gave the king complete control over fiscal issues. He could determine the weight and fineness of the coins, even deflate or reflate the economy by changing them, and he gained each time the coins were called in and re-issued by charging the moneyers for their new dies or lowering the silver content of the coins. The royal monopoly over the coinage was almost unique in Europe; in complexity and controls it was bettered only by the Byzantine Empire.[5] The coins minted were silver pennies or *sceatas*; all other denominations, such as shillings, marks or pounds, were only units of account rather than actual coins. Silver pennies were to be minted in millions during Edgar's reign and by later kings.

So great was the demand for silver that it had to be imported. In the 960s a mine was found at Rammelsburg in the Harz Mountains of Germany, after which coins made of German silver became very widespread. Many of England's mints and largest towns were in the eastern half of the country, where there was greater economic activity as it was nearer to the Continent and was where silver was brought in from abroad. This import of precious metal was to become even more necessary, as a later source would have been needed to meet the demands for coins with which to pay off the Danes in Aethelred's reign.

Edgar as king must have been immensely rich by the standards of the time. In cash and treasures, tenth-century kings were richly endowed, and could raise larger sums in direct taxation than could most of their medieval post-Conquest successors. Though there is no evidence of heavy taxation under Edgar, the payments which his son Aethelred II was forced to make to the Danes under Swein Forkbeard and Cnut are testimony to the amount of bullion in circulation, just as the vast quantities of silver pennies demonstrate the power of the state. That Aethelred could demand payment from his people is evidence of the effectiveness of what can only be described as a bureaucracy, capable of assessing estates, in terms of hides or carucates, and demanding *geld* for the king levied against each of these units of taxation. He could, because of the work of Aethelstan but especially of Edgar, demand payment in coin of the current issue. Because of Edgar's system of *renovatio monetae* there was available an abundant current silver coinage.[6]

The king derived income from the profits of justice; the fines levied were divided in the ratio of two parts to the king and one to the ealdorman. He had the benefit of the *feorm*, fixed renders of corn, meat, bread and other provisions from royal manors sufficient to supply the needs of the court for a set number of days. By the tenth century these had been consolidated into fixed renders, probably in money terms, paid to the sheriff. Alfred the Great, as Bishop Asser reveals, could turn these renders into money if he did not receive them in kind, then could send money to distant monasteries.

There were many other customary dues, not only from royal estates but from others estates and from boroughs.

All kings from earliest times had a 'gold hoard'. In the tenth century King Eadred is recorded as lodging documentary records and inherited treasure for safe keeping with Dunstan at Glastonbury. Other ready money travelled with the king, since the court was peripatetic. By Cnut's reign the place for the deposit of wealth, records and relics was known as the king's *haligdom* or 'store of holy things'.[7] By the eleventh century, and possibly earlier, the king's treasure was held at Winchester and in the care of his chamberlains. Only after the Conquest was there an official known as a treasurer. But it is certain that some kind of accounting procedure went on, probably the responsibility of the royal reeves.

The real question is how the system originated by which estates assessed in hides (or carucates) came to be used to levy a land tax. It is evident that when estates changed hands, as sales of land, leases, gifts and bequests, they were measured in hides or similar units; the practice can be traced back for decades, if not centuries, before the tenth century. Yet the first reference to a monetary levy came in 991 when 10,000 pounds was paid as tribute to the Danes. That must have been collected from assessed estates, unless it came directly out of the king's treasure.

The next reference is more precise. In 1002, according to the *Peterborough Chronicle* E, 'In this year the king and his Witan decided to pay tribute to the fleet... and they were paid 24,000 pounds'. This futile measure was repeated over and over again, culminating in a payment of 72,000 pounds in 1018. That made a total of 206,000 pounds in all, paid over twenty-seven years. This was *gafol*, or tribute, known in post-Conquest times as *Danegeld*. It should be carefully distinguished from the payments called *heregeld* made in 1014 and 1041, which were the wages of the crews of mercenary fleets employed by the Anglo-Scandinavian kings. This system was abandoned by Edward the Confessor in 1050 and 1051 when he ceased hiring the crews, though the Peterborough chronicler confuses the matter by assuming that this was the 'tax which King Aethelred had instituted to buy off the Danes', commenting that it was thirty-nine years since he did so.

Estates had been assessed in hides for decades, and the custom of describing the size of an estate in hides went back at least to the eighth century. That assessments were of long standing is demonstrated by the anomalies which survived into the eleventh century; some estates were over-assessed and others clearly under-assessed. Some royal estates, mainly in the ancient heartland of Wessex, Wiltshire, Dorset, Hampshire and Somerset, seem never to have had customary taxes converted into geld at all, though the geld assessment had been introduced into the rest of England as a result of conquests during the tenth century.[8]

What seems to have been going on was a long-drawn-out process of converting customary dues into money payments. It seems, therefore, that the decisive steps for the territorialisation and clarification of burdens had begun under Edward the Elder and had been extended elsewhere as Wessex expanded. The culmination was in response to the demands made necessary by the renewed Danish invasions in Aethelred's reign, and it was from his reign at the latest that Old English kings became accustomed to meet any occasion for special expenditure by levying a general land tax, the geld.

Under this system, responsibility for apportioning the tax in terms of hides was transmitted downwards, first to the shire (already, as documents like the *Tribal Hidage* and the *Burghal Hidage* show, assessed in hundreds of hides), then to the individual hundred (or wapentake in the Danelaw), and thence to the individual estate, or possibly to the vill (especially in the Danelaw with its sokes and berewicks). It might even be that the possibility of assessment was in the minds of the king's Witan during the process of the creation of the territorial units themselves. Edgar reformed the coinage, a sign in itself of attention to the need for reliable money which had to be made available so that the tax could be paid. Kings create money so that they can receive their dues in cash of standardised value.[9] The hidage, or carucatage, of an estate was an artificial assessment, unrelated to capacity to pay: a 'rateable value' or notional number of hides assigned to the individual estate, via the hundred and the shire. Land had been assessed in this way originally as a basis for the levying of fyrd duty – so many men from so many hides – or as the basis of levying bridgework and of course the construction of burhs. Was it possibly the case that these burdens (or part of them) were commuted into a cash levy, the geld, in time of peace when the need to build burhs or serve in the fyrd was no longer necessary? If that is so – and it is only a hypothesis and not susceptible to direct proof – then the necessary period of peace within which the system might have been worked out points to the reign of Edgar.

## LAW AND ORDER

Providing for the security of his people was a fundamental aspect of Edgar's government. He was to do this through strict law enforcement and sound judicial institutions, which fit securely into the pattern of development in Anglo-Saxon institutions during the tenth century. What Edgar did was to build on the foundations laid by his predecessors and run the system they had originated at full power. By doing so, as the absence of disorder and the maintenance of peace indicates, Edgar became, as far as internal public security was concerned, the 'peacemaker'.

The starting point for an analysis of the situation lies in the *Hundred Ordinance*, printed in earlier collections of Old English laws as the law code I Edgar.[10] This text gives the somewhat misleading impression that the hundred was a new thing. The hundred court to which it refers is then also referred to in the text of II Edgar, which was certainly Edgar's work. This reference is misleading because the hundred as an institution, though not referred to as a court, existed in King Edmund's reign.[11] Furthermore, the division of shires into hundreds of hides (but not units of 100 hides) was very much older. Another law,[12] issued by Edward the Elder, refers to a monthly meeting at which every reeve was to hold a 'gemot'[13] every four weeks for the purpose of securing every man his 'folkright'. The *Hundred Ordinance* is descriptive rather than prescriptive, and declares what the rules are for the administration of the hundred. As it refers back to Edmund's law it is evidently issued later than his reign.

It could have been issued under Eadwig, though this is unlikely given his reputation for poor government, or it could be the work of Eadred. But no codes of law bearing the names of these two kings have survived. Most authorities tend to accept Edgar as the likely originator,[14] though this is by no means certain. What is certain is that the hundred, together with other local courts to which the text refers, operated under Edgar's government in the prescribed manner. The document itself reads as though issued by a council of magnates, unless the use of 'we have declared' and 'it is our will' indicates use of the royal 'we' as in other codes issued by Edgar. The regulations to be observed are concerned with measures for dealing with theft and its prevention.

The code conventionally numbered III Edgar refers back to what may be the *Hundred Ordinance* in clause 5: 'the hundred court shall be attended as has been previously ordained'. It goes on in the same clause to lay down that a court shall be held in all boroughs three times a year and that a shire court shall meet twice a year. The latter is to be presided over by the ealdorman and the local bishop. There is appeal to the king if the law is too oppressive, but only after justice has not been made available in the locality. Although this looks like new lawmaking, it may in fact be restating existing practice. What is new about this is that it has been put in writing, becoming *lex scripta* rather than *verbum regis*.[15] Much of the code is concerned with the prevention of theft and with dealing with men of bad reputation who fail to attend court.

As with most codes in the tenth century, Edgar is not actually necessarily making law so much as codifying existing practice so that it will be consistently followed in future. The law codes deal with hundreds as administrative units in the legal system, areas which, like shires and boroughs, had their own courts, though they also had other functions. A hundred was a unit of assessment for taxation, assessed fiscally at 100 hides. This did not mean that it contained 100 equal pieces of land of so many acres, only that the area in question, probably centred on a royal estate controlled by a reeve, paid the tax due on 100 tax units called hides.

A hundred also seems to have been a unit in the formation of the Fyrd, the national army. References are few, but it appears that the men of a particular hundred acted together in battle with their own standard. Aethelweard the Chronicler, who was in a position to know, describes the shire levies as hundreds, and in the eleventh century it was recorded that the men of Swineshead, Huntingdonshire, 'paid geld in the hundred and went with it against the enemy'.[16] It can safely be assumed that the men of other hundreds served in the same manner and had been doing so for many years.

It also looks as though a real innovation developed in Edgar's day, by which hundreds were grouped together in threes for specific purposes. One of those purposes was connected with the raising of money and/or men from groups of hundreds in order to provide warships or ships' crews for Edgar's navy. These groups of three hundreds could also have involved the grant of rights of jurisdiction over the inhabitants of the hundreds to bishops or abbots, so that the courts became episcopal or abbatial courts, as at Worcester (Oswaldslow) or at Ely.

If this is so, then Edgar was experimenting with various ways of making his government more effective. His reign is generally taken as a time when English administration reached its formal stage of completion.

The three units of that administration appear together in his legislation: shire, borough and hundred. Some even argue that the borough, that is the burh, had become a primary unit of government. This had come about as a result of the burh-building in Wessex and Mercia which meant that shires, especially those newly created, were controlled from the burhs; the shire courts began to meet in the burhs, or boroughs, which could provide them with protection against Viking attacks. Aethelstan's codes speak as though all courts were borough courts.[17] But under Edgar the shire as a separate unit was revived, as his code separated the meetings of shire and borough court. By Edgar's day, all England south of the Humber had a common structure. Shire courts were meetings of the shire thegns of an English king who, through those shire courts, were making a fixed annual payment to the king, a fixed render or yearly money payment. Consideration of the development of the tax system in the tenth century leads to the interesting speculation that Edgar was responsible for the introduction of the geld.

In 962 Edgar issued what is conventionally known as his fourth code. It can be precisely dated because it opens with the statement that Edgar has been considering what remedy could be found 'for the plague which has greatly afflicted and reduced his people throughout the length and breadth of his dominion', and according to the Winchester A text of the *Chronicles*, in 962 there was 'a very great pestilence among men'.

It is now thought that the *Hundred Ordinance* cannot be numbered as I Edgar since it cannot be shown definitely to have been his work. It is also clear that the texts usually printed as II and III Edgar are the ecclesiastical and secular halves of one code. If that is accepted then II and III Edgar together form his first code, and it then follows that the code printed as IV Edgar would be his second. It is also possible that the latter code may not be quite complete because other legislation, not found in these codes, was attributed to Edgar by early writers. Either that, or, which is by no means unlikely, there was at least one other code which has not survived. A particularly ferocious ordinance, with horrifyingly savage penalties involving mutilation, is attributed to Edgar in a work by Lantfred, a monk of Old Minster, Winchester.[18]

Edgar's extant laws are harsh enough; a man without 'surety' (*borh*), meaning a lord or associates who can guarantee his good behaviour, if found guilty of theft or treason,[19] 'whatever refuge he seeks shall never be able to save his life, unless the king grant that it be spared'; and a man accused of false witness 'shall forfeit his tongue'. Herdsmen involved in unauthorised purchase of cattle 'shall undergo the lash';[20] and a thief 'shall forfeit his head'. Earlier kings had allowed scalping, loss of the little finger or loss of a hand or foot.[21]

Lantfred, who wrote around 975, and the *Narratio Metrica de Sancto Swithuno*[22] from *c.*1000 (the content of most of which is repeated in Cnut's laws)[23] refers to a savage edict of King Edgar. Lantfred's version reads:

> At the command of the glorious king Edgar a law... was promulgated throughout England, to serve as a deterrent against all sorts of crime... that if any thief or robber were found anywhere in the homeland, he would be tortured at length [*excruciaretur diutius*] by having his eyes put out, his hands cut off, his ears torn off, his nostrils carved open, and his feet removed, and finally, with the skin and hair of his head shaved off [scalped] he would be abandoned in the open fields, dead in respect of all his limbs, to be devoured by wild beasts and birds and the hounds of the night.

These authors clearly believed Edgar did this. It is supported by William of Malmesbury's remarks:

> He permitted no man, no matter what his rank, to evade laws with impunity. In his day therefore, there was no secret thief, no public robber, unless such as preferred to lose his life in attacking the property of others.[24]

The motive, from such a religious-minded king, was to allow the guilty party time to repent of his sins which immediate execution did not permit. A tale, intended to illustrate the miracles of St Swithun, related that one man, said to be innocent, had been convicted and punished in this fashion. He was persuaded that the relics of St Swithun would restore his hearing, though there was no hope of his sight. The saint duly restored both. The story is found in the metrical account of St Swithun's miracles by Wulfstan, precentor of Winchester, written just at the end of the tenth century.

That Edgar's rule could be harsh when deemed necessary is illustrated by two rare incidents recorded in the *Chronicles.* The *Peterborough Chronicle,* under the year 966, in recording the appointment of Oslac as earl in Northumbria, comments that Thored Gunnarsson[25] ravaged and devastated Westmorland. It is unlikely that he was in rebellion and was probably acting on royal orders because he was later made an earl in Deira, northern Northumbria.[26] Ravaging in this manner was the usual way of enforcing the king's orders on a recalcitrant population. (For example, in 1041 King Harthacnut 'had all Worcestershire ravaged on account of his two housecarls, who were collecting the formidable tax when that people killed them within the market town, inside the minster'.) In 969 Edgar ordered Thanet to be ravaged to avenge the ill treatment of York merchants.[27]

Archbishop Wulfstan was to make Edgar's laws a basis for Cnut to follow,[28] though Cnut was much more inclined to resort to capital punishment. Curiously, despite Lantfred's evidence, the extant laws of Edgar show little interest in mutilation as a punishment. It is probable that Lantfred and Wulfstan were referring to a lost edict, issued late in Edgar's reign. There is other evidence of lost legislation. Edgar's edict on the coinage is only known about from the chronicle of Roger of Wendover in the thirteenth century.[29]

No legislation from Edgar's reign survives after 962, yet he cannot have been doing nothing. There was a tradition of administrative direction by oral and verbal instruction. Much of what Edgar did, as indeed is also the case with his eleventh-century successor, Edward the Confessor, must have been issued in this way and has left little trace simply because it never proceeded beyond the spoken word. But that does not mean that no action followed; as the Roman adage has it, 'the will of the prince has the force of law'. The Confessor was said to have 'abrogated bad laws, with his council of the wise (Witan), established good ones and filled with joy all Britain over which he ruled'.[30] So the Codes II to IV Edgar may be no more than a representative sample of written laws issued in his name. Laws seem to have been published in written form in the late Anglo-Saxon state and at least some of the ruling class must have been able to read and understand them.[31]

The tenth-century kings were also concerned with what might be termed 'police' matters, which were the function of self-help groups rather than of an organised force. Men were expected to organise themselves in groups of ten, known as 'tithings',[32] although in later times these came to be regarded as territorial divisions of the hundred. The Ordinance of the Hundred, which operated in Edgar's day, in discussing the hundred's role in the pursuit of thieves, required the 'chief official of the hundred' to inform 'the chief officials of the tithings', so that everyone could go out in pursuit 'until they succeed in coming upon the thief'. This indicates that one of the main functions of a meeting of the hundred was the bringing of thieves to justice.

It is not completely clear from the *Hundred Ordinance* whether this referred to groups of ten men, or to subdivisions of the hundred, but the latter sense came to predominate.[33] Neglect of duty to the hundred meant fines, thirty pence payable at the hundred court, doubled at a second offence (when half went to the hundred and half to the man's lord), ten shillings for a third, and outlawry, unless pardoned by the king, for a fourth. If a group of ten men was a tithing, it could be the case that the district they occupied was equivalent to a vill or settlement, in which case the reeves of the vill mentioned in Aethelred's codes might be the tithingmen under another name, the more substantial men of the vill from whom, led by their priest and reeve, evidence was taken during the Domesday inquest of 1089.[34]

## THE PEACE GILD AND THE TITHING

Not all information about legal developments comes from 'official' documents. An organisation was current in Aethelstan's day which must have influenced the developments which led to the demand for tithings. There is a memorandum which records the measures taken for the carrying out of Aethelstan's law on tithings by a body described as the 'peace-gild of London'.[35] To this body belonged bishops and reeves attached to, or owning property in, London. They seem to have 'belonged' to the city in the sense of sharing responsibility for its defences and of owing suit of court in London.[36] The rank and file members of the gild were those living in a region which took in all of Middlesex and possibly Surrey and part of Hertfordshire.

Like later associations of a similar kind, the gild made provision for the spiritual welfare of its members, but the chief object of this gild was secular. Its aim was the maintenance of public peace, and it devised an elaborate organisation for the pursuit of thieves and for compensation for injured persons defrayed from its common purse. The members, significantly, were divided into groups of ten, one of whom acted as headman. The various headmen then formed a standing committee to account for the money contributed to a hundred composed of ten subgroups. The headman of the hundred then acted as head of the committee. They met once a month during the gild feast, to ensure that the gild statutes were being observed. It reveals the capacity for self-organisation and co-operation among the men of the English countryside which is not evident from royal documents. The king's law was being carried out, not by his official representatives, but by a voluntary organisation of free men. It raises the question of how many other royal edicts were put into effect by such co-operative action.

In later decades and elsewhere in the country, kings such as Edgar found it necessary to insist on obedience to their commands by prescribing what was to be done. He required all men to see to it that they had surety, that thieves be pursued by all men, and that the officials of the hundreds and tithings be informed so that they could pursue thieves with all speed.[37]

Cnut was to require all free men over the age of twelve to belong to a tithing and to a hundred if they were to have the right to defend themselves against criminal charges. In its developed form the tithing had to produce to the court for trial any member of the tithing involved in wrong doing or be fined for failure to do so. Lords, in order to avoid having to guarantee payment of fines themselves, had put pressure on their men to seek security (borh) among their neighbours, so surety and tithing were combined. All peasants were to be members of a tithing and could no longer choose their own pledges. After the Norman Conquest this became known as Frankpledge. Cnut is unlikely to have been the originator of this requirement; like other kings he was codifying existing custom.

Aethelred's seventh code refers only to the heads of tithings who, with the priest and reeve of each village, were to see that alms-giving and fasting laws were obeyed. It is quite conceivable that Edgar had originally enforced membership of a tithing in this way. He had a gift for systematisation. Shire, hundred and borough all provided places where good witnesses were to be found; panels of thirty-six in large boroughs, and of twelve in small boroughs and in each hundred.[38] Breach of the peace, given under his hand and seal, was punished severely, even more so in the Danelaw than elsewhere in England.

Further north there was a situation best seen as a semblance of political unity under a single ruler, while kings acquiesced in simply being overlords beyond the River Welland. There the English kings could appoint ealdormen or earls and have bishops consecrated, and they received the profits of lordship. Otherwise they had little interest in the North and rarely went there, though Edgar penetrated as far as York and Chester. Edgar found that he had quite enough to do in southern England in reviving Benedictine monasticism, though he also devoted time and energy to the defence of his kingdom.[39]

## EDGAR AND THE DANELAW

One of the most interesting aspects of Edgar's administrative and legislative system was the approach taken to the Danelaw. In 962 Edgar laid down detailed prescriptions for avoiding the wrath of God and bringing about the cessation of the plague, enjoining the payment of tithes, regulating procedures for buying and selling in boroughs, and so on.[40] He first insists that some laws must apply to the whole nation, 'to the English, Danes and Britons in every part of my dominions',[41] and insists on his own royal prerogatives 'in every borough and every shire'. He then goes on to lay down that 'the rights of the laity be maintained among the Danes in accordance with the best constitution which they can determine upon'.[42] Among the English, 'the additions which I and my councillors have made to the laws of my ancestors shall be observed for the benefit of the whole nation'. The clause about the Danes is repeated.[43] He adds, 'I have always granted you such a concession and will continue to do so as long as my life lasts, because of the loyalty which you have constantly professed to me'. Edgar also insists that 'I desire that this one decree, relating to investigations such as these (into the witnessing of the buying and selling of cattle) shall apply equally to us all, for the security and protection of the whole population'.[44] So the Danes are definitely brought within the sphere of English lawmaking.

The whole of this code is then to be promulgated by Earl Oslac among the Danes and by the Ealdormen Aelfhere and Aethelwine among the English.[45] In the case of Oslac, 'all the people dwelling in his earldom shall promote the observance of this [law]', while the ealdormen 'shall distribute them in all directions so that this measure shall be known to both rich and poor'. Oslac was said to have been made an ealdorman in 966, according to *Peterborough Chronicle* E, though he was already styled '*dux*' as early as 963.[46] He remained in power until he was unexpectedly banished just as Edgar died. The two events may have been connected but no reason for the banishment has been unearthed. This code of Edgar had therefore to have been issued in or after 964.

The Danes certainly lived very much under their own laws, and their territorial administrative unit below that of the shire was the 'wapentake'. (The name derives from the Old Norse *vapnatak* via Old English *waepentaec*, meaning the shaking of weapons to signify assent or dissent at an open-air meeting; it is usually taken to be of Scandinavian origin.)[47] The effect of Edgar's grant of privileges to the Danes was to leave the vast area known in the eleventh century as 'Danelagh'[48] (Danelaw) to be ruled under the Crown by the Anglo-Danish gentry who had inherited their lands under royal protection.

The Danelaw developed further during the tenth century with the incorporation of Northumbria into the Kingdom of England, together with the acceptance of the customs of York. An accommodation had to be found between English, that is West Saxon and Mercian, laws and methods of government, and the way of life of Danes and Norsemen settled in the North. They were protected by the Crown in return for acquiescence in English rule, and had, as Edgar states, been loyal to him from the time he became 'King of the Mercians and the Northumbrians' in 957.

In the mid-tenth century the Danelaw had been divided into several units, with shires in the southern Danelaw, which Edward the Elder had recovered, and ealdormanries, soon to be known as earldoms, for Yorkshire and Northumbria. The latter change came about under Edgar. The ruling elite was connected to the ealdormen and to the Archbishops of York. These archbishops were drawn from the Mercian Danelaw. Peterborough was to provide bishops for Durham.

A range of words was used in Latin charters to denote the position of ealdorman or earl: *princeps, comes, dux* and *praefectus*, literally prince, count, duke and prefect.[49] They were men of high rank, some of collateral royal descent and/or quasi-regal status. In effect they were local rulers acting in the king's name and on his behalf. Edgar appointed North Midland nobles to York in an effort to bring it more firmly into his kingdom. It was perhaps Danish influence that gradually caused the replacement of the Old English 'ealdorman' (which gave the language the later term 'alderman') by the word 'earl', from a combination of Old English 'eorl' and Danish 'jarl'.

The Danes, south of the Humber, and Northumbrians, south of the Tees, remained loyal to Edgar, attending his court and witnessing his charters. Unlike the West Saxons and Mercians they were unaccustomed to obeying written law and could not have been expected to surrender their way of life, nor could they be expelled or exterminated. A *modus vivendi* must have been arrived at from the time they 'bowed' to Eadred. Aethelstan and Edward the Elder had divided the Five Boroughs into shires (though Stamford never became the centre of its own shire), and hundreds were introduced there for justice, police and eventually taxation over several decades.[50] All their rulers submitted to Edgar, the one man who alone had the acknowledged and undisputed right to call himself king, just as the evidence suggests that they had acknowledged King Aethelstan. Among those attending Aethelstan's court at Lifton in Devon on 12 November 936[51] were seven lords with Danish names (such as Guthrum or Scule), possibly descendants of those who had led the Danish armies in eastern England. There had been no wholesale replacement of Danes by Englishmen.

The presence of men like those changed the character of the king's court, which explains the readiness with which Edgar was accepted in the Danelaw and in Northumbria in 957 and his willingness to make concessions to the Danes in his law codes in 962. The exact degree of Danish settlement cannot be realistically estimated, but there had been a considerable influx into the North and East of England during the ninth and early tenth centuries. Some presumably left after the area was taken over by the West Saxon kings, but most would have remained.

Edward the Elder had allowed Danes to retain their estates, which they only lost if they were late in submitting to the king. Efforts were made to assimilate them, especially in York and the North in the 950s and 960s. It was probably at this time that the confederacy later known as the Five Boroughs was established, probably as a regional system for the defence of the southern provinces of York. In allowing the Danes to make 'such good laws as they may best decide on', Edgar encouraged the formation of the confederacy, 'because of your loyalty which you have always shown me'. He certainly meant by this Earl Oslac 'and all the army dwelling in his ealdormanry'.

The Five Boroughs retained their own courts, even though presided over by an ealdorman or king's reeve, and the wapentake court operated with a body of twelve thegns who swore an oath not to accuse the innocent or shield the guilty. They had to go out and arrest men of ill-repute on behalf of the reeve. The use of a panel of twelve is a Scandinavian custom, as the Scandinavians calculated on a duodecimal system (Wessex and Mercia used a decimal base). Edgar borrowed from this Scandinavian concept. His code of 962 required that twelve standing witnesses be chosen in every hundred, who were to swear not to deny what they had witnessed nor declare in testimony anything they had not seen or witnessed.[52]

Further evidence of Danish influence during Edgar's reign lies in the development in the Danelaw of a type of lordship which came to be known as sake and soke (from *sacne*, 'cause', and *socne*, 'suit'), by which men, known later as sokemen, fell under a lord's jurisdiction as president of the hundred court in receipt of a grant from the king of the profits of justice.[53]

The phrase was devised because Old English had no single word for the concept. The first use of the phrase is in a charter of Eadwig from 956 granting an estate in Southwell, Nottinghamshire, to Archbishop Osketil of York. Southwell had dependent estates in eleven villages. The king says 'These are the villages which belong to Southwell with sake and soke'. This type of estate was common in the Danelaw but rare in southern England. Such an estate comprised a large central estate held by the lord with a number of dependent villages grouped round it. A soke could include as many as thirty villages. Eadwig had needed a phrase to describe the unity of the whole estate, since the lands granted were intermingled with lands belonging to other lords.[54]

Three years later Edgar also made a grant, as King of the Mercians and Northumbrians, of the estate of Howden in Yorkshire, to a matron named Quen, with eight dependent villages 'which belong to Howden with sake and soke'.[55] The phrase is used so routinely that these cases cannot be setting a precedent and the possession of such jurisdiction must already have become commonplace. Edgar's ruling that a judge who gave false judgement would forfeit his thegnship seems to refer to the holders of such jurisdiction rather than to royal reeves.

From the time that the southern Northumbrians of Yorkshire and Deira had bowed to the inevitable and fallen into line, accepting the Kings of the English as their kings, Scandinavian culture was brought within the bounds of English society. Northumbria was profoundly Scandinavian in culture, and this had been reinforced over a period of eighty years; place names, inscriptions, sculptures and decoration all illustrate this. The Scandinavian element in the population remained small, but the lordship was in Danish hands. Only in Bernicia did the English rulers manage to keep them out.

The Archdiocese of York was left poverty-stricken by its loss of lands to Viking settlers (which is why it was twinned with Worcester in Edgar's reign), and in Yorkshire the monasteries also lost their lands. Even the St Cuthbert Community was dispossessed of its estates by Scandinavian lords. These settlers were pagans, and as a result Christian clergy were displaced and the Church effectively disestablished. Kings were unable to reverse this before 1066. The acceptance by Edgar of this poor position for the Church in the North, as well as his grant of the privilege of a large measure of self-government to the Danes, helps to explain the accusations hurled at him of being too fond 'of foreign vicious customs' and of introducing 'heathen practices too eagerly' so that he 'encouraged harmful elements' to enter the country.

Yet his decree, probably dating from 962, was not wrung from him because he was a weak king or because he had confessed to an inability to dominate the Danelaw. He insisted on other laws being observed there as they were elsewhere in England, such as the use of one coinage throughout the realm. He would, however, have thought that the suppression of established Danish practices would be both difficult and purposeless and the recovery of Church lands impossible. The Danes were no longer a threat to his government, so he issued his instructions and left the Danes to carry them out in their own way.

# 5

# Ship Sokes and Sea Power

Edgar's reign was characterised by its peacefulness. An examination of his law codes and the development of tithings and the peace gild goes some way towards explaining the existence of internal peace. Similarly, his efforts to encourage the assimilation of the Danes, including granting them a measure of self-government while insisting on his right to legislate for the whole of England, permits some understanding of the rarity of internal disturbance. The English ealdormen and thegns found themselves unable to resist the king's drive to restore Benedictine monasticism. They could not, even had they wanted to, have defied his reform of the coinage or his insistence on the regular operation of the courts of Shire, Borough and Hundred. During his reign these men embraced his reforms and co-operated wholeheartedly with their king. Even after his death, an attempt to recover lands bestowed on the Church was short-lived and largely nullified by those who had most strongly supported Edgar.

There is little evidence of civil unrest during Edgar's reign. According to the *Chronicles*, the Isle of Thanet was ravaged at the king's order for having maltreated merchants from York. That the *Chronicles* mention this at all is evidence that such misbehaviour was unusual. Similarly, Earl Thored was to deal in like manner with the population of Westmorland. Presumably the Norse settlers in Cumbria had given trouble, possibly stirred up by the Irish Norse. Thored was for many years to be earl in York and his father had been an earl under Aethelstan, so he had probably been acting on Edgar's instructions in 966. Edgar was to deal with Thanet in a similar manner in 968, probably through local magnates acting on his orders.[1]

There was also peace abroad. There were no invasions and no fleet dared approach the coast of Britain. The only reference to warfare is in 965 when an English army entered North Wales and ravaged Gwynedd, according to Welsh sources. Gwynedd was then ruled by the three sons of Idwal and it is possible that they had tried to withhold tribute from Edgar. The Welsh annals name the commander as 'Alvryt' or 'Alfre', which looks like their version of Aelfhere, the Mercian ealdorman. As one source says of Edgar, he was 'powerful in arms, warlike, and defended the rights of his kingdom by his army as became a king'.[2] That same source also comments that he 'punished the wicked in every quarter' (which would seem to confirm Lantfred's account of the severity of his punishments) and 'reduced rebels to submission'. The question that arises is exactly how he defended the realm.

## EDGAR AND THE ROYAL NAVY

The answer seems to lie in his creation of a fleet, a real royal navy, capable of annual patrols of the waters around England during the fighting season, from spring to autumn. One way in which this might have been done, since eleventh-century kings are known to have done so, would have been to hire fighting seamen. Viking and Danish mercenaries were available and Edgar could certainly have raised the money. But apart from William of Malmesbury's claim that there were Saxons (from Germany), Flemings and Danes in pre-Conquest England, and Archbishop Wulfstan's complaints and criticisms of Edgar, substantiated by the entry in the *Chronicle* for 959, that he invited in foreigners with vicious customs, there is little if any evidence that he employed mercenaries.[3]

Instead, Edgar seems to have been responsible for the development of triple hundreds, termed ship sokes, under which system the number of men required to crew a warship, sixty, was raised from a group of 300 hides at the rate of one man from each five hides in the ship soke. This seems to parallel the fyrd requirement of one fighting man from each five hides, what some historians like to call the 'select fyrd', as 300 hides would provide sixty fighting men. That Edgar did this can only be deduced from a consideration of regulations regarding the maintenance of fighting ships in the reigns of Aethelred and Cnut.

The existence of ship sokes is proven from laws of Aethelred,[4] which command 'the fitting out of ships [*scipfirðrunga*] as diligently as possible, so that in every year they may all be equipped soon after Easter'. It is significant that Aethelred mentions this system in the context of an Easter assembly of the Fleet. Cnut the Great also insisted on this service: 'Whoever, with the cognizance of the shire, has performed the services demanded from a landowner both in the *scipfyrde* and in the *landfyrde*, shall hold his land freely during his life'.[5]

There is a reference to ship sokes in the post-Conquest document called *Leges Henrici Primi*. (This was not a code issued by Henry I, but in effect a lawyer's handbook.) The *Leges* state that shires were divided into hundreds and into ship sokes, *sipesocha*. Eric John connects these ship sokes to Aethelred's law of 1008, 'that a large warship was to be provided from every three hundred hides', which would have been, as was usual with much Old English legislation, a reiteration of an existing requirement.[6] Aethelred does not call these triple hundreds ship sokes. The word is not found in pre-Conquest sources, but the units referred to did exist.[7] It seems that a levy was made, termed ship scot (tax), and the earliest reference to it is when Aethelric, Bishop of Sherborne, complains (shortly after the year 1000) that he no longer receives ship scot from thirty-three hides of land belonging to 'the three hundred hides that other bishops [of Sherborne] had for their diocese'.

This not only records ship scot but also shows that the Sherborne diocese contained a triple hundred, a ship soke, since the hides in question paid the ship tax. The reference to other Bishops of Sherborne who received ship scot implies that the system extended back to the bishopric of Aethelsige, who was Bishop in Edgar's reign. Sherborne itself might not have held enough hides but it was responsible for the three hundreds of Sherborne, Yetminster and Beaminster. Ship scot cannot have been anything other than a tax for the fitting out and provisioning of ships. That suggests that the duty to provide ships had already been commuted for cash in some areas. It also shows that the triple hundred went back through at least two bishops' period of office. Bishop Aethelric wrote in the early years of the eleventh century.[8] If his account is right, then Aethelred is unlikely to have been the originator of the ship soke. Another reason why Aethelred is unlikely to have originated the system is that, according to the *Chronicles*, in 992 he had to summon the assistance of 'all the ships that were of any use', which suggests a falling off of naval preparedness during Aethelred's reign until the issue of his fifth code in 1008.[9]

At about the same period, around 1000, the canons of St Paul's in London provided a list of estates belonging to their church which were liable to produce fifty-eight shipmen. It is probable that there were originally sixty, in which case this is another example of a ship soke, belonging to the bishopric of London, a see that possessed between 300 and 350 hides. The best example, however, is the diocese of Worcester and its triple hundred of Oswaldslow. The details of a dispute between the Bishop of Worcester, Wulfstan, and the Abbot of Evesham, state that Oswaldslow's privilege included the right to 'the king's geld and service and military expeditions by land and sea'. That Oswaldslow comprised three hundreds is confirmed by the testimony of the whole shire (that is, the shire court) to the Domesday commissioners in 1086.[10]

Similar obligations are recorded elsewhere. Pershore Abbey was endowed with three hundred hides. It had its own steersman (that is, a ship commander), and a full complement of warriors.[11] The triple hundred was certainly a ship soke.[12] There are no records of Aethelstan creating triple hundreds, nor Edgar's predecessors, which increases the likelihood that they were Edgar's creation. Pershore's endowment cannot antedate its re-foundation in 972. The foundation collapsed and it lost two thirds of its lands to Westminster Abbey in the Confessor's day. Another ship soke was associated with St Benet's in Holme, Norfolk. That abbey also had its own steersman. Another possible ship soke is the borough of Winchcombe and its monastery church of St Mary's, founded in 972, which had three hundreds associated with it and rendered twenty-eight pounds.[13] Archbishop Aelfric and Bishop Aelfwold of Crediton both left a ship to King Aethelred, which suggests that there was a ship soke attached to their dioceses.[14] The Archbishop's ship was one of sixty-four oars described as 'his best ship, and the sailing tackle with it and 60 helmets and 60 coats of mail'. The bishopric of Dorchester in Oxfordshire held three hundreds in 1086: Sunbury, Thame and Dorchester.

There were groups of three hundreds elsewhere, especially in Wiltshire, associated with royal manors. Others were at Molland in Devon and Much Cowarne in Herefordshire. This suggests that there were royal ship sokes as well as ecclesiastical ones. There were also triple hundreds in Buckinghamshire and Cambridgeshire.[15] Although there is no clear indication that a ship soke was involved, it is of interest that Ely, which had access to the open sea through the Fens to the Wash, had six hundreds under its jurisdiction, attached to the manor of Sudbourne ('the six hundreds that belong to Sudbourne').[16] Domesday Book shows a holding of over 300 hides/carucates in Cambridgeshire, Norfolk and Suffolk. Interestingly, the record of Aethelwold's foundation, or re-foundation, of Ely, states that he bought 'the whole of the Isle of Ely' from the king, including 'the honour and soke of seven-and-a-half hundreds… two within the Isle and… five and a half in the province of the East Angles'.[17]

The recorded ship sokes are all associated with religious houses and none are known for sure to have been imposed on laymen, but this is a product of the nature of the evidence. As with so much that is known of Anglo-Saxon England, the evidence which survives does so because it was preserved by religious houses. Laymen simply did not keep archives, though kings did so to a limited degree. However, there are hints of possibilities. Archbishop Aelfric left a ship to the 'people' of Wiltshire and another to those of Kent. These just might be evidence of secular ship sokes, though that for Wiltshire could refer to a ship soke for Ramsbury.

Laymen did get involved in the system, though, because Aelfhelm Polga of Wratting in Cambridgeshire left a warship, a *scegð*, to Ramsey Abbey as well as lands to Ely and Westminster.[18] Elsewhere there were other customs which supported supplies for naval ships. The borough of Malmesbury, to which two hundreds were attached, had to supply provisions for the seamen (*'ad pascendos buzecarlos'*). They paid twenty shillings for this or supplied one man from each of the borough's five hides.[19] Maldon in Essex had the duty to 'provide aid with the other burgesses to find a horse for the host and in building a ship'.[20]

Lewes in Sussex has the entry: 'Their custom was, if the king wished to send his men *to patrol the sea* without him, they collected from all the men, whosoever land it was, twenty shillings, and those in charge of the arms in the ships had them'. This would again seem to confirm the standing arrangement for regular naval patrols. Then in Warwick, a long way from the sea, while ten burgesses went with the king for a campaign on land, 'if, however, the king went against his enemies by sea, they sent him either four boatswains or £4 of pennies'.[21]

Two other references are confirmation of the fact that military service in the Old English state could be both fyrd service and naval service. At Leicester the custom was that if the king 'went against an enemy by sea' then the burgesses sent him four horses as far as London 'to carry weapons and other things of which there might be need', while at Bedford the borough was assessed at half a hundred 'for military expeditions by land or sea'.[22]

Then there is the evidence from Worcester. There the Bishop had jurisdiction over three hundreds, known collectively as Oswaldslow and named after Bishop Oswald (960–992).[23] From his three hundreds he was liable for putting sixty warriors into the field in time of war. A charter purporting to create Oswaldslow is a twelfth-century forgery,[24] and so not contemporary proof of the creation of the triple hundred. However, Oswaldslow did exist[25] and is described in Domesday Book. The optimum moment for its creation would have been the moment of re-foundation during Edgar's reign, when he is most likely also to have created a triple hundred for the bishop. The charter is best treated as a twelfth-century historical recreation of a past event, with the forger probably putting together facts he knew about Oswaldslow in order to create the charter. The estates which make up the two triple hundreds of Oswaldslow and Pershore Abbey interpenetrate each other in a manner which suggests their creation at the same time, in or around 972, though Oswald's *Indiculum* (a letter to King Edgar on the subject of Oswald's leaseholds) has been dated to 964.

The existence of the triple hundred of Oswaldslow is also confirmed by this document, preserved in Hemming's *Cartulary*,[26] called the *Indiculum Libertatis de Oswaldeslowes Hundred* (Statement concerning the Liberty of the Hundred of Oswaldslow).[27] It is of Edgarian date, by Oswald, and states that he has decided that it is his duty to put on record in the form of a chirograph, for the information of the Bishops of Worcester who will be his successors, on exactly what terms he has leased the lands of the Church to his 'faithful men'.

A chirograph was a form of charter written twice on one sheet of parchment with the word 'chirograph' down the centre of the parchment, dividing the two copies from one another. The parchment was cut into two along a wavy line and the two parties to the agreement kept one half each. This prevented any alteration being made, because the two halves matched when put together and any alteration would then be revealed. The *Indiculum* refers to the 'archiductor who rules the see' of Worcester, meaning Oswald himself. The forged charter, called *Altitonantis* from its initial word, also uses the word 'archiductor'[28] to describe the bishop, and seems to quote from the *Indiculum*. It might be that the *Indiculum* was known to the forger. (The word is of Frankish origin, used of charters cast in the form of a letter, as in this case.)

It is this *Indiculum* which is referred to in Domesday Book as constituting the Liberty of Oswaldslow. It looks as though a franchise was granted by Edgar to Oswald, probably granting him his triple hundred on condition that it formed a ship soke, so that Oswald now tells the king how he has disposed of the land involved and on what terms. As there is no genuine charter from

Edgar making such a grant, it is likely that this was done by *verbum regis* with Dunstan, Aethelwold and Byrhtnoth as witnesses. It does not mean that the franchise included all the rights spelled out in the *Altitonantis* charter, which was probably concocted on the basis of the *Indiculum* and other, no longer extant, evidence to protect the rights claimed by the church of Worcester in the twelfth century. It has been argued that *Altitonantis* was based on a genuine original, much of which can be discerned in the text, although it is plainly a forgery as it stands.[29]

However, much of what is in it echoes other material relating to King Edgar's naval activities. Its preamble reads like an expansion of the sort of titles found in genuine charters and makes claims similar to those made about Edgar in the *Vita Oswaldi*. Certainly the Bishop of Worcester in Edward the Confessor's time had his own ship and a steersman, Eadric, called also the 'leader [*ductor*] of the army of the same bishop for the king's service'.[30] The charter refers to ship sokes and states that 300 hides constituted a '*naucupletio*', representing the Old English terms *scypfyllð* or *scipsocne*.[31]

The use of such terms is confirmed by later references, in Warwickshire Pipe Rolls from the reign of Henry II,[32] to an area that was equal to three Domesday hundreds and was described as a '*sibbesocha*' or '*sipesocha*'.[33] It looks as though the grant of Oswaldslow committed military and naval powers and duties to the bishop as well as judicial ones. It is evident from the many references to the holding of ship sokes by bishops that they had been given responsibilities regarding the provision of ships and fighting men for the navy.

Edgar, indeed, seems to have made provision for his fleet both by levying a ship scot, possibly by a tax on the hide, and by requiring triple hundreds. These in time became known as ship sokes, from the fact that the magnate, usually apparently a churchman, had jurisdiction (*socne*) within the three hundreds, with a duty to provide sixty men to crew a warship. The king seems, at the very least, to have imposed this obligation on bishoprics at about the same time that he was endowing revived monasteries and new foundations. Even some of the abbeys seem to have been involved. Certainly St Benet of Holme had a steersman for the abbot's ship and was associated therefore with a ship soke. That seems to have been the obverse of the coin; in return for endowing monasteries or encouraging their revival, Edgar, as a *quid pro quo*, expected the Church to support his navy.

The ship sokes were, by implication, a going concern in Aethelred's day, though he was having to insist on the responsibility being undertaken more diligently, and mentions the obligation in the context of a naval review and refit at Easter. These triple hundreds could produce sixty men to crew a warship, or sixty men for a contingent of the fyrd. This suggests that even the five hide rule might have originated in Edgar's reign. It was the rule, in some shires at least, for one fully armed and trained man to be raised for the fyrd from each block of five hides. Some historians have postulated the existence of such a system from the evidence in Domesday Book.

There is no direct contemporary evidence to link Edgar to ship sokes or a 'select fyrd' but there is evidence of an interest in naval affairs, supported by Florence of Worcester and William of Malmesbury, who both report his naval activities. It also connects Edgar to the origin of the geld, since both ship sokes and a five hide unit presuppose the commutation of service. If one fully trained warrior served for five hides then the service owed by others living on those five hides had to be commuted to a money payment to provide the wages and provisions of the warrior, who would also have needed a horse as well as arms. That would imply a levy of so many pence or shillings on the hide, payable within the boundary of a ship soke to the 'archiductor' of the soke.

It is Edgar's naval initiatives which provide the key to the peacefulness of his reign. The evidence is not contemporary but it is compelling. Both William of Malmesbury and Florence of Worcester give an account of naval activities. Under 973, in the context of Edgar's great coronation at Bath, Florence records that 'after a short time he sailed round the north part of Britain with a large fleet and landed at Chester'. From the context of a start from near Bath, probably from Bristol, 'the north part of Britain' must mean Wales if an arrival at Chester is in question. Once there, he held some kind of naval review and had himself rowed on the Dee by a number of lesser kings, six in some sources and eight according to Florence. Even the *Annales Cambriae* talk of 'a great gathering of ships at Chester by Edgar, King of the Saxons'.[34]

Under the year 975 Florence records the death of the king, and, following an encomium in which Edgar is compared to various illustrious warriors of the past, the following entry is made. This is substantially the same account as that of William of Malmesbury except that, wisely, William does not commit himself to any definite opinion about the size of Edgar's fleet. (Roger of Wendover goes further and claims four fleets.)[35] Florence says:

He collected, during his life, a fleet of 3,600 stout ships; After Easter, in every year, he used to make 1,200 of them assemble on the east, 1,200 on the west, and 1,200 on the north shore of the island. He would then sail to the western with the eastern fleet, and, sending that back, would sail to the northern with the western fleet, and dismissing it in turn, would sail with the northern fleet back to the eastern; thus every summer he used to sail round the whole island, performing this brave feat by way of defence against foreigners and for the purpose of inuring himself and his subjects to war.

The number of ships is, of course, absurd, but if the numbers are ignored, the rest of the account is quite credible. It need not necessarily have been the case that he did this every year. He might well have sailed with one fleet to the next, but not necessarily around the whole island. More likely, each fleet patrolled its own beat in a triangular pattern. It looks as though there might have been three bases: an eastern fleet possibly on the Humber, a western fleet in the Severn and a northern fleet perhaps at Chester. A regular series of patrols in the Channel, the Irish Sea and the North Sea would have been a real deterrent to the roving Viking raiders. The result was that, as Aelfric boasted, 'no fleet was ever heard of except that of our own people who held this land'.

Florence then connects these fleet manoeuvres with Edgar's activity during winter and spring. He says that the king made a regular progress 'through every province in England' (again, a pardonable exaggeration; English kings rarely went far beyond the Midland region of their kingdom) and that he enquired into 'the mode of the administration of justice and the observance of the laws'. Florence is perhaps assuming, from knowing that Witans were held in various places and that kings were peripatetic, that this was what Edgar would have done, and the truth may be not too far from it. Old English kings were more likely to have sent their ealdormen to make such enquiries about the administration of justice.

Florence can be trusted to some degree. It is held currently that among the sources relied upon by the writer usually called Florence (but who is now thought to have been the monk John, who claims to continue the chronicle after the death of his superior, Florence, in 1118) was a version of the *Anglo-Saxon Chronicle* not unlike that of the Abingdon 'D' text. If that is so, it might be that his account was derived from that lost version, though this cannot be demonstrated.[36] William of Malmesbury also records the fleet manoeuvres and so he too must have seen a source which mentioned it.[37]

What cannot be ascertained with any precision is the size of Edgar's navy. Alfred the Great is usually credited with being the 'Father' of the Royal Navy because he ordered special vessels to be constructed with which to repel Viking invaders, but he left no system by which the building of ships and the provision of a navy could be continued. The numbers of ships in Alfred's fleet were quite small. He used his vessels, which were stationed at burhs placed at intervals of twenty-five miles along the coast, to ferry men to the relief of other places when the Vikings made a landing. It is not known how many squadrons there were. His achievement was to have had a navy at all.

Fleets in the eleventh century, after Edgar's time, were not that large, and Viking or Danish fleets outnumbered them. The Viking leader Olaf Tryggvason had ninety-three ships in 991 and ninety-four in 994, and usually overwhelmed ships sent from London and East Anglia to oppose him. These English fleets were organised on the ship soke system, as references to the raising of the fleet in Aethelred's laws confirm. One clue to the size of the English fleet comes from the story of the defection of Wulfnoth, Thegn of Sussex; he persuaded the crews of twenty ships into defecting with him and was pursued by Beorhtric, brother of Eadric Streona the Ealdorman of Mercia, with eighty ships. That looks like a total fleet of 100.

It seems that fleets did not exceed about 100 ships at any stage, and it is known that Aethelred had been obliged to order the fitting out of more ships after raising 'all the ships that were of any value' in 991, implying that the fleet's readiness had been neglected since Edgar's day. Aethelred's laws had to insist on an annual refit every Easter, which supports Florence's statement that Edgar held annual reviews of his fleet and ordered summer patrols of the seas around England.[38]

It really does seem that if account is taken of his measures to ensure a constant supply of warships and fighting seamen (who might almost be termed marines) by recruiting them from triple hundreds, the ship sokes, and organising a navy as a permanent deterrent against invasion, patrolling the Channel, the Irish Sea and the North Sea, then it is Edgar rather than Alfred who was the first to create an organised Royal Navy.

# 6

# Tenth-Century Military Institutions

All kings expected the performance of military service on demand, the fyrd service. There were fines (called *fyrdwite*) for non-performance of such service. It was one of the three royal rights reserved whenever land was granted to anyone, lay or religious. Fyrd service was reserved together with the obligation to repair bridges and build fortifications; fyrdfare, brycgbot and burhbot, were the so called *trinoda necessitas* of nineteenth-century historians.

The military obligation was imposed on all free men, and in order that such service could be organised it had to be assessed, since, in the last analysis, an obligation on all free men, that is landowners, lies on the land. Sooner or later the king had to know how many men he could expect to be supplied with and how much service was due from any given area. So the obligations became territorialised, and the hide became the 'universal, artificial unit of assessment' for the exaction of taxes and military service.[1] The carucate or ploughland fulfilled the same function in Scandinavianised districts.

Military service was therefore organised from the top down, through the shires to their subdivisions, the hundreds or wapentakes, and on down to the individual *vill*, not necessarily a village in the modern sense but a unit of farmed land which might include several settlements or estates. As the shire system was completed during the tenth century, and as the hundred came to be used as an administrative and judicial unit in the second half of that century, it begins to look as though the system of choosing men of sufficient military quality, the fully armed and armoured thegns, was also made more selective. The demand was made for the production of both infantry, when the fyrd went to war on land, and sea-borne warriors (almost marines) when the fyrd went by sea, as in the late Old English kingdom it very often did.

Alfred the Great had created a mobile standing army. He divided it into two groups which took it in turns to take the field and was used in conjunction with the system of burhs. That system was certainly continued by Edward the Elder and it seems likely that it was still in being down at least to the time of Eadred. It appears that under Aethelred II royal armies had reverted to being ad hoc forces raised by the king or his ealdormen. The decline must have begun with the relaxation of military preparedness after the death of Edgar.[2]

It is logical to suggest that by the mid-tenth century, arms and armour were becoming more expensive and the minimum landed qualification for attaining the status of a thegn was becoming five hides. Therefore, kings might have considered restricting the call to fyrd service to those who possessed five hides and to require that, in some areas at least, every five hides should produce an armed warrior for the fyrd. However, the call for such a 'select fyrd' did not exclude the continued obligation for every free man to serve.

As the customs of Worcestershire, recorded in Domesday Book, made plain, 'when the king marches against the enemy, if anyone summoned by his edict stays behind... if he is free and has his sake and soke... he is at the king's mercy'.[3] Kings were therefore still insisting on their right to call out all able-bodied free men.

Similarly, if a free man who served another lord stayed away, the lord was expected to send someone else, and if no one went from that estate, then forty shillings was paid by the inhabitants of the estate as a fine to the king, with as much again to the lord. The fines could then be used to pay a stipendiary soldier.

The question then arises whether any king in particular tried to make the obligation more systematic and more widespread. It is accepted that Edgar was probably responsible for imposing the burden of the ship soke on bishoprics in possession of at least three hundred hides. That meant that sixty men were to be provided for the crew of a warship at the rate of one man for every five hides. It cannot have been entirely fortuitous that the king fixed on that ratio, since it meant that exactly 300 hides was enough to produce the crew required. It also seems that 300 hides was the minimum endowment sufficient to provide for a bishop and his establishment following the increase in the number of dioceses in Wessex under Edward the Elder. Sees with fewer than 300 hides did not survive for long and had to be amalgamated with others.

## THE FIVE HIDE SYSTEM

As five hides was already regarded as the minimum required to support a thegn, this ratio was a natural one to choose for the support of a crewman. Eadric, the steersman of the Bishop of Worcester according to Domesday, held five hides in the Oswaldslow 'and performed [military] service with the other services belonging to the king and the bishop'.[4] Other evidence suggests that the demand was made on the assumption that even fyrd service was best provided by demanding one man from five hides. Things had obviously changed at some time between the reign of Aethelstan, who required two mounted men from every ploughland (or carucate), and the beginning of a demand for one warrior from every five hides.[5] Eric John maintains that one warrior in Aethelstan's time served for every two hides.[6] He also suggests that ship sokes and five hide units were created together in Edgar's reign. If so, then Edgar's demand that every five hides produce a shipman and/or a thegn was not much heavier than Aethelstan's: if both were summoned, the ratio would have been one man to two and a half hides.

Just as it was Edgar who devised the ship soke scheme, so it could be said that he at least encouraged the trend towards a demand for one man from every five hides. This does not require the assertion that he actually thought of it. *Of Peoples' Ranks and Laws* – a work of Archbishop Wulfstan of York, the Homilist (fl. 996–1023), describing the various ranks in society as they were in the tenth century – asserts that a ceorl ( peasant farmer) might become a thegn if he had 'fully five hides of land' and had 'church and kitchen, bell house and burh gate, seat and special duty in the king's hall'.[7] Another section refers to a thegn who serves the king 'and on his summons' rides among his household. That thegn could himself have a thegn in his service who has also received five hides from the king.[8]

The link between a ratio of five hides to one man for both shipmen and soldiers would seem to be confirmed by the entry in Domesday for Exeter,[9] which reads: 'whenever an expedition went out by land or sea, this city gave [the same] service as five hides of land'.[10] What that service was is stated in the entry for Berkshire: 'if the King sent an army anywhere, only one thegn went out from [each] five hides'.[11] Similarly, Bedford, which was assessed at fifty hides (a 'half hundred'), was assessed on them 'for military service by land and sea': one man from each five hides, or ten men, as if it were also part of a ship soke.[12] Even the Borough of Stamford, which was assessed at twelve and a half hundreds or 1,250 hides, did military service by land and sea; this looks like 500 men, not merely from the borough, of course, but from the area under its soke. In the early tenth century, Stamford, like other Danelaw boroughs of the League of Five Boroughs, was the centre of an area occupied by a Danish army.[13]

Elsewhere the customs were of variable kinds, some more military than others. At Warwick and Leicester the burgesses, ten and twelve respectively, did service on land or sent four boatswains if service was by sea (Warwick) or four horses as far as London to carry weapons and other necessities (Leicester). Even Colchester in Essex rendered six pence from each house in the borough 'for the victuals of the king's soldiers or for an expedition on land or sea'. There is a constant refrain, when these burdens are recorded, that the service is by both land and sea, even for towns a long way inland. In another variation, at Maldon, also in Essex, the burgesses find 'a horse for the host' by paying four shillings, which may also be used to contribute to the building of a ship.[14]

How these obligations might be apportioned at individual level is perhaps illustrated by the entry in the *Clamores* for Lincolnshire.[15] This mentions the case of four brothers, Sighwat, Alnoth, Fenkil and Eskil, who had divided their father's land between them, holding it in 'parage' or equal shares. The entry states that 'they held it in such a way that if they were needed in the king's military expedition and Sighwat could go, the other brothers assisted him', and if he could not then the others went in turn, but Sighwat was the king's man.

Arms and armour also became more elaborate, as is illustrated by the Code of Cnut which lays down the heriots expected by the king in his day.[16] By this a king's thegn had to provide half the arms of an earl; his heriot therefore comprised four horses (two saddled and two unsaddled), two helmets and two mail coats, four spears, four shields and two swords. An ordinary thegn required only his horse and weapons, but these would have been costly enough. An earl's equipment was listed in eights and fours of every item.

By contrast, in 946 the ealdorman of Essex, Aelfgar, had to have three of everything, horses, shields, swords and spears, but no helmet or body armour. An ealdorman earlier in Edmund's reign (936–946) normally had the arms and armour of four men.[17] These men had neither helmet nor mail coat. In Edgar's reign, a lady called Aelfgifu (966–975), and the Ealdorman Aelfheah (968–971), each had to have the equipment of six men.[18] The ealdorman

Aelfgar appears to equate in status and wealth to a king's thegn in later reigns. The demands had clearly increased, which supports the idea that Edgar might have begun to insist on better-armed soldiers, so increasing the pressure for one man to serve from five hides. The thegnhood was becoming a well-armed military elite.

It has therefore been maintained by some historians that ship sokes and the five hide unit evolved together in Edgar's reign. The evidence for a five hide system is found in Domesday Book records of the customs of the boroughs. The various texts show that the five hide unit was quite widespread, but do not show that it was universal. Indeed, much of the evidence looks as though it was the result of bargains struck between the burgesses and an earlier king or kings. As these boroughs evolved militarily from the time that Alfred and Edward the Elder built fortifications in them, it would seem that the various military burdens imposed on them, and on the estates around them owned by the burgesses, resulted from the demands of tenth-century kings. According to William of Malmesbury, in an appreciation of Edgar's activities, 'military discipline was tightened properly'.[19] That suggests that he took an interest in military as well as naval arrangements. Some places had naval burdens which point to Edgar's reign: for instance, 'every year' Dover gave the king twenty ships for fifteen days, each with twenty-one men, which indicates some sort of naval patrol. The same was done at Sandwich and probably Romney, where the king had the right to every other kind of service and the burgesses were excused most other customary dues 'by reason of service at sea'.[20]

The command structure also points to a systematically organised military service. The original system seems to have expected the ealdorman in charge of a shire to lead the shire levy, which continued into the tenth century until Edward the Elder began to group shires, possibly in threes, under a superior grade of ealdorman. By the middle of the century it is clear that some ealdormen, men like Aelfhere of Mercia and Aethelstan Half-King of East Anglia, or the ealdormen Aethelwine and Byrhtnoth, commanded whole regions. Their status was such that in time their rank, possibly under the influence of Edgar's appointment of Scandinavians in Yorkshire and Northumbria, evolved into that of an earl — a process completed by Cnut the Great when he divided the country into four provinces, Wessex, Mercia, Northumbria and East Anglia.

These great ealdormen, like the earls who succeeded or replaced them, commanded their own military households made up of thegns, many of them of noble rank themselves. No doubt the more important king's thegns also had their own military households. In the Confessor's reign these households, especially those of the earls, were known as their 'genge'.[21] The great ealdormen were the lords of other men who commended themselves to the ealdormen in a manner that began to resemble the way in which vassals rendered homage to lords in continental Europe.

This was not yet a 'feudal' tie based on the concept of the fief (that is, an estate granted to a warrior in return for military service). Although the men of an English lord might 'bow' to him and swear an oath of fidelity known as a 'hold oath', and even receive a gift of land from their lord, this was not vassalage, though the distinction might in some cases be a very thin one. English commended men might have to render 'heriot' on death (return arms and armour to the lord), but this was not what the Normans called 'relief'; it did not involve the return to the lord of a fief because English thegns did not hold their land exclusively in return for military service. Some might hold land under a lord on a lease, typically for three lives. At the end of the third life the estate, legally speaking, had to be returned to the lord, though after anything up to 100 years it might prove difficult for the lord to recover the land or to refuse to renew the lease.

Below the level of the shire, led by an ealdorman, came the hundred. This also had to be led into battle, commanded by its hundredman, or, as Aethelweard the Chronicler had translated it, its 'centurion'.[22] In Huntingdonshire it was recorded that in Swineshead (Bedfordshire, but near Kimbolton), the men 'paid geld in the hundred and went against the enemy with them'.[23] They were led into battle under their own standards.

As for the size of the Old English army, that depends in part on how widespread the system of a five hide quota extended (there is some indication that in the Danelaw area it was a six carucate system),[24] and on the extent to which the king had a right to call on not only every thegn but possibly every freeman to fight. Not only that, it was also the case that individual lords furnished their own contingents, and of course soldiers, or ships crews, might be hired. The five hide rule might not have applied where hides were very large, or where, as in Berkshire, the hide was smaller than those in some other shires. However, the existence of such a rule is underpinned by the establishment of ship sokes, which seem to demonstrate a tendency by the kings to seek to recruit a more effective, better-armed and trained class of warrior. By the eleventh century, under the influence of the Scandinavian dynasty of Cnut, there was a class of almost professional soldiers, the *huscarls* or housecarls, who seem to have been mercenary troops in the households of the king and of other great lords.

The selection of five hides, or six carucates, was perhaps governed by the fact that this represented an area comprising the territory of a small village which might also be the estate of a median thegn. If the five hide idea is taken to be very widespread, and assuming at the least that every thegn, if still in possession of five hides, could receive a personal summons from the king, then a simple calculation based on the number of recorded hides and carucates would provide an estimate of the number of potential soldiers. One estimate is that there were 80,000 hides, making 16,000 men. A more moderate estimate is some 70,000 hides, sulungs[25] or carucates, giving a figure of 14,000 men.[26]

That would leave room for a great deal of flexibility in the size of detachments summoned to fight and allow for repeated summonses calling up relays of men. It was because of this flexibility that King Harold was able to call out the fyrd at least three times during 1066, despite losses at Fulford and Stamford Bridge.[27]

7

# Men, Monks and Monasteries

The dominating theme of the reign of King Edgar is his re-introduction of Benedictine monasticism under the influence of Dunstan, Abbot of Glastonbury and Archbishop of Canterbury, Aethelwold, Abbot of Abingdon and Bishop of Winchester, and Oswald, Bishop of Worcester and Archbishop of York. The king and the three churchmen together with a number of powerful ealdormen, notably Aethelwine (ealdorman of East Anglia and known as *Amicus Dei* or Friend of God) set about restoring previous foundations badly affected by the events of the Viking wars and founding new ones.

This outburst of religious activity, the 'monastic revival' of the tenth century, did not develop out of nowhere and had a prolonged and vital pre-history. Yet to read the accounts of the movement provided by monastic writers, especially the authors of the Lives of the three monk-bishops, is to be exposed to accounts dedicated to the achievements of these men at the expense of what had gone before. Their account maintains that monasticism had virtually disappeared from England during the ninth century. It is a 'Benedictine' view of the condition of the Church.

The result is a temptation, to which many historians have succumbed, to dwell on the push that Edgar gave to reform.[1] The achievement, great though it was, must not be exaggerated, and the limitations of Edgar's achievement reveal those inherent in his position as the heir of the West Saxon dynasty.

The vast majority of foundations or re-foundations were in Wessex itself. On the western side of the country, Worcester was the furthest monastery to the north, with none in western Mercia. To the east, there were no foundations further east than Ely, such that East Anglia and Essex had none, nor were there any further north than Crowland. In fact, north and east of Watling Street saw no foundations other than the remarkable group of

Fenland monasteries: Peterborough, Ely, Ramsey, Thorney and Crowland. No attempt was made to revive monasticism in the North-East, the home of the Venerable Bede at Jarrow. The reason is not far to seek. In those regions neither the king of the House of Wessex nor his ealdormanic supporters held land which could be acquired for the endowment of monasteries.

Monasteries were plentiful before the Vikings came. Many had disappeared by the beginning of the tenth century. North of the Fenland they died out completely; only Lindisfarne and the Community of St Cuthbert survived in English Northumbria. In Alfred's Wessex many of the smaller houses either disappeared or fell into lay hands and life according to the monastic rule vanished or became scarcely recognisable as such. In some houses the 'abbot' was a layman and in others the lay owner appointed the abbot, often a member of his family.

Edward the Elder's foundation of New Minster, Winchester, depended on foreign scholars such as Grimbald of St Bertin. New Minster was not founded on reformed Benedictine lines and its secular clerks soon earned a poor reputation in the eyes of reformers. It looks as though the reformers' complaint that monasticism, as they understood it, had vanished has some justification. Glastonbury was a house of clerks owned by the king. Dunstan made no attempt to impose reformed Benedictine practice there as he did not have the king's support to do so. Worcester was not monastic at all.[2]

The 'abbots' who witness charters seem to have had 'monasteries' given to them by the kings; some may well in fact have been laymen. Thus houses which had not become ruins were occupied by clerks who performed the liturgy, probably in a rather perfunctory manner, and instructed their own children so that they could succeed them. The monasteries were not run on Benedictine lines. This was the *saecularum prioratus* of which the reformers complained, the holding of the office of a prior by worldly men.

It looks as though the Viking age had caused a decline in regular Church practice. Monasticism collapsed in some areas or declined in others, with the education of the clergy suffering in consequence from this, especially as much Church property passed into lay hands.

The damage incurred by the Church went further than the decline of monasticism. Episcopal succession collapsed completely in Northumbria, Mercia and much of East Anglia. Dioceses were abandoned to paganism or to the sporadic efforts of local clergy, and even in Wessex the bishops had allowed all educational provision to lapse. Yet there is evidence for the survival of monastic or quasi-monastic houses, suggesting that some had escaped complete dissolution or that they had begun to revive in the early tenth century.

A century later the situation had been transformed, with Benedictine monasteries everywhere in Wessex and into the Midlands, and some slight signs of reform penetrating even Northumbria. Bishoprics were reorganised, as bishops and their households, their *familia*, were increasingly likely to adopt a monastic pattern of life and many bishops were themselves monks.

The reign of Edgar was later presented as the recovery of a 'golden age', that of the seventh and eighth centuries as depicted by Bede. This view gave Alfred very little credit, despite his revival of Athelney and Shaftesbury, and overlooked the fact that Alfred's son, Edward the Elder, built both New Minster and Nunnaminster (a convent for Nuns) at Winchester. But of course these were not Benedictine Houses. That is, they did not follow the Rule or way of life laid down by St Benedict of Nursia, the father of Western monasticism. The kings had also given financial support to other houses, Glastonbury, Malmesbury, Abingdon, as well as cathedral churches which were always central to royal interest and patronage.

It is possible that it was from Athelney that the bishops of the 920s and 930s came. There were certainly more developments in religious revival in the reign preceding that of Edgar than the reformers were prepared to admit. A line of progression can be traced from Archbishop Plegmund to the time of Archbishop Oda. Alfred the Great's ecclesiastical and educational initiatives had to wait until the reign of Edgar to reach their full potential. Before then, the English clergy had been reluctant to accept the discipline necessary for the achievement of reform and the revival of monasticism.

It was once thought that there was little evidence of continuing literary activity in the first half of the tenth century, but the proliferation of charters, especially in the reign of Aethelstan, as well as of written codes of law and the existence of something like an organised royal secretariat, is evidence that men in the service of the West Saxon kings were either able to read (and write) or employed those who could. Some historians have accused Edward the Elder of a lack of learning, yet Asser insists that he was educated.[3] The king's son Aethelstan was a collector of books as well as of relics, and took steps to encourage learning.

The line of development had begun with the re-establishment of literacy, and had seen efforts to establish an aristocracy literate at least in English and a Latin-reading clergy. The next steps were the revival of the spirit and institutions of Christianity, a credible episcopate, with recruitment from outside Wessex and beginning with Plegmund, and a new generation of bishops able to carry out the necessary reforms.

Under Aethelstan the availability of clergy to staff the royal household and a royal secretariat demonstrates that there was now a pool of educated and trained clergy, and from their ranks came the candidates for high office. All that was needed was a king who could provide the peaceful conditions in the country at large which would allow those with a taste for monastic life to adopt it, and Edgar was to provide the necessary conditions and royal support. The result was nothing less than the rebuilding of the Church in southern England.

The continental input was to have its importance in a somewhat indirect manner. Various English clerics had continental contacts and several spent time at Ghent or Fleury. Ghent was the focus of reform emanating from Lotharingia, but Fleury was much the more important. It was regarded as the citadel of St Benedict, *arcisterium Sancti Benedicti*, which engendered reform elsewhere.

A major recruit was Oswald, nephew of Archbishop Oda. By means of money and influence, the archbishop secured for him election to a community at Winchester, possibly New Minster. There he found himself obliged to tolerate the rules of the old monasticism as he could not reform them. Even as an abbot, Oswald was unable to get his way and so resigned in disgust. That proved to be a blessing in disguise, for he went off to Fleury and remained there as an ordinary monk for several years. This experience equipped him to become one of the three English monks with first-hand knowledge of the reformed Benedictine monasticism as practised in an established monastery.[4]

The other two most influential reformers, Dunstan and Aethelwold, were both tonsured in Aethelstan's reign, committed themselves to reform, and formed part of the circle which included a Frankish reforming element at court. It was Aelfheah, priest, monk and Bishop of Winchester (not the archbishop of that name), who tonsured both Dunstan and Aethelwold at the king's command.[5]

The impression one gets of Dunstan is that he was a man one either loved or loathed. In 943 Edmund made Dunstan Abbot of Glastonbury, where he remained for fifteen years.[6] After Edgar came to power in Mercia, Dunstan became a bishop, and when Edgar became King of all England he made Dunstan Archbishop of Canterbury. Aethelwold became a monk at Glastonbury, claiming that it was the only monastery in England, but as there was no hint of Benedictine reform there, Dunstan did not have a free hand, otherwise he would certainly have imposed real Benedictine discipline. Aethelwold, not entirely pleased, tried to secure permission to leave and seek a stricter community, possibly Fleury. But Eadred was now king, a friend to Dunstan and more sympathetic to the reform. Dunstan, with the aid of the queen mother, prevailed upon the king to prevent Aethelwold from leaving by giving him the derelict abbey of Abingdon to revive and reform.[7]

Dunstan was born in about 909 in Somerset. His uncle was apparently Bishop Aethelhelm of Wells and Canterbury, who brought Dunstan to Aethelstan's court. There Dunstan fell under the influence of Aelfheah of Glastonbury, Bishop of Winchester after 934, another bishop with royal connections. He saw to it that Dunstan was ordained in 937 and possibly recommended that he become an abbot in 939.

Dunstan was joined by his friend from the royal court, Aethelwold, and they made Glastonbury a centre for 'men of high birth and eager spirit', almost an English Cluny but without its missionary spirit.[8] Dunstan's involvement in the political disputes after Eadred's death led to his exile at St Peter's in Ghent, then under Abbot Womar, where he came into contact with the spirit of continental reform. (It was at about this time that Oswald went to Fleury, the reformed Cluniac abbey on the Loire.) Dunstan, recalled by Edgar when King of Mercia, was Bishop of both Worcester and London before becoming Archbishop of Canterbury in 960.[9]

What is known of Aethelwold is found in Wulfstan of Worcester's *Vita Aethelwoldi*. He was born between 904 and 909 and entered Aethelstan's royal household some time between 924 and 938. He was then ordained by Aelfheah some time between 934 and 27 October 939. He was therefore at Glastonbury shortly before 939 and from there was made Abbot of Abingdon before 23 November 955. He built a church at Abingdon between 957 and 963. He was then elected to Winchester on 29 November 963.[10] When King Edgar intervened to reinforce Aethelwold's 'cleansing' of Winchester he sent his personal representative, the king's thegn Wulfstan of Dalham. Aethelwold certainly seems to have had strong royal connections as the royal family repeatedly intervened in his career.

The third of the trio is Oswald, who was Bishop of Worcester from 961–992 and Archbishop of York from 971. Like Aethelwold, he was a great founder and re-founder of monasteries. His own subsequent wealth suggests that his family, of Anglo-Danish origin, was both powerful and wealthy. He was the nephew of Archbishop Oda of Canterbury and was raised in the household of his uncle. He was trained and ordained a monk at Fleury in the 950s where he remained until his uncle's death in 958 and was then appointed bishop in 961. What is known of him comes from the *Vita Oswaldi* by Byrhtferth of Ramsey, written between 997 and 1002.[11]

It was in the reign of King Edgar that these three really became prominent. Dunstan had been brought back from St Peter's in Ghent by Edgar when he was King of Mercia. As soon as he became King of all England on the death of Eadwig, Edgar rejected the late king's choice for Archbishop of Canterbury and nominated Dunstan, who almost immediately went off to Rome to secure a pallium, returning to England early in 961. He was to be archbishop until his death in 988, almost thirty years, yet little is recorded of his activities as archbishop.

Aethelwold had been engaged in reforming and building up Abingdon, assisted by three other monks from Glastonbury, Osgar, Foldbriht and Frithegar. These three were to follow him to Winchester after his promotion to bishop in 963, where he remained for the next twenty-one years. While at Abingdon, however, Aethelwold had for a time been tutor to Edgar and no doubt made sure that he was aware of Dunstan's merits.

Oswald was actually appointed to the bishopric of Worcester in 961, ahead of Aethelwold, who had to wait until 963 for a bishopric. After ten years at Worcester, Oswald became Archbishop of York in 971, and held both sees in plurality until his death in 992, just over thirty years.

## MONASTIC REFORM BEGINS

The real period of reform did not begin until 963, when Edgar had reached the age of twenty-one and had probably shaken off the control over his actions by the ealdormen and thegns who had put him into power. It must be remembered that he was a youth of only sixteen when he became king of the whole country and that he would have been obliged to accept the advice offered to him with the ominous example of Eadwig before him. In any case, it would have been essential to put himself into an unassailable position before any radical changes could be made in church or state. That might be the answer to the puzzle of the *Hundred Ordinance*, issued perhaps by the Witan using Edgar's authority, but not an actual royal ordinance like the later codes. The text of the *Hundred Ordinance* which has survived may have been taken from a text which is not now extant. The law-making voice of this text is in the first person plural (we) whereas II, III and IV Edgar are clearly identified as his work. The king repeatedly says, 'It is my will' or 'My will is'.

Neither Dunstan nor Oswald had attempted a full reform of Glastonbury or Worcester respectively until after Aethelwold had initiated his cleansing of Winchester. Dunstan had made no attempt at all to introduce monasticism at Christchurch, whereas at Abingdon, Aethelwold had already imposed a rigorous regime, increasing the house's endowments and building a new church. Now, with the king's support, he expelled from the Old Minster the clerks (secular clergy) whom he found there, replacing them with some of his Benedictines from Abingdon.

Yet it was from Dunstan, who as Archbishop of Canterbury had the king's ear, that enthusiasm for reform spread, and it was he who ensured that the king listened to the case for reform. So the drive to reform monasticism spread out and the monasteries were reformed, especially by doing what Oda had tried and failed to do, enforcing celibacy and removing married clergy. These latter found themselves given the option of losing their prebends and rather comfortable way of life or of separating from their wives and becoming monks. It must have been a considerable shock for the rather hedonistic cathedral clergy.

Aethelwold spearheaded the attack. He was harsh and a zealot, in contrast to the less forceful manner of Oswald, who was a born administrator and appears to have brought monks in at Worcester more gradually. Aethelwold regarded the cathedral clergy as unclean, probably precisely because they were married.

The *Anglo-Saxon Chronicles* provide contradictory accounts of what happened. According to the *Winchester Chronicle*, King Edgar took the initiative, driving the clerks out of both the Old and New Minsters and from Chertsey and 'Middleton' (Milton Abbas). He then planted monks in these houses in their place and made Aethelgar abbot at New Minster, Ordberht at Chertsey and Cyneweard at Milton Abbas.[12] The *Peterborough Chronicle* E, on the other hand, says that Aethelwold drove out the 'clerks from the Bishopric; for that they would keep no rule; and he settled there monks', and that this was in the year after he became bishop, that is 964.

Edgar is further credited with having established 'many monasteries', which is an observation based on hindsight. Only about thirty-two have since been identified. The Peterborough text also claims that Aethelwold 'established two abbeys, one of monks and the other, Nunnaminster, of nuns, both at Winchester'. In fact both already existed. The bishop is being credited with what were actually the works of Edward the Elder and Aethelstan. What Aethelwold was responsible for was the conversion of both houses to the full Benedictine Rule. The Winchester A version of the *Chronicle* is tenth-century evidence, whereas the Peterborough E version is an early twelfth-century copy of an older text, probably from St Augustine's Canterbury, made to replace the original lost in a fire. It is therefore not quite so authoritative for the tenth century as the Winchester text. The entry for 963 is taken from Hugh Candidus, who wrote a *History of Peterborough* in the mid-twelfth century.[13] His work could easily have been used by the scribe who copied and interpolated the text of *Peterborough Chronicle* E.[14]

The order of events in Peterborough E has Aethelwold ask King Edgar to grant him 'all the monasteries which the heathen had destroyed because he wished to restore them, and the king cheerfully agreed'. It goes on to record the restoration of Ely and Peterborough (under its older name of Medeshamstede) which allows the scribe to give his explanation of how Peterborough came to rule the eight hundreds of Oundle in a manner excluding any interference by earls or sheriffs, so creating a Liberty (the origin of the Soke of Peterborough) rather like that claimed by Worcester and called Oswaldslow.

The scribe provides an alleged charter of King Edgar dated 972 for Peterborough. This is S 787 and is largely regarded as spurious, concocted no doubt after the Conquest when it became essential for abbeys to hang on to their lands in the face of Norman acquisitiveness. One way of doing so was to manufacture suitable charters, and the other was to claim the creation of an ecclesiastical privilege called a Liberty from which all other authorities apart from the abbot were excluded. That way they could exclude the interference of sheriffs like Urse d'Abetot of Worcestershire or Picot of Cambridgeshire. (Oswaldslow was unusual in that the Bishop's claim was entered in Domesday Book, having been authenticated or endorsed by the Shire Court.)[15]

What is not in doubt is that Aethelwold and King Edgar began the revival with the reform of the Old Minster, and Eric John suggests that the date was 20 February 964. The *Vita Aethelwoldi* makes it plain that Aethelwold acted with royal authority, 'given authorisation [*licencia*] by King Edgar'.[16] The problem that arises is when and where that permission was granted. Eric John argues that Aethelwold went ahead and reformed the Old Minster and then, afterwards, got retroactive permission from King Edgar, together with authority to reform other monasteries. The clerks, he suggests, objected, naturally, and complained to the king, who then dismissed their appeal at a synod held at Easter 964, which gave permission for the expulsion of all clerks and their replacement by monks. That, after all, had been the aim of the reform party from the beginning, and Aethelwold's action at Winchester would have been the catalyst triggering the king's response. Other historians are less certain that it was what Eric John calls an 'Act of State' involving a council of bishops and abbots as well as the king.

The Easter synod of 964 is recorded in the *Vita Oswaldi*,[17] which claims that Edgar ordered the establishment of more than forty monasteries. Florence of Worcester, after mentioning Aethelwold's succession to the See of Winchester, appears to be following the *Chronicles* in saying that Aethelwold 'filled the Old Minster with monks, the clerks being expelled by the king's orders'. Florence believed that the Bishop was the king's 'chief counsellor and took the chief part in persuading him to expel clerks from the monasteries and cause monks and nuns to be placed therein'.[18] Florence also assigns the reform of Milton Abbas and the New Minster at Winchester to 964. That Florence had no other independent sources for this period would seem to be confirmed by the lack of entries for 961–962 and 965–966, coinciding with blanks in the *Chronicles*.

If Florence is right to assign Aethelwold's initial action to 963, then the king, as Eric John suggests, gave his consent at a Witan held at Christmas (if the custom of thrice-yearly courts recorded in the eleventh century can safely be accepted as having been the practice in the tenth century).[19] But Florence might have been mistaken about the date, which depends on the text of the *Altitonantis Charter* which is now regarded as a twelfth-century forgery. The expulsions must really be assigned to the Gloucester Witan of 964.

In Eadmer's version of the *Life of Dunstan* the clerks are said to have objected to Aethelwold's harshness. The Ramsey account includes the decision in an Easter Court.[20] That gives no date, which leads others to argue that it was part of the meeting at which the *Regularis Concordia* was imposed, the 'synodal council at Winchester'. That is inherently unlikely since the imposition of the Rule implies that there were already a substantial number of monasteries, that the Rule was being interpreted differently in a number of them, and that it was now necessary to impose some sort of order on incipient chaos. A decision to expel clerks and bring in monks does not fit the situation. The decision in 964 was a decision to impose Benedictine monasticism in place of secular clerks.

From 964 onwards the reform was rolled out all over southern England. Edgar frequently took a leading role himself. He placed (Benedictine) nuns at the monastery of Romsey, Hampshire, previously built by Edward the Elder.[21] Then in 968 Edgar appointed Sideman as abbot at Exeter, which was also reformed on Benedictine lines.

At Winchester the allegation had been that the clerks lived a hedonistic, even (in the eyes of the reformers) immoral life; many were married, and they were accused of slackness in their religious observance, neglecting services, and avoiding even saying Mass. The source for this is Aelfric's *Life of Aethelwold*:

> Now at that time, in the Old Minster where the seat of the bishop was, there were clerks of evil manners, beset by pride, insolence, and evil-living, in so much that some of them disdained to celebrate their Masses in their turn. They married wives contrary to the law, and then repudiated them and took others; they were given over to gluttony and drunkenness.

Unable to tolerate this, Aethelwold, after receiving the king's authority to do so, expelled them and brought in monks from Abingdon. As the clerks proved reluctant to vacate the buildings, Edgar sent his personal aide, the thegn Wulfstan of Dalham (near Newmarket, Suffolk), his *sequipedus* (one who followed in the king's footsteps or sat at the foot of his throne). He was privy to the king's secrets, a *secretis* in the Latin phrase of the time, what was later termed a privy councillor.[22]

Wulfstan is known to have been a discthegn or steward and a king's reeve or praefectus, steward in fact of Queen Eadgifu's East Anglian estates.[23] He was much more than a local magnate. He had a career which began well before the intervention at Worcester in 964 and lasted until his death in 973 or 974, and he was a substantial landowner with unusual powers which extended beyond his home locality. He is found convening the Ely Hundreds and holding a court there, and had presided at a Cambridge court in the time of Aethelstan Half-King when Aethelwine was the local ealdorman. As a reeve he was involved in the forfeiture of an estate at Barley in Hertfordshire and even presided over a meeting of three hundreds in Norfolk, at Kelling. He could give instructions from the king to Bishop Aethelwold in Cambridgeshire in the matter of estates at Eye in Suffolk and Horningsea in Cambridgeshire, and withhold an estate from the bishop during his own lifetime. He died before his master King Edgar, and is typical of the kind of agent used by Edgar to maintain his rule over England in a manner which his successors were apparently unable to imitate.[24]

It was on 21 February 964 that Wulfstan commanded the clerks of Winchester either to 'give place to the monks or to accept the monastic habit'.[25] The clerks, however, cursed the idea of becoming monks and left, although three of them were later said to have changed their minds and become monks.

So incensed were the clerks that it was even believed that an attempt was made to poison Aethelwold's wine. But as the story is embellished by the reference to the saying of Christ, 'And if ye shall drink any harmful thing it shall not hurt you', and attributes the Bishop's recovery to his faith, this is more likely to have been an improving tale to illustrate his holiness. Aethelwold is then reported to have proceeded to expel clerks from the New Minster as well as the Old.

There is a foundation charter for the New Minster, which if genuine marks the re-foundation by Aethelwold as a fully Benedictine house.[26] It is in book form, written in letters of gold, and has an image of King Edgar presenting the charter to Christ. It is dated 966.

After that, Aethelwold went on to carry the Benedictine message into the Fens, re-founding monasteries at Ely in 970, Peterborough in 966 and Thorney in 972, which in itself seems to bear witness to a revival of Christianity among those of Danish descent living in the Fens. Aethelwold had obviously seen the opportunity for monastic life presented by the fen islands. There had been monasteries there since the seventh century. In the eighth century some had followed the Benedictine Rule but practice remained diverse. There was to be a similar risk of diversity of practice in the tenth century.[27]

Oswald had moved to Worcester after his elevation as Bishop there, and asked the king for an alternative site for a new monastery. He was offered three sites, of which Ely and St Albans were two. Then, following a visit of inspection, he accepted Ramsey in 965, offered to him by ealdorman Aethelwine. Later, in 970, he revived Pershore and helped in the re-foundation of Winchcombe with his colleague Germanus, the first prior at Westbury and first abbot of Ramsbury.

Oswald had begun to attempt the conversion of Worcester to the monastic rule, and either he was unwilling to employ the forceful means adopted by

Aethelwold or, as some argue, preferred to employ the technique of 'natural wastage'. That is, he gradually replaced clerks with monks as the former aged and died or were persuaded to adopt the monastic habit. He then tried the alternative of starting from scratch with a proven band of monks, mainly from Westbury. There is little clear evidence of monks at Worcester before 977.

Eric John insists, on the doubtful basis of the *Altitonantis Charter*, currently rejected as a valid tenth-century source, that Oswald's introduction of monks at Worcester was as violent and sudden as that of Aethelwold at Winchester. Other evidence suggests that the whole community only changed gradually, with two main periods of recruitment, 964–965 and 969–970.[28] One suggestion is that there were clerks at St Peter's, Worcester, and monks at St Mary's.[29] There were both clerks and monks present at Oswald's funeral in 992. So perhaps at Worcester, because it was a bishopric as well as a monastic house, Oswald preferred to have both sorts of clergy available. It was at Worcester that Oswald seems to have created a triple hundred, known as Oswaldslow, and to have adopted a policy of leasing, or more exactly loaning, Church lands to his tenants on terms which he spelt out in the famous *Indiculum*, or letter, addressed to King Edgar.

William of Malmesbury was of the opinion that not all secular clergy were bad. He says:

> Oswald realised that there was material for good in the mind of the secular clergy there [at Worcester] if only there was someone who knew how to encourage it and bring it to life and so, instead of putting them off by violent methods, he won them over by skilfully including them in his religious ambitions.

Oswald therefore allowed the original church at Worcester, St Peter's, to continue to function, and built a second, St Mary's, where he established monks. William adds that the nobles, following the example of their king, competed with one another in offering Oswald endowments for monasteries, both for the foundation of new houses and the restoration of those in a decayed state.

In carrying out their ambition to spread Benedictine monasticism, the reformers certainly affected adversely the interests of local magnates. Oswald's insistence on demanding leases either severed or curtailed the links already existing between those thegns who accepted his terms and the local ealdorman, Aelfhere of Mercia (who was to lead a reaction after Edgar's death against the impact that monastic reform had had on pre-existing landowning).[30]

Oswald's tenants were, according to the *Indiculum*, to 'swear that... they will be humbly subject to the commands of the bishop', and were then granted leases. They were to perform their services in subjection to the will of Oswald himself or of an officer (the *ductor exercitus*) who administered the bishop's ship soke. In effect the leases made Oswald's men his vassals so that they were no longer the men of the ealdorman, Aelfhere. If that were the case, it would explain Aelfhere's reaction after the death of Edgar. As ealdorman he would still have held the burh and been responsible for its military obligations.

Perhaps the introduction of controlled leases or loans of land for three lives was Oswald's way of dealing with what the reformers complained about so bitterly, *saecularum prioratus*, by which they seem to have meant secular control over monastic land which allowed laymen to appoint the clergy to the benefices and even nominate the abbot or the prior. In some cases the abbot or prior remained a layman. The monks preferred the patronage and protection afforded them by the king, who could also intervene in the appointment of an abbot.[31] Such intervention was acceptable from a king exercising his *dominium* but not from a layman exercising 'secular priorship'. Royal dominion was seen as quasi-sacramental, because a king was anointed, and what he could do therefore differed from anything a secular magnate could do.

Lay control, and even the existence of lay abbots, had, the reformers complained, allowed the clergy to become idle and dissolute and to ignore the Rule of St Benedict. These communities of clerics were not necessarily even in holy orders, and lived luxurious and unprofitable lives. When expelled for refusing to become monks they were not permitted to take their landed property with them and had to look to their families for support. The manner in which they lost their lands was, as the records of the *Liber Eliensis* seem to show, a fruitful source of disputes under later kings, especially Aethelred II, when automatic royal support was not available to the monks. There is even some speculation that the problem arose from attempts by the reformers to suppress existing book-right, where land was held by book, that is a charter from a previous king. The suppression of book-right meant that families lost their title to land and every diocese had a number of ejected clerks and disgruntled lay tenants who had lost their estates, many possibly related to each other.

The *Liber Eliensis* is a somewhat miscellaneous volume, containing material of all kinds collected at different times. Particularly notable, as far as the tenth century is concerned, are the records of lawsuits, originally in the vernacular, made by or commissioned by Aethelwold himself, the *Libellus Aethelwoldi*. The *Libellus* casts valuable light on the legal proceedings which followed the death of King Edgar. Other new abbeys have left very little in the way of archive material.

Edgar had intended a general policy of endowment. The first *Life of Oswald* claims that he gave the entire lands of the Church in England to the monks, but in fact what could be done at each abbey differed. There could be no real uniformity simply because the king's authority or lordship varied in its intensity in different parts of the country. Kent was handled very carefully and it is not clear whether Dunstan introduced full Benedictine reform there. A wealthy Canterbury monk, Werhard, left his property to the cathedral community but the land did not become the property of the whole community. Instead the land remained the property of the archbishop.[32]

Ely was re-founded in 970, with Byrhtnoth as abbot, and was attractive to the reform party because of its association with St Aethelthryth (Etheldreda) whose body lay near the high altar of the church. Monastic life there had probably been destroyed during the Danish invasions, and the lands of the house in the 960s were in the hands of the king. As elsewhere, the church and remaining buildings were in the hands of a community of clerks, one of whom, Aelfhelm, wrote the account of miracles found in the *Liber Eliensis*.[33] It is probable that local ealdormen and thegns hoped that a revived monastery would renew society in the Fens, acting as a social, political and economic centre. The *Liber Eliensis* reveals that there were tensions aroused by the re-foundation but they were easily overcome by the influence of its powerful supporters. The documents in the *Liber Eliensis* show that the abbey became a powerful focal point for the region.

King Edgar allowed the abbot to define the limits of the Isle of Ely 'by a prejudged boundary line encircling it'.[34] He also granted that the hundred courts were to meet fortnightly (not monthly as elsewhere) either at Ely or at Witchford, that is 'all the people of the two hundreds of the Isle'. The compiler of the *Liber* was making this the basis of the claim, made in the twelfth century, that Ely had a privilege or Liberty such that no one else

MEN, MONKS AND MONASTERIES                                    105

might hold a court within the Isle, and that this applied also to the five and a half hundreds of Wicklow in Suffolk, the one and a half hundreds of Dereham in Norfolk, and the trithing of Winston in Suffolk. It is unlikely that any privilege was granted in the tenth century to Ely or any other abbey of the kind claimed by churches in the twelfth century in their resistance to the encroachments of the barons. Wicklow was probably not a ship soke, as far as evidence goes, but it included Sutton Hoo, had the monks but known. The East Anglian ealdorman was Aethelwine and the monks rented the Liberty to him to run for them.[35] There is no evidence of clerics being dispossessed at Ely, but evidence in the *Liber Eliensis* shows that, at the death of Edgar, men who thought themselves illegally deprived of estates did try to sue the monks.

Under Edgar there were piecemeal grants of land and grants of blocks of hundreds, as to Ely and Peterborough, which allowed them all royal dues and services and the profits of justice, often in order that they might prove to be more dutiful royal agents than the Danish thegns of the area, so that the privileges granted to Fenland monasteries had a political as well as a religious purpose. Kings after Edgar did not continue this rather dangerous policy, for the monarchy, of retreating from direct rule over groups of hundreds and foregoing the revenue from them for the benefit of the monks. But it was a check on the power of provincial magnates, who normally dominated the hundred courts and received the grant of royal dues levied on their lands. This might also have been the policy in the Danelaw to counterbalance the grant, which he is known to have made, of the privilege for the Danes of making some of their own laws.[36] Edgar not only strengthened the Church but also his own power. His appointment of Oswald as Archbishop of York was intended to strengthen royal control over the former Kingdom of York.

From these Edgarian foundations and re-foundations the Benedictine reform continued to expand. More monasteries were reformed down to the year 1000 and several years beyond. When Bury St Edmunds was re-founded in 1022, monks moved from Ely to join the new community. The continuation of reform over a period of around fifty years accounts for the tradition that Edgar founded some sixty monasteries and nunneries, but not all of them were reformed during his lifetime. Some thirty-four monasteries can be accounted for, to which six or seven nunneries can be added, making about forty.[37]

## EDGAR AND THE PAPACY

Edgar did not, it would seem, act solely on his own royal authority, although he used it to good effect and the success of the reform reveals the extent of his political control over his kingdom. He also had papal backing. The Letter of Pope John XII (955–964), if it can be accepted as genuine, says that Edgar asked *through Dunstan* 'for permission to eject secular canons from the Old Minster at Winchester'.[38] The letter gives the required permission. Some assign the letter to John XIII, but he was not Pope until October 965 and the clerks were actually ejected in February 964. The letter is not confirmation of an event which has already taken place. If it was from John XII then it was sent before his deposition on 4 December 963, rather than during his brief re-occupation of the papacy from February to May 964. He calls Aethelwold his *coepiscopus* or fellow bishop, and need not have waited to do that until after Aethelwold's consecration on 29 November 963. Many accept the letter as genuine, as it agrees with the papal formulae found in the *Liber Diurnus*.[39]

It is highly possible that Dunstan, who had obtained his pallium from Pope John XII, returning to England in 961, had obtained a letter from the Pope authorising Aethelwold's appointment as Bishop of Winchester. The previous Bishop of Worcester, Aelfsige, been nominated to Canterbury by Eadwig and died on the journey to Rome.

One other papal intervention is reported, the grant of privileges to Glastonbury by John XIII (965–971), probably at Dunstan's request. Otherwise, reform came from the monks themselves, led by Dunstan, Aethelwold and Oswald with the support of King Edgar. In what may have been a response to the papal letters, Edgar enforced the payment of *Rome-feoh* or Peter's Pence, also called hearth penny, an offering of alms for the upkeep of the papacy which appears to have become customary during the ninth century. Edgar's penalties were severe, including the order that a man who failed to pay by the correct time, St Peter's Day (29 June), was to take his offering to Rome in person and pay thirty pence in addition, then pay 120 shillings to the king upon his return.

It is not known whether the penalty was ever applied. Repeat offenders were to pay 200 shillings, or on a third offence forfeit all their possessions. It is another indication of the draconian aspect of Edgar's rule exemplified by the physical punishments reported by Lantfred.[40] Aethelred and Cnut were to repeat the 120 shilling penalty without the requirement to go to Rome or the possibility of higher penalties.[41] It demonstrates the importance these kings attached to good relations with Rome, and was a welcome source of revenue valued at Rome.

Despite the destruction wrought by the coming of the Danes, Christianity north of Watling Street and into East Anglia had not been entirely obliterated. The Five Boroughs between the Welland and the Humber were regarded as Christian in 942 despite the traces of pagan cults found elsewhere. Further north some monasteries may have been burnt to ruins or deserted, crippled by the loss of their endowments, just like those in Wessex and English Mercia, but those that survived were more like colleges of clerks who no longer stressed the three principles of monastic life, celibacy, poverty and community life. The clerks were accustomed to marry, to be non-resident and to own private property. The Rule of St Benedict had not taken so firm a root as to supplant the older, Celtic idea of monasticism, and the rules followed were very diverse.

Some improvements had been effected by men such as Archbishop Oda, whose work may have been unfairly overshadowed by the success of Dunstan and his circle. Oda had required the repair of ruined churches and issued disciplinary canons in an effort to get clergy and laity alike to accept their spiritual responsibilities.[42] In Yorkshire a few estates went to the reformed southern houses such as Ramsey and Peterborough. Otherwise the main sign of ecclesiastical progress had been the revival of church building. The St Cuthbert Community also went in for church building on its estates, mainly in Northumbria with less attention to Lancashire. Some attempt was made to revive communal life at St John's in Beverley, at Durham and at York itself, but efforts to convert Durham to Benedictine monasticism were rejected by the clerks.

## THE *REGULARIS CONCORDIA*

The climax of the Benedictine movement's progress in southern England came with the imposition at a great synod at Winchester, in about 973, of the *Regularis Concordia*, the Agreement on the Rule. (Attempts to backdate this to the synod of 964, the *'synodale concilium Wintoniae'*, have not met with acceptance.) The document was the major formulation of the Benedictine reform and was, as suggested by its title, *Regularis Concordia Anglicae Nationis monachorum sanctimonialiumque*, intended to establish uniform observance binding on all monks in England on the basis of the Rule of St Benedict, and so consolidate the reform.

Dunstan is traditionally held responsible for the *Regularis Concordia*, but there is clear evidence that it was the work of Aethelwold, at the direct bidding of King Edgar. Aelfric says that the document was compiled by Aethelwold and it bears traces of influences from both Cluniac and Lotharingian usages.[43] It is written in his usual style and the prologue and epilogue reveal the mutually profitable alliance between King Edgar and his Queen Aelfthryth on the one hand and the monastics on the other. The property of religious houses is guaranteed against secular interests. Edgar, in about 971, had also commissioned Aethelwold to translate the Rule of St Benedict into English.

The *Regularis Concordia* consists of twelve chapters detailing liturgical observance throughout the year and laying down rules for monastic life and the organisation of the cloister or enclosure. It shows clear evidence of the use of continental and Carolingian exemplars, especially Fleury. A notable English theme is the requirement for a series of daily intercessions on behalf of the king and royal family. It includes an Easter Office with all the marks of an early prototype of liturgical drama, and the three prayers for the Veneration of the Cross on Good Friday.[44] Also, unusually, it includes a mode of election of the abbot, subject only to the royal prerogative. It adds that if the monastery serves a cathedral, the monks shall elect their own bishop.

The *Regularis Concordia* opens with what looks like a royal title: '*Gloriosus etenim Eadgar, Christi opitulante gratia Anglorum caeterarumque gentium intra ambitum Britannicae insulae degentum rex egregius*', that is, 'Edgar, by the abundant grace of Christ, the splendid and excellent king of the English and of the rest of the peoples dwelling within the ambit of the British Isles'. This echoes the charter S 827 for Winchester and the text goes on to state that Edgar has decided to summon a synod in order to impose the uniform observance of the Rule. The opening protocol of the 964 synod had probably been similar in tone, beginning '*Rex autem armipotens Eadgar etc*' (Edgar King, powerful in armed might). At that synod, Edgar had played a significant role, his character was delineated and his speech on that occasion recorded in the *Vita Oswaldi*.[45] But 964 is too early for the imposition of the *Regularis Concordia*, which had become necessary because the various houses which had been re-founded or set up *ab initio* were producing their own variations on the Rule. It was necessary to introduce order to prevent incipient chaos.[46]

STRATHCLYDE

Bamburgh

NORTHUMBRIA

CUMBRIANS

Northern Fleet

YORK

Eastern Fleet

Chester

THE DANELAW

GWYNEDD

Stamford

EAST
ANGLIA

POWYS

Peterborough

Thetford

Watling
Street

Cambridge

Worcester

former Danelaw treaty line

Hereford

MERCIA

DYFED

Oxford

Maldon

GWENT

Gloucester

Abingdon

LONDON

Malmesbury

Canterbury

Bath

Kingston

Sandwich

WESSEX

Dover

Western Fleet

WINCHESTER

Exeter

Hastings

Pevensey

Isle of Wight

1 England in the reign of Edgar.

2 St Mary's Chapel, Kingston, in which Eadred, Edward the Martyr and Aethelred are stated to have been crowned.

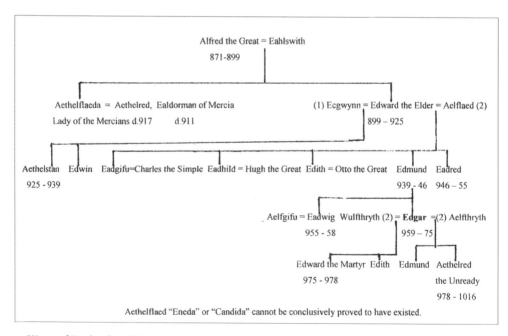

Alfred the Great = Eahlswith
871-899

Aethelflaeda = Aethelred, Ealdorman of Mercia
Lady of the Mercians d.917        d.911

(1) Ecgwynn = Edward the Elder = Aelflaed (2)
899 – 925

Aethelstan  Edwin  Eadgifu=Charles the Simple  Eadhild = Hugh the Great  Edith = Otto the Great  Edmund  Eadred
925 - 939                                                                                      939 - 46  946 – 55

Aelfgifu = Eadwig  Wulfthryth (2) = Edgar =(2) Aelfthryth
955 - 58                        959 – 75

Edward the Martyr  Edith  Edmund  Aethelred
975 - 978                              the Unready
                                       978 - 1016

Aethelflaed "Eneda" or "Candida" cannot be conclusively proved to have existed.

3  Kings of England and Wessex, 987–1016.

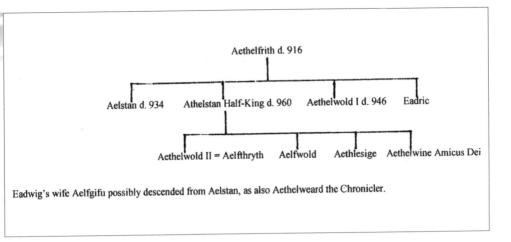

Eadwig's wife Aelfgifu possibly descended from Aelstan, as also Aethelweard the Chronicler.

4 Aethelstan Half-King and his family.

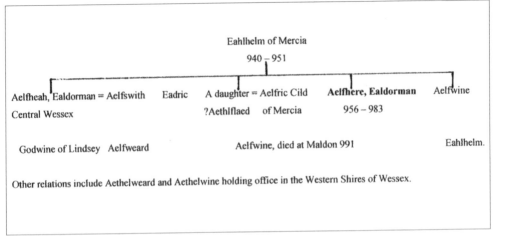

Other relations include Aethelweard and Aethelwine holding office in the Western Shires of Wessex.

5 The family of Aelfhere, Ealdorman of Mercia.

6 England and Wales around AD 910.

*Right:* 7 Saxon crucifix from around 1015 in Romsey Abbey, Hampshire.

*Below:* 8 Saxon crucifix in St Anne's Chapel, Romsey Abbey, *c.* 967. The crucifix is said to be the gift of King Edgar himself.

*Above left:* 9 Saxon chancel apse foundations, alongside the north wall of Romsey Abbey.

*Above right:* 10 The Anglo-Saxon porch and tower of St Peter's church in Titchfield, Hampshire.

11 All Saints, Brixworth, Northamptonshire. The Saxon windows of the porticus, made of Roman bricks.

*Above left:* 12 All Saints, Brixworth. The narthex door, also made of Roman bricks.

*Above right:* 13 All Saints, Brixworth. The triumphal arch into the apse.

14 All Saints, Brixworth. The west end of the nave, showing the original main entrance from the narthex.

15 Saxon tower of the church of
Earl's Barton, Northamptonshire.

16 North Elmham, Norfolk. Ruins of the Norman chapel showing the semi-circular apse,
probably dating from the original Anglo-Saxon cathedral.

*Above:* 17 Archbishop Dunstan.

*Right:* 18 King Edgar.

There had been variations. Dunstan's monasteries followed the simplest and most English interpretation. Aethelwold was more austere and borrowed elements from Fleury and Corbie. Oswald's houses followed a form derived from Fleury alone. It would seem that Fleury in particular was the spiritual centre from which Aethelwold drew a great deal of support. The use of hymns in the Rule follows the regulations of Fleury, while Canterbury, as one might expect, followed Ghent, since Dunstan had spent his exile there.[47]

So the reforms had spread from Europe as well as arising in England from the impulse originally given by Alfred the Great. The tenth century saw some of its finest minds standing for discipline and order and setting themselves to serve their fellow men. The reform movement was not a purely 'other-worldly' one, it had profound political implications, and was necessary for the consolidation and survival of society. Kings and their nobles had perhaps become acutely aware of the need for order. That in itself accounts for the tenth-century outburst of law-making by kings like Aethelstan, Edgar and Aethelred. These rulers were no doubt sincere in their Christian faith, as their devotion to relics and support for monastic reform shows. The monarchy and the Church allied with each other to deal with the problem of lawless men, and drove society to accept order.

While Aethelwold and Oswald, each in his own way, concentrated on monastic reform, Dunstan appears to have given his attention to the Church in general, holding ecclesiastical synods in his province and ordering the regular meeting of diocesan synods. With little success, he urged celibacy upon country clerics by preaching regularly and seeking to raise the standard of morality. His disciplinary canons are severe and forbid concubinage and marriage within the forbidden degrees of affinity and consanguinity.

The leaders of reform were all monks, and monks were to provide the Church with bishops and abbots.[48] Aethelwold, by re-organising and re-founding the Fenland monasteries, restored monasticism to the southern Danelaw. His monasteries were subjected to the full Benedictine Rule, though they never became part of the Cluniac Order. The *Regularis Concordia* had been drawn up by him and benefited from the advice of Cluniac and Lotharingian monks.

The Benedictine Rule prescribed manual labour and religious observance, but as this had become unenforceable by the tenth century the reformers were insisting on greater liturgical observance with longer attendance at church, elaborate music and ceremonial, though the *Regularis Concordia* can be seen as attempting to curb excesses in this area. The Rule allowed simple and sufficient diet, ample time for sleep and a disciplined but not over-austere way of life. There were long hours in church but time was made for manuscript production and the cultivation of arts and sciences. Two consequences followed from the reform: the monasteries and episcopal sees attracted large gifts of land, creating a balance of power between the nobility and the Church, and this growth of estates brought about a new kind of land tenure, leasehold grants as pioneered by Oswald at Worcester.[49]

Much of the information upon which knowledge of the monastic reform is founded comes from the collection of surviving diplomas, commonly known as charters. Most of these were what were known in the vernacular as 'landbooks'. This form of charter acted as the title deeds for land said to have been 'booked' to an individual by some lord, usually the king. The Church held many such in the years before the tenth century and they provided it with title to their land. But in the reign of Edgar, during the period when the monasteries were being revived, a number of diplomas were created which are not landbooks at all; they do not create title to land, although they are modelled on existing charters. They are all too easily dismissed as forgeries because they do not quite conform to the usual pattern.

Instead, they are about other matters of interest to the Church. They concern themselves with the conversion of separate, privately owned, estates into communal monastic property, and they are concerned also with the rights of the monks to manage their estates as they wished to do. They may include matters of specific interest, such as the right way to elect an abbot or a bishop. They vary in layout in such cases, but all follow a common procedure with the aim not of electing the right man but of keeping out the wrong one.[50]

The key figure in the tenth and into the eleventh centuries, before the Gregorian reforms, was the king. He was held to have dominion in these matters of the choice of bishops and abbots because he was seen as a type of Good Shepherd, and that made his intervention acceptable, whereas a magnate's mere *prioratus* was wrong. The king's intervention did not increase royal power, as he did not directly chose the new clerics, only approved of them. The new abbots mainly came from the ranks of men known to Aethelwold or Oswald.

The problems presented by charters are well documented and those from the tenth century have been well studied. Most of those that survive are the title deeds of estates preserved by monasteries as proof of ownership. The study of them can aid in tracing the development of royal, and noble, power; a king's dealings with his magnates, lay and ecclesiastical; and his handling of religious, economic and military affairs. Witness lists are a useful guide to the composition of the royal household and of the Witan.

Even those charters which are regarded as suspicious, or outright forgeries, can provide useful information if treated with circumspection. The information in such a charter could have been invented at the time of fabrication or it could have derived from an earlier source. Since such sources are not always discoverable, such information has to be treated with caution if uncorroborated. Charters could in fact be replaced if lost. One, issued by Aethelstan[51] and preserved in the Register of Burton Abbey, was a confirmation issued by the king who 'ordered this book of inheritance to be written anew... because that ancient book of inheritance we had not'. It had presumably been lost.

Among the tenth-century charters are a number referred to as *Orthodoxum* charters, from the first word of the preamble. They grant wide privileges to reformed houses, especially those connected to Aethelwold, and share common formulae. Some are probably forged, but those of King Aethelred to Abingdon in 993, and of Edgar to Pershore in 972, are seen as authentic by some authorities though regarded with suspicion by others.[52] Another charter of this sort, the 'foundation charter' of Ely,[53] may in fact be authentic. In its present form it could be the work of Aelfric of Eynsham 'the homilist'. It could be a forgery or an altered original, but is more likely to be the work of a leading monastic scholar.[54] Authorities differ about all these charters which grant privileges to monasteries founded or re-founded under Edgar, though most are very sceptical about their authenticity.

Charters were written and drafted by leading ecclesiastics, the bishops and abbots, often using monks from their own scriptoria in episcopal households or monasteries, as well as clerical members of the royal household who might even have constituted a royal writing office (possibly a proto-chancery). Many are astonishingly consistent in layout and appearance. In Edgar's time two groups have been identified, called Dunstan A, as originating in the Glastonbury scriptorium or written by Glastonbury clerics, and Dunstan B because of their associations with Dunstan himself.[55] Those who wrote them worked in monastic scriptoria but could be seconded to the royal court to serve the king and his Witan, so furnishing a royal secretariat.

This constant movement of personnel to the royal court from monasteries and back again probably accounts for the difficulty historians have in deciding whether there was a permanent body which could be called a Chancery. It seems to be agreed that a secretariat did exist under Aethelstan and his immediate successors, but that Edgar's policy was more relaxed. It is less certain that he retained a permanent writing staff since he could rely on the assistance of his monastic bishops. It is also thought that the use of Carolingian script (minuscule) was closely associated with the progress of monastic reform, as the dominance of the Canterbury scriptorium seems to show.[56]

Foundation charters, or those granting monastic privileges, were not the usual landbooks and were the work of scribes drafting and writing them on behalf of the recipients, so benefiting the monasteries. They do not fit the standard criteria by which authentic landbooks are judged. It cannot be claimed that they are all genuine, only that more of them than is currently thought acceptable might have a genuine original behind them, and that some may be more or less authentic.

## AELFHERE AND THE 'MADNESS'

After Edgar died there occurred what most historians have termed an 'anti-monastic reaction', a period when it was alleged that some monasteries, mainly in Mercia, were seized, the monks expelled and replaced by secular clergy, and their lands possibly returned to their previous owners. This was inspired by Ealdorman Aelfhere and his supporters. Then Ealdorman Aethelwine *Amicus Dei* and his brothers opposed the movement and brought it to an end. The problem is that there is only one known example of such action. A charter in the archives of Ramsey claims that Germanus, Abbot of Winchcombe, Gloucestershire, was expelled. The case is only known because he took refuge at Ramsey.

The sources call this a time of 'madness' and say that it spread from the West to the East Midlands until it was checked. The picture is an over-simplification of a complex situation. Evidence from other sources, such as the *Liber Eliensis*, reveal that it was more a case of the seizure of disputed lands which were alleged to have been, in some sense, wrongfully taken from previous land-holding men and bestowed on the monasteries. Some of these men were now alleging that they had not really consented to the transaction. The case at Ely, involving Hatfield, saw Aethelwine himself dispute the right of the monks to hold the land. The case was settled when the monks handed over three separate pieces of land amounting to forty-one hides, in exchange for the forty hides at Hatfield.

It rather seems as though the real problem was one of sharp practice on the part of King Edgar and his monastic supporters. They seem to have acquired land at what looks like less than market value. The owners, feeling hard done by, were now trying to obtain a fair price. These claimants were not always honest themselves. At Ely, Aethelwold had bought twelve hides at Linden (part of Haddenham, Cambridgeshire) with its dependencies of Hill and Witcham, for one hundred mancuses (25 shillings) and a fine horse and some land at Bishampton in Worcestershire. This had been done before witnesses at Cambridge. After Edgar's death, the seller, Leofric of Brandon, tried to have the sale annulled, but the Lawmen of Cambridge, who had been witnesses, found against him.[57]

In another case, too involved to describe in full, land at Stretham near Ely had been bought by Aethelwold and the sale was challenged by one Aelfwold of Mardleybury in Hertfordshire, alleging that violence had been used against him to secure the sale. After the case had been fully set out, Abbot Byrhtnoth added two pounds to the original purchase price of twenty mancuses. It might be that this was thought to be a fairer price.[58] Ely records a number of other such cases, and in several of them the matter is settled by the monks paying a little more for the land.[59]

It looks as though the so-called reaction against the monks was political and economic rather than an attack on monasticism as such. It was a necessary check on the drift of land into monastic hands and examples from Ely and Ramsey suggest that this had already gone too far, allowing religious interests in some shires to outweigh secular ones. This weakened the influence and power of local thegns on whom the king's officers relied for the maintenance of public order. Thegns obviously resented the intrusion of a monastic landlord between themselves and the king.

That Aethelwine and Aelfhere had reached an agreement is suggested by the settlement of the Downham case from Ely at what is called 'a General Meeting... convened in London', at which there were magnates of all kinds from all regions of the country. The thegn at the centre of the dispute, called Leofsige, had forcibly seized lands at 'Peterborough and Oundle and Kettering from God and St Peter [Ely]' so that they could not be cultivated. Aethelwold laid out his case before the assembly and won it. Leofsige had to pay compensation and, for the violence, pay 'to the king the amount of his *wergild*'. There was then another meeting at Northampton, for the 'whole of this region', at which the Bishop's lands at Peterborough, Oundle and Kettering were restored to him. These meetings look very like meetings of the Witan.[60] It was in this manner that the widespread uproar over land ownership was eventually settled. There had been something of a 'territorial revolution' under Edgar, with large amounts of land transferred to the possession of the monasteries, and the balance of power had been disturbed.

These disputes at Ely, and the meetings at which they were settled, took place 'when the affairs of the kingdom were in turmoil'; they are certainly part of the general settlement of disputes following Edgar's death. They testify to the degree of control he exercised while he lived. It was not the all-out attack on monasticism depicted in the *Chronicles*.[61] The monastic writers say that Aelfhere 'and many others broke God's law and impeded the monastic rule and dissolved monasteries and drove away monks and put to flight God's servants'. They claim that widows were robbed and many wrongs and injustices arose. The style of the annal in the *Chronicle* is that of Archbishop Wulfstan, possibly indicating that it was written after AD 1000. The annal in the *Peterborough Chronicle* E is the only evidence claiming the overthrow of monasticism by Aelfhere. Archbishop Wulfstan was using the conflicts after Edgar's death as the reason God's vengeance had been visited on the English people in the form of the return of the Danes.

There is little concrete evidence for real damage, nor any sign of the dissolution of any monastery. The evidence from Ely, as from Ramsey, is of harassment and lawsuits to recover lands, not all of which were successful. The faction led by Aethelwine seems to have put an end to it, perhaps by intervening personally in cases, and profiting by it as the *Liber Eliensis* reveals.

# 8

# England in the Reign of Edgar

In Edgar's reign, the four pillars of medieval society were clearly visible: kingship, lordship, community and family. Equally clearly to be observed were the three strands of society as envisaged by the Benedictine reformers, in the form of the adage 'some must fight and some must work and some must pray'.

It is extraordinarily difficult to recover a complete picture of what this meant for English society. There is a lack of the material needed, not so much because of neglect by those who lived in pre-Conquest England, but because of the attitude of contempt for the past adopted by the Norman conquerors. They interpreted the past in a manner which cast aspersions on the character of the people and their rulers and took little care to preserve accurate copies of such documents as survived their coming. Scribes had no hesitation in altering charters to adapt them for their own purposes, so reducing their value as evidence of pre-Conquest practice.[1]

Contempt was also expressed by the way in which the Normans sought to wipe out all traces of Anglo-Saxon architectural achievement. Wherever they went the Normans sought to erase the buildings of the past. That they were not entirely successful was not for want of trying. The long-lived Bishop Wulfstan of Worcester is said to have wept at the abandonment of the former church erected in 960. The extent of the conquerors' success is plain to see. The imprint of Norman architecture blots out the preceding Anglo-Saxon heritage.

There are no really informative traces of thegnly or ealdormanic residences, nor royal ones for that matter. There are scarcely any remains of the defences erected around burhs. The layout of many towns and boroughs has been altered, often, as Domesday Book reports, by the wholesale destruction of houses and streets to make way for Norman castles and Norman cathedrals. At Lincoln, for example, the property of the prominent citizen of Lincoln, Toki, some thirty messuages (houses with land attached) were destroyed by the Norman bishop Remigius when he moved the seat of his bishopric from Dorchester to Lincoln, so that he could build Lincoln Cathedral on the site. There are no 'Saxon' monastic buildings because the Normans simply cleared the site before rebuilding on a grander scale. The number of churches destroyed to foundation level was considerable.[2] Major sites were deliberately destroyed and important tenth-century buildings have therefore been lost.

The residences of thegns and ealdormen might, in some cases at least, lie beneath the great Norman castles (where these are not built over the remains of town houses), or even be buried under the mounds of motte and bailey castles. Even if excavation were possible, little would remain, as those residences were mainly built of wood. They comprised a great hall, rather like a tithe barn, with built-in chambers (such as a bower), a kitchen and then outbuildings. They had a palisaded defensive ring work around them and a fortified 'burh gate'. There might also be a bell tower. This picture is based on the excavations at Goltho in Lincolnshire. The oval earthwork around the Norman keep at Castle Rising in Norfolk is also probably pre-Conquest.[3]

Nonetheless, much can still be said about English life in Edgar's day: about the various ranks of society, the development of boroughs, the regulation of trade, and the imposition by this strong king of law and order. Military and naval institutions have already been explored and the Benedictine monastic reform described.

Anglo-Saxon, that is tenth-century English, law emphasised correct procedure with elaborate formulae and much formality. Persons and personal property were protected by fines and compensation, such as the *wergild* payable to the kin of a slain man which varied according to his social rank. Courts tended to pay more attention to groups rather than individuals, who required either kin or peer groups to vouch for them as compurgators or oath-helpers. They supported a man's oath with their own oaths. The number of oath-helpers needed varied with the nature of the accusation and the value of each oath varied with the status of the giver. They also had to guarantee the payment of fines or act as sureties.[4]

## LAW MAKING IN THE TENTH CENTURY

Kings in the tenth century made laws in an impressive manner. Although four codes are attributed, in printed sources, to Edgar, they can safely be reduced to two. The *Hundred Ordinance* may not be of royal provenance in the copies that have survived and II Edgar and III Edgar are now thought to be the secular and religious sections of one code. But Edgar appears to have made much more law than has survived in written form. There is, for example, the set of severe punishments described by Lantfred. In the Code 'IV Edgar' there is a reference to provisions made 'for the improvement of public security' by his councillors; these were very acceptable to the king, and he orders them to be 'continually observed among you'. Yet no such provisions are to be found in any extant laws of Edgar, unless the reference is to the *Hundred Ordinance*.[5] Like Edward the Confessor, Edgar had a reputation for law-making which seems to depend not so much on written law (there is no genuine law code attributed to the Confessor) but on the *verbum regis*, the king's (spoken) word. The English took very literally the maxim *quod principi voluit, habet vigorem legis*: the will of the prince has the force of law. This was verbal law-making witnessed by the Witan. The important thing was always the king's oral decree, what he actually said.[6]

It is by a king's laws that his success is usually judged, the degree, that is, to which he was able to bring about peace, prosperity and the common good. It is argued that much of the law of the tenth century was built upon the foundation of Alfred's law, as represented by his *Domboc* and which remained in force throughout the tenth century.[7]

His successor, Aethelstan, had shown through his law codes that a king should be seen to govern; they show the extent to which he could drive his officials to do their duty. It is not only by law codes that Edgar's government can be judged, but by the contents of his charters and of the saint's lives, which reveal the extent to which he was successful, where his predecessors had failed, in suppressing wrongdoing and maintaining social order.[8] They reveal a state of affairs where the king's will was obeyed without fear of contradiction, which explains why his reign was renowned for its peacefulness. William of Malmesbury states that under Edgar 'the greed of thieves and the double-dealing of money-changers was suppressed by capital punishment'.[9] Edgar issued a remarkably uniform series of charters, and even the northern provinces of his realms are represented in the witness lists, an indication that his writ ran even in Northumbria.

His legislation is impressive, even though it does not reach the heights of Alfred's codes and is quite small when compared to those of his successor Aethelred II. The two surviving codes and the reports of other legislation which is not found in written form reveal those aspects of his work which were of concern to the king and his Witan and seen as in need of re-statement, modification or reform. Thus he and his Witan laid down regulations for the regular payment of tithes to the Church and for the observance of Sunday as a day of rest. He regulated the proceedings in the courts of justice to ensure the punishment of those who gave false witness, meaning perjurers, and issued regulations for the buying and selling of cattle.

It is by no means impossible that some of Edgar's actual legislation has not survived in written form simply because it was superseded or re-issued in somewhat milder terms by Aethelred. That king is found providing the only documentary proof of the existence of a ship fyrd and supports the idea of an annual review of the navy. Like Edgar, Aethelred enforces the payment of Peter's Pence, and repeats the demand for improvement of the currency, correction of weights and measures and so on. It is probable that other legislation by Aethelred repeats laws passed by Edgar, but in the absence of documentary evidence, none has been identified as yet. Cnut repeated Edgar's punishments by mutilation applied to ears, eyes, and feet.

Edgar emphasised regularity of administration rather than spelling out the substance of the law. This was often perhaps taken for granted, as ealdormen at shire courts are found administering law without explicit reference to any law code at all. On the other hand, most records of court cases concern disputes over land rather than the application of the criminal law. Ealdormen are found simply applying the law as they themselves understood it. Edgar himself was more concerned with the universality and efficiency of the administration, insisting on the proper operation of the procedures of law (so avoiding maladministration) which were not necessarily new in themselves but which might not have been properly observed under his predecessors, especially Eadwig. Courts were ordered to meet regularly, and reeves were told to 'deal in the manner prescribed by the aforesaid ordinance with everyone who fails to perform this and who by any remissness on his part consents to violate the solemn declaration of my councillors'. He insists that 'the laws of my ancestors shall be observed'.[10]

So Edgar required every man to provide a surety, a guarantor of his good behaviour, to hold him to his duty in shire, hundred and borough, and perhaps even at the level of the vill (which was a subdivision of the hundred and a unit in the system of taxation).[11] Courts had to be regularly convened and properly operated. All transactions in them had to be properly witnessed and offenders relentlessly pursued. Edgar insists successfully on the enforcement of the rules he has added to 'the decrees of my ancestors'.[12] That explains Aelfric's description of him as 'the strongest of all kings over the English nation',[13] and that of another author who writes that he 'oppressed evildoers everywhere and subdued tyrants'.[14]

His insistence on uniform practice is found wherever he turned his attention. He required a uniform standard of coinage and of weights and measures. Then he demanded uniform religious observance from the newly reformed and re-established Benedictine monasteries, whose abbots and abbesses were urged to 'be of one mind'.

The degree of his success is perhaps best measured by the fact that despite the destructive impact of renewed Danish invasions in Aethelred's reign, the single English state created by Edgar successfully withstood the attacks and survived them more or less intact. Its comprehensive system of administration remained fully operative under Cnut and his successors, under Edward the Confessor and Harold II and under the Normans. The structure of the State remained substantially the same.

## FINANCIAL REFORM

Edgar's financial reforms enabled his successor Aethelred II to raise and pay the enormous sums required for Danegelds and Heregelds. Indeed Aethelred raised these sums so easily, without introducing any administrative legislation, that it does indeed look as though the assessment system, by which every estate and every borough was assessed in hides or carucates upon which the tax could be levied, was already in existence before the Danes arrived.[15]

The 'Danegelds' (as they were later named) were extraordinary taxation, as was the Heregeld, a levy to pay a standing army or a permanent force of warships. It should be distinguished from what Domesday Book repeatedly calls 'the common geld' or 'the king's geld'.[16] So, Stigand, Archbishop of Canterbury under Edward the Confessor, had full rights in Guildford 'except when the common geld is laid on the town, which none can escape'.[17] The lawmen at Stamford and the men of Hertford had similar obligations. At Stamford[18] the borough 'paid geld for twelve and a half hundreds for military service and for Danegeld' and the lawmen had sake and soke 'excepting geld and heriot'. At Hertford,[19] seven houses of the men there 'rendered no customary due except the king's geld'. Furthermore, in Berkshire the common geld was seven pence on the hide, payable in two halves of three and a half pence at Christmas and at Pentecost. It looks as though there was a standard geld, collected when the king required it to be collected, not necessarily an annual tax. What Domesday Book does not state is when this system began, but it does seem to distinguish between ordinary geld, used to pay the costs of the fyrd, and Danegeld, the tribute paid by Aethelred.

As with Edgar's other legislation (the swingeing punishments, the system of ship sokes and the details of his reform of the coinage) for which no written edicts have survived, it might be the case that, by his reign at the earliest, a uniform levy was customary on all hides and carucates. According to the *Liber Eliensis*,[20] possibly during Edward the Martyr's reign shortly after Edgar's death, or even before the latter king died, a certain thegn called Aelfric 'was burdened with a heavy imposition of tax'; as he could not pay it he had to sell land to Aethelwold and Abbot Byrhtnoth in order to raise the money. This suggests that the geld was already being levied. Edgar certainly had a Witan of talented individuals, men like Dunstan and Oswald and ealdormen like Aethelwine and Aelfhere, quite capable of exploiting the system of assessment by levying money in lieu of actual service, which, as a result of the peace engendered by his naval policy, would not otherwise have been needed. Edgar was certainly responsible for a great deal of systematisation and for the exploitation of a wealthy economy, as his secular and religious policies went hand in hand.[21]

His administration was carried out by agents of his government at three levels. Over whole regions of England there operated the great ealdormen. After 964 the North was assigned to the Dane Oslac. Western Mercia was in the hands of Ealdorman Aelfhere, and Eastern Mercia and East Anglia were administered by Aethelwine and his supporting ealdormen. Wessex was directly under the control of its king. In all areas there were subordinate ealdormen in charge, it seems, of one or more shires. These were the members of the great families which supported the monarchy, forming an extended cousinhood connected to the royal family by blood, by marriage and by fostering, or, at the very least, by commendation.

It may have extended downwards into the ranks of the administrators of the second rank, the king's thegns (like Aelfric Cild or Eadric, 'one of Ealdorman Aethelwine's high ranking men')[22] and his reeves, and sideways into the families of the archbishops, bishops, abbots and abbesses. Great thegns, like Wulfstan of Dalham, could be used almost like Carolingian *missi dominici*, the legates and agents of the Carolingian kings. Below such men as

Wulfstan of Dalham came the serried ranks of the many and various reeves with charge over vill and estate, over hundred and wapentake, over royal estates and over boroughs and ports. They were rather like those 'maids of all work', the Tudor Justices of the Peace.

England was being run in such a way, as some historians have estimated, that a high proportion of the population was involved in administration in a more than merely passive sense. At Leominster, for example, the figure was about five per cent.[23] Nothing much changes, or so it appears.

All these men were involved in assessing the capacity of the land to provide revenue for the king. It is known that the assessment of land in hides can be traced back to the seventh century and was used mainly in the eighth as the basis for the levy of men for the fyrd, because 'some must fight', and then for the construction of fortifications, the burhs, which Alfred the Great was instrumental in developing in a rigorous and systematic manner. Even bridges and perhaps royal roads were maintained by a levy on assessed estates, probably originally and mainly in the form of forced or obligatory labour.

By the tenth century every piece of land was under assessment, and that assessment was related to the institution known as the hundred, which in turn integrated into the judicial system, as well as forming part of the military and naval systems in the form of fyrd contingents and ship sokes. By the eleventh century this had come to mean a rate of one pound for forty days' service, when a pound was the expected revenue a landed lord could expect from one hide in one year.[24]

The hundred became the basis of the geld collection even when it did not actually amount to one hundred hides. One variation on the normal, or at least common, system operated in East Anglia, where assessment lay not on the hundred but on the vill, and was paid at the rate of so many pence contributed by the vill to a geld pound levied on the hundred. The document known as the *County Hidage* apparently relates to the assessment of hidated shires in Mercia and Wiltshire some time after the reign of Edward the Elder, that is any time between Aethelstan and Edgar. That document seems to show that assessment in hides or carucates followed the division of areas reclaimed from the Danes into shires. The Midland shires are so uniformly constructed around a more or less central borough, the 'burh' built by Edward the Elder or by Aethelflaed, that the system is clearly artificial. Maitland's analysis of the *County Hidage* also clearly reveals the artificial nature of its assessments.[25]

The lowest social or legal organisation in tenth-century England was, or so it seems, the vill. Hundreds were composed of a mosaic of such units which were then the basic units of taxation. The geld levy was raised not by lordships and manors but vill by vill. A vill was not necessarily identical to one particular settlement or village, though it could be; most were groups of settlements. Where a vill and a large settlement coincided, the area later became known as a village. There may be a connection here between this system (bearing in mind the East Anglian variation where vills paid so many pence to the pound, rather than the more usual pence to the hide) and the social and agricultural institution in the Danelaw of the 'soke', where a number of outlying settlements (even as many as thirty, known variously as berewicks or sokelands) owed customary dues and suit of court to a central vill.

Research in Northamptonshire suggests that the assessment on the hide, in some shires at least, was made by counting the number of yardlands or virgates (from Latin *virga*, a rod), which were quarters of a hide. Thus the inhabitant of a vill paid the reeve so many pence according to the number of yardlands he cultivated. The reeve here might be the agent of the lord of the vill, where there was such a lord, or of the central vill of the hundred. If resident in a vill, the reeve might act as the head man of it.

It was the social and economic, and for that matter legal, depression of the men and women living within the vills (especially where these came to form a Norman manor) into semi-bondage, tied to the soil and unable to leave the service of their lord, the new Norman owner, which made the word *villanus* — one who lives within a vill — into the equivalent of the word 'serf' (*servus*). It was when men fought back against this servitude and resorted to outlawry rather than remain on the manor that the word 'villain' (a *villanus*) acquired its criminal associations.[26] In pre-Conquest England free men were plentiful. Domesday Book, in astonishment, records the many men who held their land so freely that 'they could go with their land to whatsoever lord they wished'. These were the holders of one, two or three hides or mere fractions of a hide, or even of a number of acres, called in 1086 villans, cottars or bordars. Their status was well below that of a sokeman, a man who owed service and suit of court to his lord but was otherwise free.

The shire, hundred and borough are all mentioned in Edgar's extant legislation, but the vill — which, unlike the other institutions, had no public court — is not mentioned, nor is it in any other pre-Conquest document. It must have existed in practice, and might well have evolved like the hundredal system during the tenth century.[27] Interestingly enough, it was during the tenth century that the ealdormen ceased to be mere shire officials, and by the year 1000 they are found to be running many shires. Accordingly, from Edgar's reign onwards, reeves were given charge of shires, though not yet formally called *scir-gerefa* or sheriff. The earliest reference, in Aethelred's reign, is to a *scir-man*.[28]

The conclusion which might be drawn is that a major change took place in the organisation of power in the tenth century, though exactly when is not yet clear. Edgar was responsible for a great deal of systematic organisation and it is not implausible to attribute these developments to his reign, though much of the work might have resulted from ealdormen, bishops or abbots making logical adaptations to a developing and increasingly more sophisticated administrative and financial system. Edgar's reign saw the construction of a uniform system of government and an increasingly royal judicial system. The scale and scope of his known innovations, as well as of those which can plausibly be attributed to him – setting the administration of justice in shire, borough and hundred on a firm footing, reforming the coinage and the system of weights and measures, putting in place a royal navy and the means to support it, the ship sokes, even the development of the assessment system into a tax system, the geld – demonstrates his power and explains his reputation.[29]

His power is demonstrated by the success of his policy towards the Danelaw. So successful was it that his successor, Aethelred II, was able to legislate quite freely for the area. Edgar himself acted with great diplomacy and tact. The Danish settlers were not used to written laws or the customs so familiar to the Anglo-Saxons and could not, therefore, be expected to surrender their established way of life.[30] Nor could they be either eliminated or expelled, so they had to be accommodated and a *modus vivendi* or *via media* found: one which would give wider significance to the institutions of kingship and government, rather than merely continuing with established ancient customs. Edgar had to act with consummate statecraft to achieve his ends and cope with the new conditions brought about by the conquest of the North by his predecessors. The great 'coronation' at Bath in 973 would certainly have played its part in this.

All of this ought not, perhaps, to be attributed in its entirety to Edgar himself since direct evidence is lacking, other than the fact that the Danelaw and Northumbria remained peaceful and there were no uprisings. There is nothing remotely resembling a Life of this king, either from contemporary sources or from others shortly after his death (though there seems to have been some sort of account of the life of Aethelstan which lies behind William of Malmesbury's account of his reign). The ideas and methods might well have originated with his advisers, men like Dunstan, Oswald and Aethelwine. But it should not be forgotten that these men were either chosen or kept in office by Edgar and that it was his personality which held the whole edifice together. Aethelred II, his son, had powerful and wily advisers too, and some of Edgar's men remained with Aethelred into the 990s, but in the end he was unable to hold his government together. He could not even maintain Edgar's naval dispositions and so failed to repulse Swein Forkbeard's invasion.

## THE UNIFICATION OF ENGLAND

The year 955 had seen the end of the first stage of unification, the creation of a single kingdom of England from the Channel to the Firth of Forth, with West Saxons, Mercians, Northumbrians, East Anglians, Danes and Britons all under the rule of one dynasty. The peace of Edgar's reign in part reflects the military success of his predecessors which left him free to concentrate on his monastic reform, with its tremendous political overtones, and the creation of a uniform administration which, after 958, had to be created by largely ignoring old boundaries and limitations. For instance, the former ancient divisions of Mercia were ignored. Shropshire was formed of an artificial union of lands once divided between people called the Magonsaetn and the Wreocensaetan, and Warwickshire was formed by joining lands south of the Forest of Arden to the former kingdom of the Hwicce.[31] These were the old provinces and regions of Mercia. Stenton pointed out that it would have needed a strong king to do this and suggested Edward the Elder, but there is no real evidence that he did so. The more settled times under Edgar are a more likely period for this to be accomplished. Edgar also brought about the conditions under which the Five Boroughs (originally Danish military areas dominated by jarls and holds and their armies) were divided into shires on the West Saxon model, and were then further subdivided into hundreds or wapentakes.

It was in the Danish areas that distinctive usages and customs survived, especially in legal matters. It was here that the institution of groups of twelve lawmen or *judices* (judges) had arisen for the declaration and interpretation of law and custom. It was no wonder that Edgar openly acknowledged, and perhaps even learned something from, these customs and sought to avoid confrontation with the Danes over them, so much so that later writers vilified him for being too ready to accept pagan behaviour.[32] He readily legislated for Wessex and Mercia but was much more canny in his approach to the Danelaw. This did not prevent him from legislating when necessary for the whole realm. A good example of that is his coinage reform and the reform of weights and measures.

It was probably in the early 950s or 960s that the confederacy later known as the Five Boroughs was established, possibly as a result of that very policy of toleration associated with Edgar. It may have been a kind of regional defence system for the southern provinces of York, and might even owe something to the inspiration of Archbishop Oswald, who was himself a member of the Danish family of Archbishop Oda of Canterbury (Oda had negotiated a truce with Archbishop Wulfstan of York concerning the Five Boroughs).

Edgar had allowed the Danes to 'make such good laws as they best decide on',[33] and granted that concession 'because of the loyalty which you have always shown me'. They had certainly shown loyalty in supporting him when he became 'King of the Mercians and the Northumbrians' in 956. The identity of these Danes is revealed by Edgar's command in that same code that 'Earl Oslac and all the *here* [army] dwelling in his ealdormanry are to give their support that this law may be enforced'. So the Danes of the former kingdom of York, now under Oslac's rule, are incorporated into the kingdom of the English as the king legislated for 'all the nation, whether Englishmen, Danes or Britons in every part of my dominion'.[34]

Edgar, early in his reign, had held a Witan at York, after the death of an earl called Osulf (of the House of Bamburgh). The king was unwilling to allow such a vast area to be inherited by one person and so he divided the earldom into two parts, giving the land from the Humber to the Tees to Oslac and that from the Tees to Mireforth (Mirkfjord, the Firth of Forth) to Eadwulf Evil-Cild.[35] The king did this to prevent discord arising in the North due to the aspirations of the inhabitants to recover their former liberty.[36] This was also the occasion when Edgar ceded Lothian to Kenneth II of Scotland. In that manner Edgar relieved himself of the necessity of imposing his rule on the area.

The area of the Five Boroughs never quite became anything so definite as to deserve the label 'federation'. It remained a matter of informal co-operation in the interpretation and application of custom in that region.

The divisions called 'trithings' or thirds (origin of the Yorkshire Ridings), were units of local government involving the grouping of wapentakes, but these latter units soon came merely to correspond in powers and functions to the English hundreds. More significant were the groupings of estates called sokes, in which settlements around a central capital town had to pay suit of court there and render all customs including the geld. The sokes seem to have performed a role not unlike that of a royal vill, but were held by king's thegns and other magnates. They remained territorial units down as far as the thirteenth century. It was in such local adaptations that much of the devolved nature of local government in the Danelaw consisted.[37]

Edgar's decree[38] was not a concession wrung from a weak king who could not enforce his will, nor a confession of any inability to dominate the Danelaw. That domination was no doubt accomplished through an impressive demonstration of overwhelming military might which lies behind Florence of Worcester's insistence that Edgar made a winter peregrination through his territories, no doubt accompanied by his magnates, the ealdormen and king's thegns, with their attendant retinues.

Edgar preferred to see the suppression of Danish practices as both difficult and purposeless, and therefore unnecessary, since they were no longer a threat. It is thought that he issued instructions and left the Danes to carry them out in their own way, and up to a point this seems to be so.[39] He certainly insisted on the enforcement of Christian duty to support the Church, through tithes and through Rome Scot or Peter's Pence, saying, 'it is my will that these ecclesiastical dues be everywhere alike throughout my dominion'.[40] He insisted also that the rights of lay people were to be maintained 'in every province, at the best standard which can be devised' so that his royal dignity remained unimpaired, and then added that lay rights were to be maintained 'among the Danes in accordance with the best laws which they can determine upon'. It was not such a huge concession as some seem to believe, because the royal reeves were expected to deal harshly with those who failed to obey the ordinance or violated the 'solemn declaration of my councillors'.[41] Edgar insisted on maintaining his 'royal prerogatives as my father did'. Buying and selling was to be properly witnessed 'in borough or in wapentake' and the Danes were to 'continue to observe the best laws which they can determine upon', which he explicitly calls a concession and adds that 'I desire that this one decree relating to the investigations such as these shall apply equally to us all for the protection and security of the whole population'. His concessions are hedged about with limitations preserving the royal prerogative.[42] Earl Oslac is specifically charged with enforcing the decree in his earldom.

The reign cannot have been a period of totally even development. There was doubtless much confusion and faltering arising from the need to absorb the foreign element in society represented by the Danish settlers. Edgar readily acknowledged the limits of his authority, just as Aethelstan had made concessions to the Scots, in order to preserve the semblance of political unity, and Edgar acquiesced in being seen more as an overlord than a king beyond the River Welland. Yet he could appoint the Archbishop of York and other bishops, and appoint ealdormen with vice-regal powers, as is indicated by the use of the word 'earl' rather than 'ealdorman'. The old English spelling was *eorl*, from the contrast made between men of higher birth, the 'eorlish' (meaning noble) and other free men, who were 'ceorlish' (of lower status).[43]

How those he appointed exercised their powers was a matter for them. Earl Thored resorted to ravaging in Westmorland, devastating the homes and farms of the people as a punishment for their disobedience to the king. Edgar rarely went north, where he had few royal vills, but he did hold a Witan at York and held a ceremonial naval gathering at Chester, which his successors do not appear to have been able to do.[44] It is not clear that the apparent limitations on royal authority or power in the North, beyond Watling Street, differed from similar limitations to the south of it, where Edgar, like his predecessor Eadwig, found that he had to make gifts of estates to his supporters to ensure their loyalty. In Edgar's case, of course, the main beneficiary of this political generosity was the Church.

An important point is that although a notable cluster of new and re-established monasteries was set up in the Fens of East Anglia, there were no such institutions provided for the northern Danelaw. York was administered ecclesiastically from Worcester, Lincoln was administered from Dorchester and East Anglia from the See of London. It may be that the kingdom of the English, deriving its powers from those of the former kingdom of Wessex, lacked the resources needed to extend its administration directly into the northern areas. Developed government was a long time in reaching the North, and even Cnut and William the Conqueror in their turns found it a difficult area to govern. One possibility is that the machinery of government south of Watling Street, especially in Mercia, had been destroyed or very severely weakened by the ninth-century Viking invasions, and that government had to be re-built there and in the southern Danelaw first before it could be extended further north. The rebuilding was achieved

ENGLAND IN THE REIGN OF EDGAR

in Edgar's reign, through the further division of Mercia and the southern Danelaw into shires, and those shires into hundreds or wapentakes.

Edgar's laws and his charters, and the abbeys he founded or re-founded, are important memorials to his government. He issued some quite detailed laws, many of interest to historians of social conditions. He legislated about lords and lordship, especially about those who, in almost fourteenth- or fifteenth-century language, might be described as providing 'maintenance' for their men, protecting them in court and elsewhere in defiance of right and justice. Thus Edgar had to allow the proviso that although men were expected to appear before the hundred court at the appointed time, they might be 'prevented by a summons from [their] lord'.[45]

Edgar was the first to recognise boroughs as centres of trade.[46] Overall he was concerned to deal with the perennial problem of theft, an insoluble problem in early societies.

Like other kings, Edgar was definite also about what ealdormen could not do.[47] They were not empowered to mint coinage or issue charters, nor hold their own courts (they presided over shire and hundred), and there was no tier of local government higher than that of the shire. There were no counts or margraves in England with powers independent of the king, as in continental states. Ealdormanries and earldoms were not actually provincial governments (when Tostig Godwinson in the Confessor's reign tried to behave like a provincial governor he provoked a rebellion which overthrew him) and royal control over local institutions meant that the ealdormen could not develop their area of competence into a principality. Similar institutions did this on the Continent, where the Count of Rouen eventually became the Duke of Normandy.

Edgar, in fact, seems to have acted to reduce or prevent the likelihood of any ealdormanry, even in East Anglia where Aethelstan had been 'half-king', from developing in that direction. He built up the numbers and importance of the king's thegns, possibly in order to provide a counterbalance to the power of the ealdormen. He certainly endowed his 'faithful ministers' with land and, as one charter puts it, 'I have determined with the counsel of my magnates [opibus] to endow my faithful thegns out of the wealth given me by God'. That is another example of legislation by *verbum regis* not found in a formal law code.[48] The king's thegns (*ministri*) are found in attendance in all parts of the kingdom and some of them rose to become ealdormen. Others remained purely local or provincial magnates, visiting only the courts held at Winchester or Canterbury.[49]

The thegns co-operated with the king at shire courts, of which they formed the 'Witan', and it was to them as a body in the shire that writs, whether spoken or in writing, were addressed. The king's thegns were the characteristic servants of the tenth-century monarchy, a corps of provincial *ministeriales* (royal officers in general), much more at the king's mercy and more responsive to his mandates than the ealdormen. They rode on the king's errands with his writ and summons.[50] They could intervene in shire courts and other local meetings, proclaiming royal ordinances, and they could advise and co-operate in the execution of them. Think of the Witan at Thundersfield 'to which Aelfheah Stybbe and Brihtnoth son of Odda came, bringing the king's word to the moot'.[51] So to be a king's thegn was to be his servant.

Below the thegnage, even when economic disaster had reduced a thegn's actual holding in land below that of the five necessary hides (the rank was heritable once acquired), came the ceorls or free farmers. They formed the real basis of English society and far outnumbered all other ranks. They had a *wergild*, the legal value of their life if slain, of 200 shillings (£10) where a thegn had one of 1,200 shillings (£60). But they filled an honourable and responsible position in the state and were indeed those of whom it was said, 'some must work'. And they did most of it.

The law protected a ceorl's home and family and the peace of his household against intruders. Ceorls owed limited personal service in the fyrd in an emergency and in time of war, bearing a free man's arms of sword, spear and shield. They joined with others of their class in contributing to the king's feorm, the food-rent, and were independent masters of a peasant or farming household.

A ceorl's land-holding or tenement was originally at least the land unit known as a hide, in origin enough land to support a ceorl and his family. By the tenth century the hide had become a unit of assessment or of account, like a rateable value, upon which tax could be levied or from which service could be demanded.[52] As the holder of a number of hides a ceorl was liable to fyrd service, the obligations of burh construction and bridge work, and a contribution to the geld. What cannot be ascertained is the number of acres which constituted a hide, as this varied considerably according to the fertility of the soil and to the accuracy of the assessment. It is clear that in many places there had been 'beneficial hidation': the assessment had been artificially reduced, possibly as a reward for outstanding service. In the sources, hides can vary from forty acres in Wiltshire to 120 acres in Cambridgeshire and the eastern shires. Documentary references to estates assessed in multiples of five, ten or twenty shillings make it quite clear that by the tenth century the system had become almost wholly artificial.

The king's 'farm' (*feorm*) was that quantity of provisions which, traditionally at least, was reckoned to be sufficient to maintain the king and his normal retinue for twenty-four hours. It was rendered once a year from a group of settlements or vills to the nearest royal vill in the district within which they lay. This render was then applied to the king's use by his reeve. Kings could travel from one royal vill to the next, consuming the accumulated produce. That from vills they did not visit might be transported to another vill, or to Winchester, or, for more distant estates, simply sold in the nearest market. Other services could be demanded; some have already been mentioned, and others were often agricultural or related to the sport of medieval kings, hunting.

Royal estates could be distributed as rewards to faithful servants, and a king had to be known as a good giver, either of land or of precious objects: rings, bracelets, fine weapons and cloth, and of course the relics of saints. Royal estates, because of this, had fallen into the hands of ealdormen and thegns and, especially in Edgar's reign, into those of bishops and abbots.

Along with the land went the entitlement to the customary services and dues which it rendered, always excepting the three essentials which kings always reserved to themselves: bridge-work, burh-work, and fyrd service. It has been suggested, somewhat controversially, that even some kind of devolution had occurred of a right to fyrd service in a limited number of cases. It had been given to ecclesiastics rather then lay lords, as in the case of the liberties or privileges (later known as franchises), that is, the triple hundreds liable to fyrd service and ship service in Edgar's time. Some argue that this handed over the right to demand such services to the bishops and/ or abbots. Of course, even if it did, they could only raise the fyrd or perform ship service at the king's command.

Most of the services which went with a gift of land were agricultural, in the widest sense; cartage and carrying services, building on royal estates, work on the lord's home farm (the demesne), and so on. Even the king's *feorm* itself might end up in the hands of an ealdorman. The recipients of such grants were in turn able to and expected to reward their own faithful men. A great lord might recruit men to his service by means of an outright grant of land, even if made in return for a pledge of loyalty. This was not the grant of a feudal benefice, as on the Continent, which was a revocable or conditional grant in return for future service. The English commended man expected to be rewarded for having performed service for a lord, though the lord no doubt hoped that gratitude would hold the man to his oath of fidelity, especially as kings in the tenth century expected every man to have a 'lord'.

A variation on this seems to have developed more thoroughly during the tenth century, and its future spread probably owes something to the example set by Oswald of Worcester. Precisely because, as a bishop and monk, he saw himself as holding the lands of the See of Worcester and the abbey as their custodian who would one day pass them on to his successor, Oswald chose to endow his *fideles* not by outright grants, which would have reduced the Church's total landholding, but by developing a more legally binding version of that form of 'bookland' (land granted under the terms of a diploma or charter, the book) which was in fact a lease, or to be even more precise, a loan. He drew up a set of conditions binding on his men, who therefore became his tenants (literally men who hold the land), and to make doubly sure he wrote a letter, an *Indiculum*, to Edgar spelling out what he had done.

What was required of the men commended to Oswald (or required of them as the recipients of loan land) is illustrated from the conditions imposed by him. At Worcester the tenants were required to 'fulfil the law of riding as riding men should', that is, carry out all sorts of commissions for the bishop, including acting as messengers and as mounted escorts, as well as performing miscellaneous agricultural services and some services relating to hunting. The land was 'booked' (at least in part) to the Church rather than the Crown and some men were now three steps away from the king, owing service to a great ecclesiastic, or nobleman, and to the superior tenant, the riding man. The king was lord over his magnates and they in turn were lords over the riding men, who were then lords over their subtenants. In the course of time some of this service became military, especially where there were triple hundreds or ship sokes.

The tenants agreed to hold the land for the term of a number of 'lives', being their own lifetime and that of their heirs. In the case of family men, especially laymen, that would naturally mean their son and grandson in the case of a grant for three lives, or only the son if for two. Some no doubt accepted a single lifetime grant, which would certainly have applied to those who were clerics – members of the monastic community who were not yet monks, preferring to remain secular priests.[53] The monks, rather ingenuously, call the leases 'landbooks' which they were not. A landbook gave the land to the recipient (or sold it) whereas these agreements were for a limited duration and at the end, in theory at least, were expected to revert to the ownership of the Church. In practice it proved very difficult to recover land which had been so leased as written evidence was not always accepted in the courts of shire and hundred.

Some men might even have held the estates in question by book, and Oswald might have been attempting to restrict the rights of his men in order to protect the Church's holdings with the leases, trying to define what were previously only customary obligations. Quite a few of the tenants were members of Oswald's 'connection', for example kinsmen or his commended men, while others were new tenants. He had important military obligations to fulfil and so needed to have a supply of reliable men. The tenants might even have been the crew of his ship.

All this so far has been concerned with the doings of men, since so much of the material which survives is about just that. But women were a vital factor in society, especially within the family, though a few took part in political life and had a fair share of influence in the eyes of the law. Of the wives and daughters of ceorls little is known, but of women of the middle and upper ranks something can be said. They could own land, make wills, and appear in shire and hundred court. At one recorded court case, as well as an abbot, a priest, an aetheling of the royal family and eight other men, there were present two abbesses and six other ladies as well as many good thegns and women. In this instance it was a woman who brought the case and won it. The *Liber Eliensis* (from Ely) records the decision of the daughter of a nobleman who refused marriage to a man called Guthmund, brother of Abbot Wulfric of Ely. Guthmund did not hold forty hides of land and was thus not a noble of the first rank, called a *procer* – that is, one close to the king, a counsellor.[54]

A distinction was made between three forms of marriage. This was not a simple matter because the real aim of marriage was the procreation of heirs. Christian marriage, involving consent and dowry, was not that different from the Danish form except for the involvement of the Church. Both involved a stable but not necessarily indissoluble union.[55] The third form was concubinage. The term 'concubine' could always be applied to a rival's wife in order to discredit him or her. The marriages of those of high birth were seen as more legitimate. So Church condemnation of concubinage led on in due course to the condemnation of divorce as well as of adultery. The law removed privileges from concubines and their children were regarded as illegitimate. The use of the terms 'concubine' and 'concubinage' had the effect of blackening the reputation of marriage *more danico*. It was at this point that the ranks of religious women could be recruited from abandoned wives as well as widows.[56]

The activities of noble women were quite varied and were such as befitted their rank. The daughters of Edward the Elder excelled in needlework, spinning and weaving. Other women were skilled in embroidery or wove tapestries. They learned all the necessary skills for running a household and directing servants. Widows remained important, especially as landowners, as in the case of a matron called Quen who was granted land at Howden and Old Drax in South Yorkshire by King Edgar.[57] The estate had eight other dependent settlements which belonged to Howden 'with sake and soke'. The king grants this in quite a routine way, and to a woman, and not as though creating a precedent. For a person to hold land in that way, with the implication that the people of the settlements owed suit of court at Howden, or at least that the landowner received the profits of justice, suggests that such privileges were readily granted.[58] It is noteworthy that even a woman could hold such an estate with soke and sake. The phrase (*socu et sacu*) had already been recorded in a charter of Eadwig granting Southwell in Nottinghamshire to the Archbishop of York, Oscytel, with eleven contingent settlements, a typical Danelaw 'soke'.[59]

Anglo-Saxon law in the tenth century emphasised correct procedure with elaborate formulae and much formality. Persons and personal property were protected by fines and a system of compensation known as bot, wer and wite, that is, the making of amends or compensation for injury, the value put on a man's life and his oath, and payment as a punishment.[60] A man's *wergild* was payable to his kin if slain and varied according to his social rank. Courts tended to pay more attention to groups than to individuals, who were required to be members of a kin or of a peer group (a tithing) which would vouch for them as compurgators or oath-helpers to support a man's oath with theirs. The number needed depended on the nature of the accusation, the value of each oath and the status of the accused. Such groups also guaranteed payment of fines and acted as sureties.[61]

Something, then, has been said about the nature of English society and life during the reign of Edgar. It is known that boroughs developed further during Edgar's sixteen years of peace (though details are scarce), trade was regulated, as his law codes show,[62] and he had imposed strong patterns of law and order. More needs to be said about the operation of his government, the position of the queen as it developed in his reign, the influence of religious belief on the politics of the reign, the kind of state he ruled and the glorious manner in which his reign reached its highest point in 973.

# 9

# The Witan and the Household

The early kings had found it necessary to consult, and were supported and consulted by, a council. This was composed not only of their own natural supporters and closest and most intimate friends, or members of their personal household if they were of noble status, but also of great land holders. These were men who, by family, status or wealth, felt themselves to have, and were recognised as having, the right to advise kings and to be consulted by them.

This body naturally included all ealdormen and king's thegns, especially those who were recognised as 'nearest to the king'. That meant his closest and most trustworthy servants, and, in the Christian period, the archbishops, bishops and abbots and even some abbesses.

When meeting to deliberate on the affairs of the realm, to approve, sanction or witness the promulgation of codes of law, to witness and consent to grants of land and privileges, to sit in judgement in lawsuits involving great men of the kingdom, the council became known as the Witenagemot or meeting of the wise. These 'wise men' (*sapientes* in Latin), or Witan, from *wita*, one who knows, were thus those who by rank, wealth or experience were thought qualified to advise kings. When used in this way, 'Witan' means the King's Council.

It was often difficult to establish whether a particular meeting was a secular or ecclesiastical occasion. Some sessions of the Witan dealt exclusively with religious affairs, as the contents of some law codes issued in the tenth century, especially by Edgar, show.

Charters issued by Aethelstan, a predecessor of Edgar, reveal that the Witan in his day had been greatly enlarged. It included many sorts of great men and many more of them. No document survives which describes what the Witan was, so what is known about it has to be teased out from the various references to it. It was certainly not an organised constitutional body governed by precise rules of procedure, nor did it meet in regular sessions at appointed times or at a specific location. It met as and when the king had need of it. Nor was it a representative assembly of any kind, though no doubt its members felt that they were in some way the embodiment of English opinion.

There could even be present princes from other parts of the island of Britain outside the borders of England. Hywel Dda the Good, of Dyfed in South Wales, witnesses a charter of Aethelstan from 934 giving thirty hides at Frome in Somerset to the Old Minster at Winchester. He is there alongside the Archbishops of Canterbury and York, fifteen other bishops, all the ealdormen and fifteen *ministri* or thegns. At Colchester in 931 some fifty lay nobles of differing ranks were present, an indication of the large size of Aethelstan's Witans. Overall it is known that there were some seventy meetings of the Witan in the tenth and eleventh centuries, though that only covers those of which some record survives.

Repeated consultation by kings over a long period of time must have led the members to withdraw or refuse consent on occasion. One recorded case is the refusal of those present in 1051 to authorise the use of force against Earl Godwin. But how often consent was withheld cannot be known, possibly because when consent could not be obtained no record was kept of a negative decision.

There has been some debate among historians over whether the Witan actually elected, or even deposed, a king. Such evidence of 'election' as survives seems only to show approval of the choice of the obvious successor, often after a rival had been removed by death. Edgar was 'elected' King of all England when Eadwig died, but then there was no other candidate. Edward the Martyr was elected when Edgar died despite the existence of Aethelred, called explicitly in one source Edgar's legitimate son, but Edward's election might have come about because in 975 Aethelred would have been too young for kingship.

Certainly the Witan of Mercia withdrew consent, to an extent, in 956 and chose Edgar for king north of the Thames, but Eadwig remained King of the English and continued to issue coins in the North. That was an exceptional situation and might reflect some deathbed provision by King Eadred, that Edgar should be King in Mercia when he came of age.

In a crisis it was the strongest and most able candidate who was 'elected', the man most fitted to rule and with the most overt support. There was no question of a vote of any kind. Generally the last will and testament of a previous king might be decisive or the heir might have been recognised in some way during his father's lifetime. Mostly the Witan simply seem to have accepted the most logical candidate.

Men readily attended the Witan because it gave access to the king and his patronage and the rewards which flowed from it. How it operated is illustrated by two charters. Some time between 955 and 968 a thegn called Aethelstan of Sunbury came to the king and 'bade a doom of him', and as a result the Mercian Witan 'doomed him the land'.[1] Of another estate it was recorded in a charter that the owner, Ecgferth, had forfeited it and the king, though asked, could not alter the decision because 'it is a doom'.[2] So the characteristic function of the Witan was the giving of judgement and, with that, the maintenance of justice and equity.[3]

Earlier Witans had been largely ceremonial rather than legislative, and it is only under Edgar that edicts are found common to all the 'nations' within the boundaries of his kingdom of England.[4] Thus precautions were to be taken against theft and fraud and were to be binding on the whole of England.[5] The clause reads, 'the following Edict shall be common to every folk, Angles and Danes and Britons in every quarter of my realm'. Further it was enacted that 'My Witan and I have chosen what the penalty shall be among the English', while the Danes were to 'choose according to their law' what it would be. But punishment there would be everywhere.[6]

Some members of the Witan were also members of the royal household, the king's supporting staff and companions and his servants. It was an essential component of royal government because it was the only form of public administration which existed. The household was as old as kingship itself. Attendance upon a ruler and the opportunity to serve him personally brought with it opportunities for advancement and to influence the decisions which were made. Dunstan was promoted to the household of Aethelstan and won promotion as Abbot of Glastonbury under King Edmund. Others who served as thegns might go on to become ealdormen as they advanced in seniority or in favour with the king.

The household travelled with the king from one royal vill to another, but there were occasions when it remained in one location for a considerable period of time. There is evidence of a royal complex of buildings at Kingston upon Thames which might well have included a 'palace' or 'King's Tun', and there was a palace at Winchester close to the site of New Minster. Aethelwold, until he became Bishop of Winchester, is said to have lived in the palace for some time early in Edgar's reign. Sometime later a Bishop's residence was built at Wolvesey, possibly for Aethelwold. There was also a palace at Westminster some time before the Conquest of 1066.[7]

Few remains, if any, have been found of royal residences; they all seem to have been made of timber. Documentary evidence suggests that such a residence comprised a large oblong hall, containing private apartments for the king and queen, and a feasting hall, called the 'mead hall' by poets. Other buildings around it would provide kitchens, stables, storehouses and so on. The whole would be surrounded by a ramp and ditch and a palisade, or else a stone wall. The hall called 'Heorot' in the poem *Beowulf* would have been typical. The poet's description reads, 'It came into his mind that he would command the construction of a huge mead hall... Heorot he named it whose word ruled a wide empire'. It had high arched gables and is described as a stately building. It was decorated with gold plates nailed to the walls and had gold embroidered tapestries. There were separate chambers for Hrothgar and his queen. Such halls were much the same as other lordly residences.[8] They can be thought of as not unlike a tithe barn. At Winchester the palace would have been within the surviving Roman walls.

The essence of the household was the people who ran it. Churchly influence had moved it away from the essentially military aspect it had in earlier times, and by the tenth century it had a more sophisticated arrangement. No longer merely the assembly of the *comitatus* or military companions of the king, it contained priests and even bishops and abbots. From Alfred's time onwards, there was a trend towards building halls and chambers with separate functions and to gather together learned men who could advise the king.[9]

The sons of noblemen and even of kings might be educated at court. The charters of Eadwig show the presence at court of his foster-parent (a thegn called Aelric), since, like Edgar, he had not been brought up by his own father and mother, Edmund and his queen.[10]

King Alfred employed 'Mass-priests' (one is referred to as *sacerdos*), who kept records for him, wrote his written orders (his *gewrit*) and said Mass. Under Aethelstan it is accepted that there was an actual writing office, not yet so formal a body as to be called a 'chancery', nor presided over by an official called a Chancellor, but which was capable of drafting and writing charters, law codes and other royal documents. Alfred had organised his finances in two divisions, devoting one part of his money to Church expenditure and three parts to the cost of government, dealing with noblemen, workmen and visitors.[11]

There was a hierarchy of sorts even then, as Alfred's will shows, with some servants taking precedence or ranking higher than others. Eadred's will is even more detailed. He makes bequests to archbishops, bishops and ealdormen, and then to his seneschal, chamberlain and butler.[12] He goes on to list priests who have charge of his relics, other priests and then other members of the household.

His seneschal, then called *discthegn*, had charge of the royal table, helped by the *discifer*, later called a dapifer, a type of steward. There was a *hraeglethegn*, a type of chamberlain in charge of clothing, aided by a similar official called a *burhðegn*. There was a *byrele* or butler (*pincerna* in Latin) in charge of the drink and the vessels for it.[13] In Eadred's will,[14] one class of these servants received eighty mancuses of gold (ten pounds) while a lesser rank of official received only thirty mancuses (three pounds and eighteen pence). These latter were the stewards, *stigweards*, a kind of reeve responsible for the financial control of royal estates. They might perhaps have received the payments from other reeves when these were delivered.[15] Other household servants were called *cubicularii* or chamberlains.

If the Ely tradition is to be trusted,[16] Edgar created some sort of office very like that of the later Chancellor or *Cancellarius* but divided the responsibility into three. The abbots of Ely, Glastonbury and St Augustine's, Canterbury, were each alleged to spend one third of the year at court 'performing service with the reliquaries and other ornaments of the altar'. That suggests that they were in charge, by turns, of the king's *haligdom*.[17] This derives some colour of truth when it is recalled that Dunstan, as Abbot of Glastonbury, was given charge of Eadred's relics, treasure and documents. A similar tradition at St Albans claimed that their abbot, Aelfric, was *cancellarius* to King Aethelred. He might have done a similar job for that king. This word does not carry the meaning of 'Chancellor' until after the Norman Conquest.

In Aethelred's time, if not earlier, the king had a kind of notary, called a *scrinarius*, who wrote documents for him. One charter of Aethelred claims to have been written 'by the pen and ink and hand of the notary and *scrinarius* of Aethelred, King of the English'. Such an official, like the earlier household priests, had charge of the relics. Aethelred also had a *scriptor* or writer called Aelfwine.[18]

None of these officials belong to anything remotely resembling the officials of the great departments of state which developed in the twelfth and thirteenth centuries. Royal courts in the tenth century were always on the move and personnel remained fluid, ad hoc and variable. It is possible that some sort of treasury had developed, since the vast quantities of coin from taxation, customary dues and the profits of justice must have exceeded expenditure. The excess had to have been stored somewhere rather than all of it travelling with the king. Later evidence from the eleventh century suggests that if there was a treasury anywhere it was at Winchester, so this could well have been developing in Edgar's time.

This gradual elaboration of the Household is another example of the 'Carolingian' note struck by the developing English monarchy, and it was from the writing office in the Household that the language voicing 'imperial' pretensions had emanated.[19] There must also have been influence on the English administration from contact with the court of Otto the Great in Germany, Edgar's uncle by marriage. Court life in England was becoming more dignified and formal. Ealdormen and thegns congregated at court as a distinct part of it and this gave rise to a more hierarchical structure, observable in the witness lists of charters. There was a distinct order of precedence among the witnesses that must have caused a similar order amongst the Household men themselves, as King Eadred's will reveals.

# 10

# Queenship, Marriage and Motherhood

Women in the tenth century had a more prominent status among the very highest in the land than in previous centuries, especially the queens. Eadgifu, third wife of Edward the Elder, remained a key figure in the reigns of her sons Edmund and Eadred, and was deeply involved in the succession dispute when Eadred died. Although she lost her lands in Eadwig's reign, she was rewarded by her grandson, Edgar, whose succession she had helped to secure.[1] She was daughter to ealdorman Sigehelm of Kent and married King Edward the Elder in 919. Of little prominence under her husband and under Aethelstan, who was not her son, she became prominent with the accession of Edmund, who was her son, becoming one of the most important queens of the era. She was a stalwart supporter of Dunstan and Aethelwold, whose careers may well have owed something to her influence. She displayed great interest in Church reform and was involved in the extension of Wessex and its power. Her large estates in Kent made her a quasi-regent there. She is last noted in 966 at the time of the birth of Edgar's second son, demonstrating family unity.[2]

Kings' wives were ecclesiastical patronesses and could influence Church appointments. After Eadgifu's death (c.966–967) the most influential woman was Queen Aelfthryth, conventionally regarded as Edgar's second wife, who became more influential early in the reign of her son Aethelred, deriving her power from having been anointed and from being both a king's widow and the mother of the reigning king. Queens are prominent as mothers or wives to their sons and husbands.

It seems that Edgar might well have followed the example of his grandfather Edward the Elder in taking up to three wives, though the exact circumstances of his matrimonial entanglements are difficult if not impossible to unravel. It may be that at least one of his wives was through what became known as a marriage *more danico*, a hand-fast marriage with the consent of the bride's family but without the witness of the Church. If it was, that might help to account for Edgar's reputation as a lover of 'pagan ways'. As the *Chronicle* states under 959, 'Yet he did one ill-deed greatly! He loved evil foreign customs and brought too firmly heathen manners within this land'.[3] But Geoffrey Gaimar seems to have been both accurate and acute when he says of Edgar, 'the King was devoted to women'.[4]

The queen of Edgar's elder brother Eadwig was unpopular with monastic writers, but the real problem was a political matter rather than Eadwig's relationship to Aelfgifu. She was certainly a member of a royally descended southern English family and at first the marriage strengthened his position during the 'palace revolution' accompanying his accession in 956, when his marriage was opposed by Dunstan and Oda perhaps more for political than theological reasons. His marriage, and the prospect of that producing an heir, was a threat to the possibility of Edgar's eventual succession. Edgar's démarche or quasi-rebellion (in assuming the throne of Mercia) weakened Eadwig's position when Edgar demanded recognition as next in line to the throne, which is perhaps what setting him up as king in Mercia and Northumbria implied. Eadwig was then forced to divorce his wife on grounds of consanguinity.

English kings did not seek wives from other dynasties outside the kingdom; they married the daughters of the same local families that provided ealdormen and king's thegns, and the endowments for monasteries. So wives were of high birth and were married for political reasons rather than romantic ones. In Eadwig's case he had such poor support that his marriage did him little good in the eyes of his enemies. The growth in the power and status of these local families was becoming a significant factor in enhancing the status of queens, and it is thought that in addition to providing support such marriages threatened royal security. They could contribute to disputed successions, particularly when kings married more than once.

## THE QUEEN'S IMAGE

Aelfthryth has the title of Queen applied to her well before 973, the occasion of Edgar's alleged second coronation. Earlier queens were only designated *cwen*, rather than *hlafdige* or 'lady'.[5] The latter title brought them the benefits of additional security of status and more formal powers at court. Queens, during the ninth century, do not seem to have even been named as such. Aethelred II, Edgar's successor, had no consecrated queen during the lifetime of his mother. The marriage and anointing of Aethelred's queen, Emma of Normandy, followed the dowager queen Aelfthryth's retirement and death. Perhaps this indicates that there could only be one *anointed* queen at a time.[6]

Aelfthryth's own anointing had been part of the quasi-imperial ceremonies at Bath in 973, and is associated with the promulgation of the *Regularis Concordia*. As part of that agreement, the abbots and abbesses of the reformed monasteries were to seek the lordship of the king and queen respectively and the queen was specifically charged with the duty of being the defender and guardian of all nuns. The monks and nuns were in return required to pray daily for the welfare of the royal family. This is deemed to have been a high point in the definition of English queenship, elevating the queen to a role much closer to that of the king.

The queen's image later arose out of an interrelationship between the queen, the nunneries and the reforming churchmen, as efforts were made to redefine clerical status and distinguish it from that of the laity. There was an emphasis on chastity, required also of male clergy, as the Northumbrian Priests' Law shows, because of their role in the offering of the Eucharist. Most Lives of queens were the product of religious houses founded by queens and were intended to glorify the foundress. Yet, rather surprisingly, they tended to picture other royal wives as evil, scheming, avaricious or murderous, or even all of these things.[7]

Reformers were keen to make use of the queen's involvement with religious communities, just as the king himself was involved through his enhanced status as the anointed of the Lord, more legitimate and acceptable because of his combined royal and quasi-priestly role. The queen, in her turn, became more of a queen and less of a laywoman. Her status was enhanced by the growth of the cult of the Virgin Mary as 'Queen of Heaven, Lady of the World, fruitful mother of the Only Son of God', a cult illustrated in art and in manuscripts, especially those of the Winchester School. Aelfthryth was required to be above suspicion in her own conduct. There could not be any breath of scandal. Aethelwold appears to have been particularly close to Queen Aelfthryth and there developed a tradition of holy queenship.[8]

But problems developed after Edgar's death, as the king's family relationships had political consequences. (There were rival groups of magnates supporting each of Edgar's sons, with Aelfthryth at the head of Aethelred's party.) This resulted in stories being created which saw

Aelfthryth's relationship with several nunneries as threatening and exploitative. This was a result of the resentments engendered by the effects of the reforms on lay interests.[9] The atmosphere in the tenth century which gave rise to stories of immoral behaviour developed as the Church sought to condemn loose sexual practices along with Viking heathenism.[10]

What in the ninth and tenth centuries had been a form of marriage in a Germanic-based society now tended to be regarded by the Church as concubinage. Previously, marriage had been seen mainly as a business arrangement between the families concerned, involving the payment of a bride price which made the wedding legal.[11] The money, or land, went to the bride and became her dowry. The wedding itself was a feast at the bride's house, which might last a week! It would end with the bedding of the bride and various pagan ceremonies to ward off evil influences and promote fertility. The Church endeavoured to replace these celebrations with Christian ceremonies and regulations. There was a reading of the banns (designed to discourage marriage within the forbidden degrees of relationship), a blessing at the Church door (which was also meant to ward off evil and invoke God's blessing), and a prayer for fertility.

Edgar, if he contracted a less-than-formal marriage in his youth, would have participated in the less-than-Christian ceremonies. When he proposed or needed to marry Aelfthryth, Dunstan would almost certainly have required him to repent of his earlier conduct and might well have imposed a long penance of some kind, though it is not likely that it involved a ban on the wearing of a crown. The tale that Dunstan did impose such a penance was put forward by Anglo-Norman writers seeking an explanation for Edgar's apparently long-delayed coronation.

These 'Danish' marriages, as they seem to have been known, were not uncommon.[12] But the Church was increasingly insisting on the involvement of priests in the ceremonies and viewed such earlier marriages as unlawful. That made it easy for kings and others to repudiate such marriages contracted *more danico* (in the manner of the Danes), without priest or religious ceremony.

But concubinage was an institution different again from marriage 'Danish'-style. It was a form of subsidiary marriage and was quite widespread even among secular clergy.[13] The upper classes and members of the extended royal family were not averse to it. The advantage for the groom was that no dowry or bride price was involved, the couple were not betrothed (no vows were exchanged),[14] and the protection available from more formal forms of marriage for the woman and her children was greatly reduced. It was a purely sexual union, although by custom there might be some privileges and the children might inherit property if acknowledged by their father.[15]

Church condemnation followed from the regulation of marriage, which the Church taught depended for its validity on the mutual consent of husband and wife, although priestly blessing was still often seen only as desirable rather than obligatory. The Church also equated 'legal' with 'morally acceptable'.[16] But as far as kings were concerned, the repudiation of unwanted wives and subsequent remarriage flourished in all dynasties and kingdoms. Kings simply repudiated one wife to take another. This was made easier in English society by the existence of marriage *more danico*, which the Church simply affected not to recognise.[17]

Queens were expected to give advice and counsel to their kingly spouses, but the line between that and domination was a thin one. A king might be seen as impartial in his judgements, a queen hardly ever. That made for a highly charged political situation since queens, like the wives of great nobles, brought to their husband the support of the wife's family and connections. In their own way, churchmen were developing the idea of queenship as an office which allowed a woman to overcome the limitations of her sex, of motherhood, and yet a queen still had to be some man's wife, mother or daughter and the guarantor of peace and friendship between families. So the queen was seen primarily as *conlaterana regis* and in witness lists was located immediately after the archbishops. The term *conlaterana regis* means 'king's wife', literally 'she who stands at the king's side'. Aelfthryth is described in one charter as the *laterana* of Edgar.

In the tenth century the ritual for queen-making was derived from that for making an abbess, rather than from the marriage ritual which rather emphasised her role as bed-mate and the need for fertility.[18] It was not until the introduction of the third coronation service that the queen's role in sharing in the rule of the kingdom was mentioned.

There was also the contrary notion of powerful women as mothers-in-law or dowager queens, as Aelfthryth was to become in Aethelred's reign and as Eadgifu, wife of Edward the Elder, had been in the 940s. However, after 973 the anointing made the queen a sacramentally sanctioned office holder, a woman recognised as holding a secular office with the right to appear in witness lists. All power is social and the witness lists were lists of officials. Anointing gave the queen added security of status and more formal powers at court. The queen could derive even more power from her intimate access to the king's favour and from her sexual desirability, and Aelfthryth was reputed to be beautiful. Her beauty no doubt explains the jealousy that led to the attacks on her reputation and character.

Queens could now exercise patronage, and in Aelfthryth's case this was formally promulgated in the *Regularis Concordia*. This put the queen at the king's side, with joint rule over monasteries and nunneries. The queen was expected to live up to the ideas of the reformers, and was seen less as a lay woman and closer to the status of a religious woman because of her anointing. But the queen's involvement, after the death of Edgar, in the murder of her stepson Edward at Corfe, while he was on a visit to see her and her young son Aethelred, laid her reputation open to attack as the obvious hate-figure of the evil stepmother. To this was added the allegations of resentful abbesses who objected to their being expected to conform to the standards of the new monasticism and to the subsequent loss of estates, which became the communal property of their house.

The queen certainly exercised ecclesiastical patronage; the nunnery at Wherwell in Hampshire was her foundation, as was Amesbury in Wiltshire, but her takeover of Barking in Essex and the temporary expulsion of Abbess Wulfhild (until she accepted the new monasticism) caused resentment. It might not have helped that she was closely associated with Aethelwold, whose expulsion of secular clergy and conversion of their prebends or clerical livings into monastic estates was greatly resented. Wulfhild was expelled under the terms of the *Regularis Concordia* because of disputes at Barking over reform. The nuns changed this into an allegation of expropriation of nunnery lands by Aelfthryth. Then emphasis was placed at Barking and at Wherwell on her control over nunneries for her own supposedly nefarious purposes. The fact that she chose Wherwell for her place of retirement and was its patron did her no good.

The *Liber Eliensis* contains an astonishing attack on the queen's reputation. She is accused of witchcraft and lewd behaviour and of an attempt to seduce Abbot Byrhtnoth. He died around 996–999 and Aelfthryth at about the same time or a little later. The Ely record accuses her of his murder because he would not accede to her demands. She is said to have plunged red-hot knives into his chest through the armpits, yet when his body was recovered by the monks it bore no sign of any injury. The cause of death must surely have been a heart attack! They also bring up the allegation that she 'openly trapped by all her trickeries and unlawfully killed' her stepson, the martyr Edward. The whole thing is a farrago of monastic misogyny.[19]

Queen Aelfthryth had championed the reform of New Minster which was the centre of propaganda for the new monastic revival and its theology. Theological developments went hand in hand with organisational changes and the transfer of large quantities of land to monastic ownership. This had a considerable political and economic impact and serves to endorse the dictum 'all political differences are at bottom theological'.[20] There was a development in religious iconography emanating from Winchester. Aethelwold and his followers were responsible for it and were probably the advocates of Aelfthryth's anointing in 973. New Minster writings were to stress the legitimacy of Aethelred and of Aelfthryth as the king's wife as against the claims of Edward, who was supported by Dunstan.

Aelfric the Homilist was a product of Winchester, and his definition of the status of an aetheling suggests that claims to the throne were affected by the status and consecration of Aethelred's mother. He wrote, 'the cwen gives birth and the aetheling by his birth rises to the throne'. This attitude also emerges in charter references to the aethelings. Aelfthryth is the 'legitimate wife of the above king' (Edgar), and Edmund, her elder son, who died in childhood in 971, is 'legitimate son of the above king'. Edward, the first born, is only 'aetheling born of the above king'. Aethelred was born after 966 and probably before 969.[21] In ealdorman Aelfheah's will,[22] Edmund was again 'the elder aetheling, the king's son and hers'.

Aelfthryth is thus repeatedly identified as the legitimate wife of the king, as *regis coniux* and *legitima conjunx*, the king's consort and the legitimate consort.[23] The repeated stress on Aelfthryth's legitimate marriage is curious and might well be politically inspired. It implies that there was, or had been, a rival wife of Edgar who was not seen as part of a Christian marriage. It casts doubt on the idea that the mother (or mothers) of Edward and Edith (possibly the same person) was only a mistress or concubine. The offspring of a genuine marriage, even if not a Christian one, would have been recognised by many as Edgar's heir, with a claim to the throne. That explains the use of the Latin term *clito* for Edward, the equivalent of aetheling.

This stress on Aelfthryth's legitimacy as a wife is in sharp contrast to her later unsavoury reputation and is contemporary evidence. The stories attacking her are all late and probably fabricated. They arose not from any contemporary tenth-century evidence but from conflicts between nuns and male reforming clergy who emphasised the importance of chastity. The stories were elaborated as the years passed and are quite incredible. William of Malmesbury[24] accused her of seducing Edgar and of being implicated in the death of her own first husband, Aethelwold of East Anglia, son of Aethelstan Half-King and Edgar's foster-brother. His brother, Aethelwine *Amicus Dei*, was one of Edgar's chief supporters throughout his reign.

The tale, as it emerged in Anglo-Norman writers and in Gaimar, is an obvious fantasy derived from the biblical story of David and Bathsheba and the death of Uriah the Hittite. It is thought to have originated in the nunneries along with other attacks on the queen's reputation.[25] Edgar is supposed to have heard of Aelfthryth's beauty and to have sent Aethelwold to verify it. Instead the ealdorman concealed the truth because he wanted her for his own wife. Edgar was enraged when he discovered the truth and arranged for Aethelwold to be sent to York, where there was trouble, and he was killed in the fighting. Edgar then married his widow.

There is no evidence that Ealdorman Aethelwold died violently. The marriage was a fruitful one with at least one child, a son, Leofric, founder of the Abbey of St Neots. There might even have been a brother called Aethelnoth. Aethelwold simply died sometime before 964, the year in which the king married his widow.

## HOW MANY WIVES?

As for Edgar's other liaisons, all is confusion. Most of the evidence for them is late and from suspect sources. No charter evidence substantiates the existence of any wife before Aelfthryth. But some sort of relationship must be accepted in order to explain the existence of Edward and Edith. Very late sources, such as Florence and Nicholas of Worcester, write of a wife called either Aelflaed or Aethelflaed who never became queen. The name may be simply an echo of Aethelflaed, Lady of the Mercians, or of Aelflaed the first abbess of Romsey, daughter of Edward the Elder. Florence of Worcester adds the epithet 'Eneda', meaning Duck or Swan (with an implication of fair skin), and Nicholas calls her 'Candida', meaning White (or the Fair). Such confusion inspires little confidence.[26] The only slight support for the name comes from a twelfth-century list of benefactors of the New Minster, which names her as Edgar's wife, but it has little authority.

She is alleged to have been the daughter of an ealdorman of East Anglia called Ordmaer. No such ealdorman can be identified. Yet most historians prefer to accept that there was a wife before Aelfthryth and accept Aethelflaed. The thinking is that Edgar married a wife while he was King

of the Mercians, to bolster his support in that region. He would not have
expected to become King of all England as rapidly as he did and needed
support. Those who accept this might well be influenced by the case of Earl
Harold Godwinson in the Confessor's reign. He married, *more danico*, an
East Anglian lady, Edith Swan-neck, and then, when he took the throne in
1066, married, in Christian fashion, the sister of the earls Edwin and Morcar.
(Edith's existence, and by-name, might even have influenced the Norman
writers when they concocted the tale of Aelflaed Eneda.)

Some historians think Edgar had behaved similarly. If so then Edward
might have been the offspring of that union. But there are problems. Edith
the king's daughter, Saint Edith of Wilton, regarded Edward as her full
brother. Both seem to have been born between 961 and 964; neither is
likely to have been born after 964. Edward was a 'child ungrown' in 975,
that is twelve or thirteen and so born around 962–963. Edith died aged
twenty-three between 984 and 987, suggesting a birth between 961 and 963.
She might just have been the result of an extra-marital affair shortly after
Edgar's marriage in 964, but that is most unlikely given the probable timing
of Edith's birth.

As Edward was an acceptable heir, and became king, and as Edith became
an Abbess, it does look as though Edgar's relationship with their mother was
a marriage and not the result of an affair with a concubine. If so then it was
probably a marriage *more danico*, which would explain his reputation for
liking Danish ways.[27]

The story in Eadmer's version is that Edgar turned his attentions on a
young woman at Wilton nunnery who sought to evade him by wearing the
veil, that is, pretending to be a nun. He puts this after Edgar's marriage in
964 and uses it to explain the alleged penance imposed by Dunstan during
which he was not allowed to wear his crown. This is an eleventh-century
fabrication meant to explain the idea of a delayed coronation, which was
then widely accepted. (In the Anglo-Norman period, women certainly did
seek to avoid marriage to predatory Norman barons seeking to legitimise
their possession of the estates of deceased Englishmen. They did, as
Archbishop Lanfranc acknowledged, take the veil to avoid marriage.)

The Anglo-Normans insist that Edgar's first wife was the daughter of
Ordmaer, but the only sign of a noble of that name is the Ordmaer who,
with his wife, left an estate at Hatfield to Edgar in their will. The bequest
was the subject of a lawsuit recorded in the *Liber Eliensis*.[28] There is no
evidence of a daughter called Aethelflaed.

The case is recorded because Edgar gave the estate to Ely and the monks' claim to it was challenged by Ealdorman Aethelwine and his brothers during the troubled time after Edgar died. They claimed the land had been 'forcibly' and therefore unjustly acquired by Edgar and that it had belonged to their father, Aethelstan Half-King. The estate was seized by the ealdorman and the monks paid him off by exchanging it for other lands at Hemingford, Wennington and Yelling in Huntingdonshire. The case had been heard at Slaughter in Gloucestershire in the presence of Aethelwine and of Ealdorman Aelfhere of Mercia, Aelfric Cild and many others. It looks very like part of the settlement between Aethelwine and Aelfhere which brought an end to the disorder that followed Edgar's death. There is no indication in any of this that Ordmaer could have been Edgar's father-in-law.

Goscelin of St Bertin, a well-regarded hagiographer, writing in the early eleventh century, produced a *Vita* of Abbess Wulfhild of Wilton. He says that *she* had been the object of Edgar's unwanted attentions, but managed to resist his advances and to direct his attention onto her kinswoman Wulfthryth, a laywoman not a nun. The relationship of the two women is possible; names in families tended to begin with a common syllable, in this case 'Wulf'. As a result of the liaison, Wulfthryth gave birth to Edith 'offshoot of princes and noble child of a noble duke'.[29] Goscelin viewed this as an informal marriage which was ended when Wulfthryth and her daughter both became nuns. There is a gift of land to Wulfthryth (as abbess) and Wilton Abbey, with confirmation of privileges, dated 974. The charter is wrong as to the date of the coronation and Edgar's age when crowned and may not be genuine in its present form, although it might record genuine tradition.[30]

Later clerical writers preferred to see Wulfthryth as a concubine rather than a wife, because attitudes to such marriages were hardening as the Church sought to take control of the institution of marriage. The Church was moving towards the definition of marriage as one of the sacraments, Matrimony, which entailed a life-long commitment. Goscelin's view tends to support the idea that Edgar might have contracted a marriage *more danico*, and that it was Wulfthryth who was his first wife and mother of both Edward and Edith. This is acceptable if the idea of an earlier marriage to the shadowy Aethelflaed is abandoned in favour of one earlier marriage which was not a Christian one, and a second in 964 which was. There might still have been some sort of earlier sexual relationship which did not produce children, which would account for the air of scandal. Later writers simply conflated both accounts, William of Malmesbury in particular putting together a tale compounded of the stories in Goscelin, Osbern and Eadmer to produce his own version.

In the absence of any contemporary evidence the above solution can only be tentatively advanced, but it does resolve most of the difficulties. The existence of an Aethelflaed Eneda/Candida cannot be proved, and she might have been invented to avoid the implication that Edgar had an affair with a nun. The Passion of St Edward[31] does assert that Edward and Edith were brother and sister, and they might well be the result of a marriage *more danico*. It has been pointed out that everything rests on the Wilton tradition because Shaftesbury was either unable or unwilling to name Edward's mother, possibly because she became a nun.[32] This suggestion does allow for the birth of Edward and Edith a few years before 964 and makes them the offspring of Edgar's hand-fast marriage to Wulfthryth. She was then put away and relegated to Wilton with her daughter. It also explains why Aelfthryth was seen as the legitimate wife and Edward as only the offspring of the king, not his legitimate son.

There is an odd tale in the records of St Peter's, Gloucester, that an estate at Hinton was the gift in 981 of an aged sister of Aethelred called 'Elfleda' (i.e. Aelflaed) in a probably fabricated list of benefactors. She was said to have been born in 943 and cannot therefore be a daughter of Edgar. Some suggest it might be a garbled memory of Edward the Elder's sister Aethelflaed or his daughter Aelflaed. It might just also be a memory of a mistress of Edgar's called Aethelflaed.

The conflicting stories and fragments of evidence do not permit a definitive answer to the puzzle. As for Queen Aelfthryth, she was born around 944, and was therefore a little younger than Edgar. She was daughter of Ordgar, a powerful noble with estates and duties in the south-west of Wessex. Her mother was said to have been of royal descent, so Aelfthryth was a political asset for Edgar, strengthening the base of his support in Wessex after he became king. She was part of the extension of West Saxon control over the Midlands and East Anglia, where she is recorded to have had extensive estates.[33]

Later on, after Edgar died, what mattered was not whether Edward's mother was some mythical wife called Aethelflaed or a nun called Wulfthryth, but the shadow such an origin cast over the legitimacy of the king's claim to the throne. The account of his 'martyrdom', which was accepted by Florence of Worcester, alleged that Edward was intended by Edgar to be his heir, but that may be mere hindsight based on the fact of his actual accession. That accession was certainly disputed. The *Vita Oswaldi* and Byrhtferth of Ramsey both say that the 'chief men of the land' wanted Edward, presumably because he was the elder aetheling while Aethelred was still a child in the care of his mother, while others preferred the 'king's younger son' because he was 'gentle in speech and in deeds'. Edward, on the other hand, inspired fear and terror. He was given to ungovernable rages, attacking men 'with dire blows and especially his own men dwelling with him'. Some historians see him as an unpleasant lout who was sanctified simply because of his unjust murder.

Eadmer claimed that his right to the throne was challenged because of his mother's status and because she was not a crowned queen. Aelfthryth might well have advanced the claims of her 'legitimate' son and appears to have been supported by Aethelwold, by her brother, Ordwulf, and by Ealdorman Aelfhere and his brother Aelfric Cild. Archbishop Dunstan is alleged to have supported Edward's claim, and he certainly carried out his coronation. Florence of Worcester adds Archbishop Oswald, an opponent of Ealdorman Aelfhere, to those who supported Edward. Aethelweard the Chronicler, a member of the royal family, was also a supporter of Edward.

Then, on 18 March 978, King Edward was slain at Corfe while visiting Aelfthryth and Aethelred. Up until then they had been, to all appearances, on friendly terms. Upon his arrival the king was surrounded by retainers of Aelfthryth, and one of them, never named, stabbed him. It was an event not unlike that which resulted in the stabbing of King Edmund in a brawl at Pucklechurch in 946. Although the queen and her son were the immediate beneficiaries, there is no evidence of a plot. Either some over-zealous supporter of Aethelred took the law into his own hands or, more likely, it was the result of personal hatred. The allegations against Aelfthryth are very late and part of the general character assassination to which her reputation was subjected.

Edward was buried with scant ceremony at Wareham, and then, after a year, Ealdorman Aelfhere moved his body to Shaftesbury. Eventually, about ten years later, miracles began to be reported and the cult of Edward, King and Martyr, began.[34] Of Edward's reign little is known other than an impression of civil disorder and an abrupt end to the endowment of monasteries.[35]

Edward's sister Edith remained a nun at Wilton for the whole of her life, despite repeated attempts to bring her out into the world and make her a queen or at least an abbess at Winchester, Barking or Amesbury. Her *Vita* by Goscelin emphasises her humility and service to others and provides anecdotes to illustrate this. Stories also highlight her royal connections and that Wilton was a royal convent. Miracles were recorded after her death and a cult developed. Her feast is 16 September and she was the principal saint at Wilton.

# II

# The Cult and Location of Relics: An Instrument of Royal Policy

Relics in the Middle Ages were, in the first instance, the mortal remains of saints and martyrs: their often mummified bodies or skeletal remains such as a head or an arm, or even a mere fragment of bone. In addition, objects closely associated with the crucifixion of Christ, such as fragments of the True Cross, were highly regarded. Places where saints had been buried or where martyrs had suffered death were also regarded as particularly holy. By contemplating such relics people were moved to pray more fervently, believing that the presence of the relics brought them closer to the object of their devotion. The saints were believed to intervene on behalf of those who prayed to them, using the power given them by God to cure the sick or punish evil-doers.

Tenth-century kings, like Edgar, not only valued relics for their own sake, though they certainly did, nor did they see them only as a means of reassuring themselves that their prayers to the saints would be answered. Relics were also a tangible way of demonstrating their piety and how closely they supported the Church. They housed their own collections of relics either in the *Haligdom* (royal relic collection) or in churches dedicated to the cult of relics. All churches had their own relics, preferably those connected with the saint or martyr to whom the church was dedicated. Some churches were the burial places of the saints whose relics they housed, and to whom, often, they were dedicated. A good example is Ely, which possessed the body of St Aethelthryth (Etheldreda).

Relics were outward symbols of kingly piety, just as they were of the piety of the people at large. Possession of a large collection of relics promoted a king's prestige. Aethelstan, for example, could demonstrate his piety and his zeal by the use he made of relics. He not only collected great numbers of them but on one occasion gave one third of his collection to Exeter, so creating a locus of gratitude to the king for his beneficence. The contents of the collection given to Exeter is recorded in a list which was kept there.

The fervent collection of relics seems to have begun, or at least to have taken off in a more determined way, during the tenth century, and in Aethelstan's reign, although Alfred the Great had ordered that his collection of relics was to accompany him everywhere.

Relics had an intrinsic value of their own, just as if they were gems or other precious objects. When Aethelstan sought to increase his collection by obtaining them from Brittany, the prior, Radbod, wrote to the king saying that he knew that the king 'valued relics more than earthly treasure'. That remark echoed the attitude of Christians from very early times, as the cult of the saints and martyrs developed as early as the second century. When Polycarp, Bishop of Smyrna in Asia Minor, was martyred by being burnt at the stake, his congregation collected his bones from the ashes because they were 'more precious than the richest jewels, and assayed above gold'.[1] The tombs of the martyrs and their places of execution attracted worshippers who came to pray there, and it became usual to celebrate the Eucharist over the tombs. Churches were later built over the tombs and it became obligatory to incorporate the relics of martyrs in the altar tables of other churches.

The cult of saints developed further because men thought that just as they might approach a king, when seeking a favour, through one of his close companions or servants, so it was right to approach Christ, seen as a King of Kings, through his saints and martyrs, including those saints, called 'confessors', who were revered for their holiness of life despite their not having been martyred. Towards the end of the tenth century, the papacy, in the person of Pope John XV (985–996), explicitly approved of the cult of relics at a council or synod held at Rome in 993, called partly to proclaim the canonisation of St Udalric. The Pope taught that when the relics of martyrs and confessors were honoured and revered, it was as though the saints themselves were the object of devotion, and that by honouring his servants, the honour redounded to the honour of the Lord God himself.[2]

To the tenth-century mind, relics, the cult of a saint, even a church dedicated to a particular saint, became the focus of religious devotion which made them channels of God's grace and power, which might cause miraculous events. So, rather remarkably, the Church not only allowed kings to amass collections of relics but seemingly encouraged it as a means of ensuring their devotion to religion. In England relics could be brought to meetings of the king's council, his Witan, and in a sense might be understood to be presiding over the proceedings, the saint or saints in question being regarded as members of the king's council.

Relics made suitable diplomatic gifts and kings and other princes habitually exchanged them, often trying to outdo one another with the splendour and importance of their gifts. The list of relics given to Exeter contained a number of relics of Frankish origin and illustrates the wide extent of Aethelstan's continental alliances. He had received relics from the King of Germany, Henry the Fowler, when a marriage was arranged between the German king's son Otto (later Emperor Otto I) and Aethelstan's sister Edith. Other relics were received when his other sisters married into continental royal or noble families.

Relics might also be moved from one cultic centre to another within the same kingdom. Aethelstan moved the body of St Oswald from Bardney in Lincolnshire to Gloucester, St Werburg from Hanbury, Staffordshire, to Chester, and St Eahlmund from Derby to Shrewsbury, all as part of the building or strengthening of burhs in those places, so moving them from Danish-controlled areas to form new centres of power in English areas.[3] In doing this he no doubt bolstered Mercian pride and increased support for his kingship. The martyred King Edmund of East Anglia was moved to Ramsey, where his *Vita* was written, and some West Saxon bishops even claimed to be related to him. This helped to bind East Anglia closer to the kingdom of England in Edgar's day.[4]

Other relics were linked to King Edmund's military campaigns. He took relics from Monkwearmouth, Jarrow and Lindisfarne. King Eadred too, in 948, burned Ripon and moved the relics of St Wilfrid to Canterbury. Even Edgar moved the relics of St David to Glastonbury as a sign of his hegemony over Wales.

The full significance of such actions is most clearly revealed in the *Tract on the Origins and Progress of the Church of Durham*.[5] It comes from the early twelfth century and explains that King Alfred and his sons had followed the advice of St Cuthbert, as conveyed no doubt by the members of the Community of St Cuthbert. As a result of doing so, St Cuthbert's promises (given in a vision) had been fulfilled and the boundaries of the kingdom of Alfred and his descendants had been extended. The promises were most fully fulfilled in Aethelstan's reign, as he 'subjugated his enemies everywhere and became the first king of the English to obtain dominion over the whole of Britain'.[6]

The Community of St Cuthbert, an association of secular priests (who might have been the clergy for whom, in part at least, the 'Northumbrian Priests' Law' was intended), was a religious association of influential men with vast estates scattered throughout Northumbria between the Tyne and the Tees. They had been ejected by Vikings from their original home of Lindisfarne, the saint's first burial place, and spent decades in search of a permanent home before settling at Durham in 991. In Aethelstan's time they were at Chester-le-Street. Their influence extended as far south as York and in the north beyond the Tweed. No wonder kings thought it wise to ensure their support.[7]

The account, in the *Libellus de Exordio* from Durham, repeats that Aethelstan ruled 'the whole length and breadth of Britain'. It again claims that he was assisted by 'the blessed Cuthbert' who interceded with God on his behalf as he had previously promised 'when he appeared to Aethelstan's grandfather Alfred... saying... By my intercession the kingdom of Britain will be conceded to your sons and placed at their disposal'.[8] The account further says that Edward the Elder had told Aethelstan of the assistance he had received in adding 'the greater part of Britain to his father's kingdom' and advising Aethelstan to be faithful to St Cuthbert. Therefore Aethelstan visited St Cuthbert's tomb while on his way to Scotland 'with the army of the whole of Britain'. There he sought the saint's patronage with many gifts, including twelve vills and ninety-six pounds of silver. So he was able to defeat Owain, King of the Cumbrians, and Constantine, King of the Scots, and 'conquered Scotland with a land army and a naval force in order to make it subject to him'.[9] This was when he campaigned as far as Dunnottar and his fleet as far as Caithness.[10] He is then recorded to have put his trust in St Cuthbert at Brunanburh. The truth behind this might be that Aethelstan had received the support and financial backing of the Community of St Cuthbert.

King Edmund is also, according only to this document, said to have asked Cuthbert's intercession and given gifts during his northern campaign. It adds the rather extravagant claim that he ravaged Strathclyde and gave it to Constantine as a fief. (Possibly an echo of the cession of Strathclyde by Aethelstan when he set a limit to English expansion.) King Eadred was also credited with visiting St Cuthbert and giving gifts on an expedition to Northumbria. Edgar is noticed only as succeeding to Eadwig; presumably neither of them was regarded as a friend of St Cuthbert.[11] The background to this is that these kings took care to cultivate the support of the Community of St Cuthbert to ensure acceptance of their rule in Northumbria and Northumbrian support against the Scots and the Vikings.

Kings, and other magnates, could be less than scrupulous in the way in which they acquired relics. Edgar simply seized a relic of St Botulph for his collection. Then there is the story of how, with Edgar's authority behind him, Abbot Byrhtferth of Ely took servants and soldiers with him to view the sarcophagus of St Wihtburh, sister of St Aethelthryth (Etheldreda) of Ely, held by the local church at Dereham. While the townspeople slept he simply loaded it onto a wagon and made off with it. He was pursued as soon as the people became aware of the theft but escaped by transferring to a boat at Brandon in Suffolk. His idea was that the saint should join her sister at Ely.[12]

Relics were brought out to be reverenced by the people on rogation days, when prayers were offered for deliverance from pestilence, famine or invasion. So that this could easily be done, and so that they could be brought to courts of law where oaths might be sworn while touching them, the relics were kept in 'feretories' (portable shrines) which could be carried in a procession. They played a part in trial by ordeal, the accused being expected to swear on the relics and so invoke the protection, or curse, of the saint whose relics they were.[13]

According to Aethelred's Seventh Code, the king ordered, during the Danish invasions, that as a special measure against Cnut, 'When the Great Army comes, everybody, out with the relics!' or more precisely 'all shall go out with the relics and from their inmost heart call earnestly upon Christ'. The word here for relics is *haligdom*. That meant a collection of relics, as when the *Liber Vitae* of New Minster refers to the king's *haligdom* and to King 'Aethelstanes gamma [gem] with the bones of Saint Sebastian'. The king himself boasted of 'all the *haligdom* that I have gotten into England by God's mercy'.

Amongst those relics were the gifts he received from Hugh Capet, Duke of the Franks, brought by Aethelstan's cousin, Adelolf of Boulogne. Apart from the usual costly things, like perfumes, gems, an onyx vase and a jewelled diadem, were the Standard of St Maurice, the Lance of Charlemagne, said to be that used at the Crucifixion, fragments of the True Cross and the Crown of Thorns set in crystal, and the Sword of Constantine with a nail from the Cross embedded in the hilt. Aethelstan obtained more relics, from Brittany, such as those of Saints Scabillion, Senator, and Paternus. Some of these relics might strike a modern reader as difficult to accept as authentic, but what mattered was the worshipper's belief that through the relic he could in some way be sure that his prayers were answered.

Monasteries appreciated the gift of relics. Westminster claimed to have been given an exotic collection of unlikely ephemera such as the Veil of the Virgin Mary, while the kings had many others which they claimed to have inherited from King Alfred.[14]

King Eadred's will shows that he had priests in his household who were entrusted with the care of relics, perhaps the same priests who also assisted in the writing of charters as well as saying Mass. The *Vita Dunstani* records that King Eadred, on his sick bed, sent the abbot back to Glastonbury so that he could bring to him the relics the king had left there in the care of the abbey. While Dunstan was still on the road back, King Eadred died, and it is claimed that Dunstan was told of the king's death by an angel at the exact moment that it occurred. The probable truth is that Dunstan knew that the king was dying and no doubt had told his escort so. (The word 'angel' in Greek actually means 'messenger'.) The real point of the story is, of course, that the royal collection of relics and documents was now so large that it was no longer carried around with the king in its entirety, and Eadred had entrusted a large part of it to Glastonbury. That might also be the truth behind the Ely story that the abbots of Ely, Glastonbury and St Augustine's, Canterbury, were appointed to divide the year between them and 'perform service with the reliquaries and other ornaments of the altar'. In an anachronistic fashion, the *Liber Eliensis* says these abbots shared the office of Chancellor, which is unlikely as there is no evidence for such an office before the reign of William the Conqueror.[15]

Saints' 'resting places' were centres of religious power and influence, as a tenth-century inventory of such places shows. It lists the places associated with St Cuthbert; his right arm was at Bamburgh and the rest of him at the New Minster in Gloucester. The locations of St Alban and St Columba are listed, then other Mercian and Northumbrian shrines. It shows a keen interest in the shrines of Viking England, and accuses Raegnald of York of being an enemy of St Cuthbert because he had seized estates belonging to his Community and implies that Raegnald's defeat at Tettenhall in 910 was due to St Cuthbert's anger.

From King Edgar's point of view, the most important relic of all was the body of St Swithun.[16] There is a medieval wall painting at Winchester, in the Morley Library, which shows the earliest known representation of Winchester Cathedral in its Romanesque form, complete with the reliquary, or shrine, of St Swithun. It pictures the shrine at the time of his 'translation' to a new site. Edgar presented the recently-discovered relics to Winchester in 971 or a little later, and the shrine was moved again to the Romanesque building in 1093.

The body had been 'miraculously discovered' during Aethelwold's construction of the westwork at Winchester, and he gave it, with Edgar's help, a magnificent *sacellum* or chapel, using 300 pounds of gold, silver and gems. The exterior showed the Passion and Resurrection of Christ, His Ascension and other religious scenes. The *Vita* of St Swithun was written up and his cult became an essential feature of worship for the new monasticism at Winchester.

Relics were certainly used to secure saintly patronage and protection in time of war. The relics of St Wendreth (Wendreda) were brought to Ely by Abbot Aelfsige, purchased from King Aethelred and taken from their shrine at March. The new shrine at Ely was adorned with gold and jewels. When Aethelred went into battle against Cnut at Ashingdon he was accompanied by monks from Ely who brought the body of St Wendreth with them. They were all killed and Cnut took the relic and gave it to Canterbury Cathedral as a sign of his gratitude for his victory.[17]

The cult of saints and their relics was closely linked to the idea of a royal cult. Glastonbury was one such cultic centre, located as it was in the 'more princely' part of the kingdom. Winchester tried hard to rival Glastonbury and both have a number of royal burials. The first royally authorised canonisations in England were those of King Edward the Martyr and of St Dunstan, followed by Aethelwold and Oswald.[18] This was all linked to the 'sacral' nature of kingship as it was envisaged in the tenth century. The hope was that it would lead people to expect God to honour the *stirps regia* or royal family. So the *Regularis Concordia* ordered daily intercession on behalf of Edgar and the royal family. A recognised form of honour to the royal blood was, of course, sainthood. This came in two forms, martyrdom (hence the cult of King Edward the Martyr and of King Edmund of East Anglia), and the class of saint called a confessor (or for women, virgins and widows), usually kings who had abandoned the throne to become a monk, of which there was no tenth-century example.[19]

Devotion to the saints inevitably gave rise to a state of mind that led a king like Edgar to accept the ideas of the monastic reformers. He founded, re-founded or reformed, according to contemporaries, about forty monasteries or convents, but only some thirty-two of them can be safely identified.

There is little archaeological evidence of the style and appearance of the building works accomplished simply because the Normans tore down what was there when they built their monasteries and cathedrals, though the buildings seen today are the result of many changes over many years.

Among those which owed their existence to Edgar and his three clerical co-workers, the best known are Peterborough, Ely and Worcester. Of the total number, however, many are now only ruins, the result of the Dissolution under Henry VIII. Even the ruins that survive are mainly Norman, because the Normans destroyed the pre-existing buildings down to foundation level.

## CHURCH ARCHITECTURE UNDER EDGAR

At Romsey in Hampshire, for example, the church founded by Edward the Elder and reformed (967) in Edgar's reign was reduced to its foundations, and the entirely Norman abbey church of St Mary and St Aethelflaed was built over them. Archaeologists have uncovered remains of the foundations. The remains of an apsidal chancel are now visible beneath the tower crossing and the remains of the north transept can be seen outside the church along the north wall. The original church had been an equal-armed cruciform church with an apse at the east end, some twenty-eight metres in length and breadth. Other surviving evidence of tenth-century worship can be seen. On a wall of the transept on the south side there is a high relief carving of Christ on the cross, dated by archaeologists to about 1000–1025. The hand of God appears from the cloud to acknowledge his son.

Even more significant is another carving of the Crucifixion with Byzantine influences. Two angels watch over Christ on the cross and two haloed figures, the Virgin Mary and St John, stand on either side. Below, two Roman soldiers offer Christ a vinegar-soaked sponge on the end of a spear. At one time the carving was gilded and the eyes would have been highlighted with precious jewels. It is of such high quality that it is quite likely that this was the actual crucifix given by King Edgar in the 960s. Edgar had his young son Edward buried at Romsey. He granted land at Edington, Wiltshire, in 968,[20] and received from the nuns 'a finely wrought dish, armlets splendidly chased and a scabbard adorned with gold'.[21]

Similarly at North Elmham, Norfolk, the original Saxon cathedral is thought to have been built where the private chapel of Bishop Herbert

Losinga was erected around 1100. As many 'Saxon' churches were of wood, and as there are references to a wooden church at North Elmham, little trace can be expected to be found. But the basic form of Losinga's chapel is that of a cruciform apsidal church with transepts, rather like that at Romsey; it is about thirty metres long with transepts fifteen metres wide. The Bishop might well have built his chapel on the same plan as the pre-existing church. There is a pre-Conquest cemetery nearby and remains of a wooden structure have been detected.[22]

Evidence of Saxon construction does survive. There are over 200 churches with varying amounts of Saxon work, from as little as a font, stone cross, carving or sundial to complete naves, some with arcading, chancels and towers. The best examples are said to be Worth in Sussex, Brixworth and Earls Barton in Northamptonshire, Bradford-upon-Avon in Wiltshire and Deerhurst in Gloucestershire. Many other churches have towers which are in at least part Saxon, as well as the round towers of Norfolk, Saxon in origin.

Deerhurst had a nave and choir, presumably with an apse, two chapels on each side of the choir and a tower at the west end. That was the usual form of a Saxon church, whether in wood or stone.[23] Deerhurst was extended on each side at some date after the tenth century. Almost all of the tenth-century church was incorporated into the later fabric. The church at Ely that preceded the cathedral had a steeple at the west end and a southern (and therefore probably a northern) aisle, and Alfred, the murdered brother of King Edward the Confessor, was buried there. It was probably larger than Deerhurst but not dissimilar.

Dunstan's Glastonbury was as large as most continental abbeys. Little is left of Aethelwold's Abingdon but it was described as being a basilica in style, with a circular chancel and a circular nave twice the diameter of the chancel. Even the tower was circular.[24]

The dominant feature of most Saxon churches was the nave, which was long and of great height in proportion to its width. Windows were set very high, providing a large expanse of wall. The walls were either hung with pictures or painted with biblical or other religious scenes. Bede ascribes such decoration to the church at Jarrow. Parish, or Minster, churches were responsible for quite a wide area of the surrounding countryside. A good example is St Peter's, Titchfield, Hampshire. Side aisles were added to the original nave in the twelfth century, but the lower part of the tower and the nave, originally narrower than at present, and shorter, survive. The original pre-Conquest church had solid walls.[25]

At York, Oswald was responsible for the construction of St Mary Bishophill, using existing Roman masonry. St Helens-on-the-Walls was built directly over Roman mosaics and there is evidence for further church building at five other churches. These were most likely funded by wealthy York burgesses. Churches were also built in the countryside, at Wharram Percy for example, and after 990 the trend was towards building in stone. The effects of reform extended well after Edgar's reign into the eleventh century.

# 12

# Kingship and Empire

Some aspects of Edgar's reign are still in need of further examination. The role of the Church in enhancing the prestige of the tenth-century monarchy, no doubt for its own purposes, must be considered. The way in which those who drafted and were responsible for the production of royal charters (from the reign of Aethelstan onwards) made use of hyperbolical and somewhat overblown royal styles and titles at the head of tenth-century diplomas is an important aspect of this role.

## CHURCHMEN, DIPLOMAS AND THE LANGUAGE OF EMPIRE

The role of the Church in producing the royal styles and titles in charters is closely linked to the Church's support for the monarchy. The archbishops and bishops (and, after 969, the abbots) figured prominently in the kings' councils, the Witans, which aided the kings in their decision-making and in the issue of royal law codes. It was the churchmen whose scribes were responsible not merely for drafting diplomas and actually producing them, but also for the language used in them.

Bishops and abbots provided the scribes needed for the production of charters and for making copies of the law codes. Without their contribution a great deal less would now be known about the reigns of these kings. One puzzle is the relative paucity of information provided by those responsible for the continuation of the *Anglo-Saxon Chronicles*. One possibility might be that the best scribes were all heavily engaged in the production of charters and other documents and that their absence from their monasteries while carrying out their duties at court hindered the continuity of effort needed to produce the *Chronicles*. Lesser scribes, left to put in what they felt was of interest, found this to be largely the affairs of the Church rather than those of the State.

That it was the churchmen and their scribes who were responsible for the language of the main body of the charters is suggested by the contrast between the high claims made for kings and the quite modest style and titles adopted by the kings themselves when signing the charters. They were, in the main, quite content to attest as *Rex Anglorum* (King of the English), rather than the elevated styles of the opening paragraphs of the charter.

There are a number of charters attributed to Edgar, mainly those bestowing privileges on newly founded or re-founded monasteries, which do not fit easily into the recognised pattern for diplomas intended as 'land-books' which give title to land. Most historians are unwilling to grant these diplomas any authenticity. Some, however, argue that they should be evaluated differently.[1] It is suggested that they are not outright forgeries but documents which may have been re-written, possibly inflated or altered, in restored monasteries, and that they were written originally by the beneficiaries themselves rather than by the king's own scriptors. They could therefore have an authentic basis. The Ely foundation charter in particular is viewed as having been translated from Old English into Latin and then translated and altered by Aelfric the Homilist. Some of what it says might therefore have been part of the original text, especially the section about sub-kings who accepted Edgar's leadership. It is supported by other evidence which asserts that Edgar overcame kings and tyrants and speaks of his ability 'to subdue kings and earls who cheerfully submitted to his rule'.[2]

One problem about the charter language is that it is for the most part confined to the charters themselves. There is little or no sign of it in the *Chronicles*, the law codes or on the coinage of these kings, so some historians argue that the charter terms are mere stylistic flourishes with no political or constitutional significance. The scribes, it is suggested, were merely seeking to use as many different ways of expressing the idea of kingship as possible by making use of every conceivable Latin term in their vocabulary.

Even the charters themselves are said to fall into two different classes: those which make use of the title *Basileus*, a borrowing from the Greek *basileos*, and those which resort to the Latin *imperator* and its derivatives such as *imperialis*. It is also the case that many of the charters in the latter category (there are seventeen of them) are regarded as spurious and forged. The condemnation is by no means universal, and historians disagree about the relative authenticity of various charters, some accepting as authentic what others reject as spurious. A number of these type two charters belong to a group known from their use of language as the 'alliterative' series, and the authenticity of those charters has been strongly defended by Dorothy Whitelock.[3]

It is quite certain that those tenth-century kings who first claimed the title of 'Kings of the English' laid claim to an imperial status, but what is not so clear is what the exact political and constitutional significance of these claims was.[4] Kings from Aethelstan onwards repeatedly claimed to rule what can only be described as an empire, and yet, for the most part, they avoided the use of the word 'emperor' or 'empire'. They were certainly described by later writers as 'emperors'. They had plenty of ways of making the claim without using the actual words. The claims can be said to have begun with Aethelstan's Lifton Charter of 931 in which he said that he was 'king of the English, raised by the right hand of the Almighty to the throne of the whole of Britain', and this sort of statement can be found in various charters, many of which are of unchallenged authenticity, from then on.[5]

King Edgar himself reveals an 'imperialist' note in his law code,[6] saying that it was to apply to 'Englishmen, Danes and Britons in every part of my dominion… and… to all of us together who live in these islands'. See also his later charters,[7] especially S 775 for 970, in which he is *'imperator augustus'*, a full Roman style. It has also been suggested that an imperial tone might not have been out of place even in 963, when Edgar was the first king for many years to hold his court at York, in the heart of the Danelaw.

Aethelstan claimed to be 'Basileus of All Albion' and 'Basileus of all the peoples living roundabout'. Janet Fairweather, translator of the *Liber Eliensis* in which *basileus* appears in its copies of charters, offers the translation 'High King of the beloved island of Albion'[8] and comments that *basileus* was used by the Greeks as the title of the Great King of Persia. It was commonly used by Greek emperors in addressing foreign kings. To people in the West it was a known title used by the emperors at Byzantium. Elsewhere it appears to have been a straightforward translation of the Old English *cyning* for king, when a charter is available in both Old English and Latin. But when associated with a claim to rule the whole island it is certainly of greater import.

Even King Eadwig, whose control over Mercia and Northumbria was reduced by their choice of Edgar for king in 956, is found boasting of being 'crowned by the imperial diadem of the Anglo-Saxons' or as 'wielding the sceptre of the whole of Britain'.[9]

So the 'imperial' claim appears to be a genuine one, promoted by the Church. That this is so is confirmed by the 'Roman' atmosphere of the coronation of 973, which is attributable to the inspiration of Dunstan and the diplomatic activities of Oswald. The argument against this interpretation, that the coronation ritual made no use of 'imperial' language, can be dismissed on the grounds that it was seen as of far more significance that Edgar was being anointed and crowned king, not just of the English, but of the whole of Britain.

## POLITICAL AND CONSTITUTIONAL CONTEXT

The context of all this will perhaps make the political and, as it would be put today, constitutional significance clearer. The 'imperial claim' was being made on two levels, perhaps even three. Firstly, the dynasty of Alfred the Great, the 'Cerdicings' or descendants of Cerdic, had become, through the conquests (not re-conquests) of Edward the Elder and his sons, Kings of all England. This meant not only the kingdoms of Wessex and Mercia, but also East Anglia and Northumbria, especially after Eadred's overthrow of the last independent kingship, the Viking kingdom of York. In that sense, Eadred's successors were kings over several different peoples, which was one of the qualifications for being regarded as an emperor.

Secondly, Strathclyde had been conquered by Aethelstan,[10] and by the end of his reign all the kingdoms of the Welsh were under his acknowledged overlordship as well, their kings accepting the obligation to attend his great courts and paying tribute. He and his successors, Edmund and Eadred, had extracted uneasy but obedient allegiance even from the kings in Scotland and the Western Isles.[11] Further ecclesiastical and political work had to await the advent of Edgar, who was 'mightiest of all the kings of the English' and who 'spread the praise of God everywhere among his people; and God subdued his enemies for him always'.[12] To the Church, Alfred and his successors were Christian kings who gained victory over the heathen and provided their people with peace.

Alfred the Great had been the first to be acknowledged as overlord by the Welsh, according to Alfred's biographer, Bishop Asser, and so set the pattern for Anglo-Welsh, if not Anglo-Celtic, relations,[13] developed further by Aethelstan and Edgar. It was Aethelstan who set the example Edgar was to follow by bringing to his court magnates from every part, not only of England but from the rest of his far-flung overlordship. It is no surprise to find that it was in Aethelstan's reign that imperial pretensions first manifested themselves.

Aethelstan's position was such that it had diplomatic repercussions. His aid was sought in continental affairs and both kings and emperors, as well as other great magnates, sought the hands of his sisters in marriage. No doubt had Aethelstan been a married man with daughters they would have been sought after also. It was Aethelstan who first put on his coins the claim to be 'Rex totius Britanniae' (King of the Whole of Britain), and legislated for a common currency to be minted in the boroughs. There was no other king in England during his reign and his overlordship extended into Wales and Scotland.

The seeds of his imperial pretensions lay in the very fact that he was King of all England (though he was not to remain unchallenged). His coins show a crowned head, the first numismatic portrayal of a crowned English king, using the *cynehelm* or royal helmet. He is also portrayed on the frontispiece of the tenth-century copy of Bede's *Life of St Cuthbert*.[14] Aethelstan is shown presenting a book to St Cuthbert, wearing a gold circlet decorated with golden orbs, possibly six. Similarly, Edgar is portrayed on the Winchester manuscript of 966, offering his charter to the New Minster at Winchester. He wears a gold circlet decorated with gold fleurets.[15] These crowns might well have been the result of artistic licence and borrowed from biblical illustrations.

All this created an atmosphere conducive to the formulation of imperial pretensions and the use of the concepts of Britannia (England and Wales combined) and Albion (which included Scotland and the islands). Overlordship became the dominant theme in the diplomas, quite independently of the use of the words 'empire' or 'emperor'.[16] Overlordship is emphasised in the *Chronicles* by the use of 'recent' (ruler), 'mundbora' (protector), or 'wine' (friend), and in the charters by words and phrases like 'gubernator et rector' (governor and ruler), 'monarchus', 'dispensator regni totius Albionis' (steward of the kingdom of the whole of Albion), 'primicerius' (chief or chieftain ), 'curagulus' (guardian), and 'dominus' (lord).[17]

The claim to imperial status had other implications. England, and more especially the whole island of Britain, was surrounded by the ocean, as the Roman Empire had been in the eyes of the Romans. At that time, to assert such status as sole ruler over all the nations within the confines (the *limes* or limits) of Britain was to exclude all continental ambitions to extend rule in this direction. From that flowed the concept of sovereignty, in the sense of excluding all exterior secular authority, the next step being to a claim to be a fully independent ruler owing no fealty to anyone other than

God Almighty. That is the sense in which Queen Elizabeth I was to claim that England was 'an empire sole and entire to itself alone' when defying Philip II, or as one charter of the tenth century expressed it, 'rex monarchus Brittaniae insulae', king and sole ruler of the island of Britain.

The king used every available means as instruments of royal propaganda. There were the diplomas, the coins, the codes of law; there was the political significance which lay behind the translation of the relics of saints (their solemn transfer from one cultic centre to another). The whole exercise culminated in three great events of Edgar's reign: the promulgation at a solemn synod of the *Regularis Concordia* which put all monks and nuns and all monasteries and nunneries under one Rule, committed to daily unceasing prayer for the king and royal family; his great solemn coronation and anointing with holy oil by no fewer than two archbishops; and the subsequent grand spectacle at Chester in the presence of the whole English fleet and assembled aristocracy when Edgar was rowed on the Dee by eight subordinate kings headed by the King of Scots.

The means by which these territories and this overlordship had been acquired and maintained was by the use and, in Edgar's case, overwhelming demonstration of military and naval force. He also used law and diplomacy, and indeed religion, to the same end.[18]

The signs of leadership over disparate groups of allies had begun with Aethelflaed, the Lady of the Mercians, who organised an alliance against Raegnald of York comprising Constantine of Scotland, Ealdred, High Reeve of Bamburgh (at that time virtually an independent ruler), and the Danes of Yorkshire. There is even a story that she recruited Welsh princes to her banner as well. Then, after Aethelstan's earlier victories in which he annexed the Yorkshire realm of Guthfrith Sihtricsson, he advanced to Eamont Bridge near Penrith on 12 July 926, where he received the homage of Constantine of Scotland, Eugenius of Strathclyde, Ealdred son of Eadwulf and several Welsh princes led apparently by Hywel Dda himself.[19] After that, he adopted the inscription on his coins of 'Rex totius Britanniae'; the verse panegyric recording his triumph speaks of 'ista perfecta Saxonia', or 'thus is the land of the Saxons made perfect'. More of the Welsh submitted at Hereford shortly afterwards and then the Cornish at Exeter. Aethelstan passed all his rights in due course to his successor Edmund and, in his turn, Edgar specifically laid claim to all the rights of his father Edmund's kingship, the 'cynescypes gerihta'.[20]

Edgar's power was to be so complete that, in addition to earning the soubriquet *Pacificus* (the Peacemaker),[21] Aelfric the Homilist was able to boast that in his time 'no fleet was ever heard of except that of our own people who held this land'. Edgar's power, like that of his predecessors, was further illustrated by the many innovations in government which originated or flowered during his reign.

The prestige of the monarchy had begun its rise under Edward the Elder, who was able to demand 'the oath and pledge which the whole nation has given' at Grateley in Hampshire. That prestige is reflected in the flowering of the range of quite extraordinary titles which were adopted by Aethelstan and his successors. It should always be remembered, when reading these titles, that a distinction is made between the monarch as King of the English (even when he occasionally subscribes as *'Basileus'* or 'High King'), and his lordship over the rest of Britain. He might, in addition to claiming to be *Basileus* of the surrounding nations, claim to be their governor or ruler, even when this is extended to the claim to be *'curagulus orbis Britanniae'*, ruler of the world of Britain. A distinction is drawn between the claim to be King of the West Saxons, the Mercians and of the Northumbrians, and to be governor or ruler of Albion.

Yet these titles cannot have rested simply on the readiness of those who drew up the kings' charters and the scribes who wrote them out to use high-flown language. The charters were witnessed by quite formidable numbers of ealdormen, king's thegns and Danish earls. From Alfred's time onwards it was expected that such men should either be able to read, at least Old English if not Latin, or to employ someone who could. The charters were probably read out in council before they were signed and witnessed. The assembled magnates gave their implicit consent to and bore witness to their understanding of the truth of such claims.

Most of these titles, for Eadwig and Edgar, are most easily found in the *Abingdon Chronicle* as printed in the Rolls series. One interesting addition to the proofs available for the adoption of these claims is found in an early charter of Eadwig's reign which he dates to *'primo anno imperii mei'*, literally 'the first year of my *imperium*',[22] which can be construed as either 'empire' or merely as 'rule'.

It still remains to discover, if at all possible, what these claims meant in practice to those on the receiving end, and, what is more, whether those who used them and wrote them in charters had a clear idea of what they meant. It might be the case, as some historians still argue,[23] that they arose from the efforts of the scribes to vary the language used to describe the king's status, because of the Anglo-Saxon love of variety for its own sake. It is suggested that there was no real non-Roman concept of Empire among the Anglo-Saxons, based on the undeniable fact that the claims, as regards nations and peoples outside the limits of what can only, even at this date, be called England, do not imply direct rule over other peoples in the sense of making laws for them or constructing methods of administration, nor of taxation. The payment of tribute is a levy extracted by force, not the collection of tax by right of legitimate government. Not to put too fine a point on it, it is extortion.

But insufficient attention is paid to the parallel situation on the Continent, where the Ottonian kings, the heirs of Henry the Fowler, were claiming the title of Emperor and saw themselves as the heirs of Charlemagne. At the same time, King Edmund, in one of his charters, refers to other kings who had become emperors and implies that he himself was one of them.[24] It is also true that Edmund's dynasty was older than any of those on the Continent.[25]

Just as Aethelstan in 937 had won the decisive victory of Brunanburh, so Henry the Fowler had crushed the Hungarians in 933, a victory which, like Aethelstan's, assured his family's succession. Otto I, the Great, succeeded in 936 and took three years to subdue the feudal magnates of central Germany. After his coronation he set about establishing what is described as a 'quasi-Carolingian' state.[26] He saw himself as a soldier of the Church and the heir of Charlemagne, and set out over a period of thirty years to reconstruct the Empire. He extended German rule east of the Elbe and into Italy as far as Rome, and in 955 finally eliminated the Hungarian threat at Lechfeld. Shortly afterwards he defeated the Slavs at Recknitz.

By 962 he was able to march into Italy, where he was crowned and proclaimed Emperor in a second coronation. Even his family was consecrated (just as Edgar was to have his queen anointed). This 'restored' empire was not really comparable to that of Charlemagne. Otto's empire derived its character from German social structure, creating a 'Holy Roman Empire', but a German one. It is notable that the papacy had accepted him as its reformer. Both Leo III and John XII allowed him to reform a clergy corrupted by simony and the exploitation of shrines and relics. Otto accepted the moral leadership of the reformed monks of Cluny.

Otto had been married, at his father's behest, to a sister of Aethelstan, but he married off his son, Otto II, to Theophano, daughter of Romanus II of Byzantium. The Byzantines had accepted the marriage as the price to be paid for retaining their Italian possessions. Otto the Great was to do no more;

he died, coincidentally enough, in 973. The parallels with developments in England are plain enough and need no elaboration, but the English dynasty had most certainly retained its family connections with the Ottonians, as Aethelweard the Chronicler shows. The English kings would have been conscious and aware of the imperial activities of Otto the Great and could not have remained uninfluenced by them. It cannot have been entirely a coincidence that imperial pretensions developed in both families in this period, nor can it have been coincidental that England was affected by the reforming movement spreading throughout Europe.

What are, for convenience, referred to as 'Carolingian' ideas and practices are found affecting both the heirs of Alfred the Great in England and those of Henry the Fowler in Germany. The parallels developed here are not exact, but they are there; and there must have been powerful influences, even if only subliminal, at work, such that similar ideas worked themselves out in the two realms in differing ways affected by the differences in the environment within which the two dynasties operated. In England, the reigns of the kings were all too short to allow the kind of consistent progress which occurred in Germany. From 878 to 975 there were seven kings in England; in Germany only two. Henry the Fowler had been king since 876 and died in 936 after a reign of sixty years. His son, Otto the Great, was in power from 936 to 973, ruling for thirty-seven years. Things might have been very different for England had there been the same degree of longevity.

Nor was the influence only one-way. Henry the Fowler took up the strategy of Alfred and Edward the Elder. He surrounded Saxony, and possibly Thuringia, with *burgen*, fortified towns, in fact 'burhs'.[27] The two courts exchanged expensive gifts. Aethelstan might well have decided to set up his secretariat or writing office after hearing of the way in which *capellani* (chaplains) accompanied the German kings, who made use of their literary skills as well as requiring them to look after their relics and say Mass.

There is one other influence at work in the development of imperial notions among the kings of Alfred's dynasty. As Eric John first pointed out, there is a sense in which the use of the word *imperator* is simply as a Latin version of the Old English *Brytenwealda*, and the Venerable Bede used *imperium* to describe the supremacy of Anglo-Saxon kings. *Imperator* was certainly a tenth-century English usage, as the *Vita Oswaldi* shows.[28] At his death, Edgar is called *'ducum et totius Albionis imperator'*,[29] 'emperor and leader of the whole of Albion'.

The usage *Brytenwealda* is of great interest. Most writers at present seem to prefer the translation 'wide ruler', but the older interpretation was 'Ruler of Britain' or even 'Britain-wielder'. It was so used in Bede's *Ecclesiastical History of the English Nation* to describe the supremacy or sovereignty at any one time of one of the seven or so kings of what it was once fashionable to call 'the Heptarchy'.[30] The *Chronicles* give the word in various forms; King Egbert of Wessex is *Bretwalda* in 828, translated variously as 'Ruler' or 'Controller of Britain'; or *Brytenwalda*, translated as 'wide ruler' but more often again as 'Ruler of Britain'. Also found are *Brytenweald* and *Bretenanweald*.[31]

The form *anweald* means 'sole ruler', and this last version would naturally read 'sole ruler of Britain'. Stenton was of the view that it should probably be translated in such a way and that it represented the Latin *Rex Britanniae*, as in Aethelbald's charter of 736.[32] He was head of a confederation of every kingdom between the Humber and the Channel.

Overlordship claims in this period, and in the tenth century, cannot be construed in feudal terms but are rather a claim to be the patron of other dependent kings. Such kings could provide safe conduct through the lands of lesser kings, approve of an under-king's grants of land, and even transfer provinces from one king to another, as when Edmund first ravaged and then ceded 'Cumberland' (possibly the Viking-held area on the Solway Firth) to the King of Scots 'on condition that he should be his fellow-worker as well by sea as by land'. Thus was an alliance sealed.[33] The relationships so formed were personal, between the 'lord' and his 'man', and ended with the death of either. The lord might well extract tribute.

## THE CEREMONIES OF OVERLORDSHIP

While these English kings did not 'give law' to those over whom they claimed hegemony, they did apparently enforce various agreements upon them. As laws were probably promulgated at great councils, the Witans, it is only too likely that various sub-kings were also present to see this law-making for the English taking place.[34] Great efforts were made to convene the magnates of the kingdom in council, usually at the major feasts of the Church: Christmas, Easter and Pentecost. The records are incomplete, but as far as they do record councils and their time of year, the result is that four councils are known to have been held at Christmas feasts during the tenth century, another four at Pentecost and thirteen at Eastertide. They are also associated with the issue of law codes; four are known to have been issued at a great feast out of the twenty-two codes issued between 899 and 1022. But if the issue of charters is viewed as a legislative action, up to one quarter were issued at great feasts.

It is known that the kings who accepted English overlordship attended councils. At Eamont in 926 there were present Constantine III, King of Scots, Hywel, King of the West Welsh, Owain, King of Gwent, Ealdred of Bamburgh, and possibly (if William of Malmesbury is to be trusted) Owain of Strathclyde-Cumbria.[35] At the great meeting summoned by Edgar at Chester in 973 there were present, according to Florence of Worcester, eight under-kings. There is also evidence of such attendance in charters where some of the under-kings acted as witnesses. A charter of 928, issued by Aethelstan at his great court held at Exeter, reveals the presence of Idwal Foel of Gwent and a prince called Hywel, probably Cornish.[36] Five Kings of the Welsh had been defeated in 927 and conceded defeat and overlordship at Hereford, calling Aethelstan *mechtern* or 'great king' and paying a huge tribute. In response to this, the poem 'Armes Prydein' called upon all Welshmen to unite with other enemies of the English and, wrongly, predicted an English defeat.[37] The grand alliance it demanded, of the Welsh, Irish, Scots and Vikings, did materialise, only to be defeated at Brunanburh.[38] At Cirencester, Aethelstan then had five Celtic kings acknowledge his supremacy in a ceremony which probably anticipated that of Edgar at Chester in 973. In the last analysis, hegemony rested not on ceremonial and the swearing of oaths but on the threat and use of military force.

Aethelstan's victory was not long lasting. The Norse Vikings took back the kingdom of York and cut southern England off from Northumbria. Edmund and Eadred had to fight hard to recover what was lost and their gains were handed on to Edgar. It was he who then consolidated English hegemony, not only reigning over Mercia and Northumbria but also regaining overlordship of the rest of the island of Britain. In so doing, he earned himself great prestige and a solemn anointing and crowning as king, not only of the English, but of the whole of Britain.

## 13

# Pomp and Circumstance

Edgar the Peacemaker's reign reached its apogee in 973 with the anointing and enthroning of the king and his queen, in a magnificent coronation ceremony at Bath. It was orchestrated and scripted by Archbishop Dunstan of Canterbury and his fellow Archbishop, Oswald of York.

## THE CORONATION OF 973

The principal accounts of the coronation ceremony are found in the *Anglo-Saxon Chronicle* for that year[1] and in the *Vita Oswaldi* by Byrhtferth of Ramsey.[2] Quite simply, Edgar was consecrated at a great assembly held, in 'Ache-mannes city' or 'at the Hot Baths', at Pentecost (11 May), 'in the thirteenth year after he succeeded to the kingdom'. Immediately afterwards he led his whole Fleet ('the whole raiding ship-army') to Chester. There, six kings, or in other accounts eight, 'pledged to be his allies on sea and on land' and rowed him down the river with the king at the helm.

This coronation has been the subject of much comment and controversy almost ever since. There is debate about its significance and about whether Edgar had received a prior consecration at the beginning of his reign, or whether, as men seem to have thought at the time and in the eleventh and twelfth centuries, his coronation had been, most unusually, delayed until he had reached the age of thirty. One view would be that he had never been previously anointed king and that this was his first and only coronation.[3]

An opposing view holds that it was inherently unlikely that Edgar could have reigned as King of the English, with all the panoply of imperial-style claims found in his charters, for almost fourteen years (959–973), totally unopposed, without having been solemnly installed as king, which would have involved his enthronement and anointing. No other tenth-century

King of the English ruled without benefit of a coronation, which would usually have taken place within two years of accession.

There is no direct evidence of an earlier coronation, but then the *Chronicles* for the early years of his reign are singularly bare. The *Winchester Chronicle* A is blank for the year 960, and for 961 records only the death of Archbishop Oda, who actually must have died around 958 since his successor-elect died on the way to Rome for his pallium in 959.[4] Then the *Abingdon Chronicles* B and C are blank from 959 to 971, the *Worcester Chronicle* D is blank from 959 to 965, the *Peterborough Chronicle* E is blank from the end of 959 to 963, and the Latin text F from Canterbury ends in 937 and only resumes in 990. Florence of Worcester only adds for 960 that Dunstan persuaded King Edgar to make Oswald Bishop of Worcester.

It was as '*coronatus et electus*', crowned and chosen, that Edgar entered the church at Bath in 973.[5] There is no reference in the text to his prior election by bishops and people. The *Chronicle*, in two versions (the *Winchester* and *Peterborough Chronicles*) using as a source a ballad written about the ceremony, says simply that Edgar 'was hallowed to king with a great company of priests and monks in attendance, *as I have been told*'. So the report is not that of an eyewitness.[6] The other versions call him 'aetheling' before the ceremony, but the scribes may be influenced by a previous entry referring to his son Edmund as an aetheling. Most kings coming to be crowned were aethelings, so the scribes are simply repeating an established formula.

Edgar's immediate predecessors, Eadred and Eadwig, were anointed by Archbishop Oda. After Edgar's death, his successors Edward and Aethelred were also anointed, Aethelred by the two archbishops assisted by ten suffragan bishops in 978. It is likely that Dunstan used the same coronation service, or *Ordo*, at all three coronations. Nonetheless, the later writers all assumed that there had been a delay in Edgar's case. They offer various explanations, none of which is convincing. Some historians avoid the point by suggesting that 973 was merely a crown-wearing. That is improbable in the light of available evidence to the contrary. Others suggest that it was some sort of 'imperial' ceremony, an idea which deserves closer examination.

Eleventh-century writers offer the fanciful excuse that Dunstan had imposed a seven-year ban on Edgar during which he was not allowed to wear his crown, and that in 973 he celebrated the end of his penance with a coronation. But he became king in 959, so a seven-year penance offers no viable explanation at all. By the twelfth century it was being argued that Edgar had indeed delayed his coronation until he had reached the mature age of thirty out of a sense of humility, feeling that he was unworthy of coronation until he had outgrown the passions of his youth.[7] This is a variation on the seven years' penance story and stresses also that Aelfthryth was an anointed queen while his first wife had not been anointed. The story, in the *Vita Dunstani*, actually supports the idea that Edgar really was the undoubted king: 'the most glorious King Edgar reigned [*regnavit*] for nineteen years; two years as king of the northern parts beyond the Thames, and then sixteen years after the death of his brother Eadwig'. It makes no distinction between Edgar's status before 973 and his status after that year.

Edgar's first wife, whether she is taken to have been Aethelflaed or Wulfthryth, was certainly not an anointed queen. Aelfthryth was not married to Edgar until 964 so could not have been anointed any earlier. Nicholas of Worcester does not actually assert that Edgar had not been crowned and anointed earlier. He stresses that Aelfthryth was the king's first *conjunx*, and was '*legaliter sibi disponsata*', his legal spouse given to him in marriage. She was the consort of the realm and Lady of England, his second and true wife (*uxor*) who received unction and a crown.

## ONE CORONATION OR TWO?

The emphasis on Edgar's having delayed coronation until of mature years derives from an argument that rests on the fact that he was 'in his twenty-ninth year' immediately before the coronation, and had reached the age of thirty when the rite was performed. It suggests that the clergy had chosen 973 for the event because the king was now thirty years of age, just as Christ began his public ministry when he was about thirty years of age and because canon law laid down that a priest or bishop ought to be thirty before he could be ordained. Ordinations were generally postponed until that age, but not exclusively so, and there were many recorded exceptions. However, Dunstan and the reformers might well have seized on the fact that the king was coming up to the age of thirty in order to emphasise the parallel some saw between kingship and priesthood, as both were the result of an anointing. The king, pupil of both Dunstan and Aethelwold, might well have thought the same. This idea is adopted by those who seek an explanation for Edgar's allegedly delayed coronation. It might well just have been an interesting coincidence and nothing more.

It is likely that all tenth-century kings were consecrated as soon as possible after their election and accession. They dated their reigns from the date of election, and this was certainly the case with Edgar. The *Chronicle* puts the coronation of 973 in 'the thirteenth year after he succeeded to the kingdom'.[8] Power and authority were reinforced by, but not wholly dependent upon, consecration. Edgar's charters, issued before 973, speak of him as 'raised up over the English people by the right hand of the Almighty'. He also dates his reign from 956 in at least three charters, one for 971 and two for 963.[9] The *Liber Eliensis* describes Edgar as in a 'God-given position of dignity'.[10] There is no hint anywhere that he was not a genuine Christian king, and in this period that term usually meant anointed.

Inspection of the events between 959 and 964 seems to show that Edgar indeed was fully king. He had assumed the government of the kingdom immediately following Eadwig's death and moved swiftly to reject Eadwig's nominee to the See of Canterbury. Dunstan was appointed instead and immediately went off to Rome to secure his pallium, returning early in 961. He also secured a privilege for Edgar from the Pope allowing him to dismiss the secular clerks from the Old Minster, Winchester. There was a great Witan at Easter 963, when the decision to eject secular clerks was endorsed and the reformation of the monasteries began in earnest.

It is not inconceivable that the newly consecrated Archbishop seized the opportunity presented by the Easter Witan, at which Aethelwold was probably made Bishop, to hold a coronation which would allow the newly anointed king to use his authority as well as that of the Pope, to deal with the burning question of monastic reform. The major matter which emerged from the Witan was the decision to remove secular clerks and bring in monks, and that rather overshadowed other events. The *Chronicles* concentrate on ecclesiastical affairs and simply do not mention secular matters at all. Even the earliest biography of Oswald concentrates on the king's action in driving out the clerks, as do the other sources.[11]

The sequence of events suggested cannot be supported from the sources in detail, but represents a probable scenario. The effect is to postulate two coronations, one early and one late. It might even be the case that there were two coronations for Aethelred, though the evidence is ambiguous. The *Abingdon Chronicle* C (and Winchester A) for 978 says: 'here in this year King Edward was martyred and his brother, the aetheling Aethelred, succeeded to the kingdom; and he was consecrated as king the same year'. The Peterborough version E agrees, saying: 'And here Aethelred succeeded to the kingdom, and very quickly after that, with great rejoicing of the councillors of the English race, was consecrated king at Kingston'.

But the Abingdon version repeats itself under the year 979: 'In this year Aethelred was consecrated king on the Sunday, fourteen days after Easter, at Kingston; and there were at his coronation two archbishops and ten diocesan bishops'. This is written as though a year had intervened between the death of Edward and the coronation. This has led some to suppose two coronations, a rapid one to secure the throne and a more magnificent one when rule had been secured. Others post-date the coronation to 979 or assume that the coronation was carried out very rapidly, as if to cover up the murder of Edward, a fortnight after Easter.[12]

There is a later example of an English king with two coronations. Henry III was crowned at Gloucester on 28 October 1216, a few days after the death of his father King John. After three years, when the country was in a more settled state, he was crowned a second time in Westminster Abbey at Whitsun, 17 May 1220. It is therefore not impossible that Edgar was anointed twice.[13] If that is so, an explanation is required of what was different about 973.

To dismiss an early coronation is to ignore important points. Edgar did not suddenly break the established tradition whereby English kings had been consecrated early in their reign. There is no parallel for such an action. Dunstan, of all people, would have appreciated the importance of the consecration involved. To defer it was to invite a challenge to the king's legitimate right to rule, as Edward's accession was to be challenged in 975. Edward's opponents argued that he had been born before Edgar had been anointed and that his mother was not an anointed queen. (Edward was probably born before 961 and so before any putative coronation in 962 or 963.)[14]

Another argument is based on the language of one version of the coronation *Ordo*.[15] The prayer in the text simply does not reflect the circumstances of 973, but echoes exactly those of 959. The prayer assumes that there has been a recent breach of concord and a division of allegiance between two peoples and hints that the king was to blame. The king is warned that he should not 'desert the royal throne, to wit, the sceptre of the Saxons, Mercians and Northumbrians'.[16] This fits exactly the occasion of Edgar's accession in 959 after the failure of Eadwig to hold the kingdoms together under one crown. The argument is that this earlier form of the *Ordo*, the First, was used for Edgar's first coronation and that the later texts were those used for Edgar's successors and for him in 973. It is the ceremony of 973 that is in need of explanation, and a coronation by Dunstan in 961, or a little later, to seal the unity of the kingdom is only too likely.

Edgar issued the first example of royal consecration charters at the very beginning of his reign, first as king of the 'Mercians and the Northumbrians', and then as King of the English (*Rex Anglorum*).[17] He claimed to be *basileus Anglorum* and *Britanniae Anglorum monarchus* (High King of the English and Monarch of the English of Britain).[18] A charter preserved by William of Malmesbury[19] is dated 'the fourteenth year of my reign'. William also says[20] that he succeeded in 959 at the age of sixteen and 'held the throne for the same number of years... with no treachery from his own people'. Edgar could compel other kings to attend his court, especially at the City of the Legions (Chester).

The evidence of the text of the *Promissio Regis* (the threefold promise required of a king before his anointing and crowning) needs also to be considered.[21] No existing text of this document is earlier than the tenth century, and the text of the second version is older than 973. It might have been available to be used for Edgar then, or earlier. The preamble states plainly that Dunstan was the officiating minister, but not at Bath, as one might expect, but at Kingston-upon-Thames. The King taking the oath is not named but is referred to as 'our lord'; this is usually taken to mean either Aethelred or Edward, who were both consecrated at Kingston. Yet the *Promissio Regis* also says that the text was to be laid on the altar by the king 'as the bishop directed him'. That looks like a reference to Dunstan when he was Bishop of London, and could point to a coronation in or after 959, probably in 961. He is referred to as Archbishop because he held that rank at the time that the scribe copied the document.[22] The text reads:

> This writing is written, letter by letter, after the writing that Dunstan, Archbishop, delivered to our lord at Cingestune (Kingston) on the day that they hallowed him king and forbade him to give any pledge except this pledge which he laid upon Christ's altar as the bishop directed him.

It goes on to spell out the duty of a hallowed king, '*gehalgodes cynges riht is*', that is, the three promises required: to ensure the peace of the Church, forbid robberies and unrighteous dealing, and to do justice and mercy in all his judgements.

From 961 onwards, Edgar certainly did do his best to fulfil pledges such as these in a manner which suggests that he had made them. His law codes are evidence for that. Wormald points out the relevance of these three promises to Edgar's policies.[23] They became a three-fold oath in the revised version of 973. The manuscripts are attributed to the hand of Dunstan. There is no *a priori* reason why he could not have used them for an earlier coronation.

Kingston had long been the scene of English coronations. It is even claimed that the stone found in the former simple tenth-century church, which still existed in the nineteenth century, was the coronation stone. That is of course quite incapable of proof.

The note struck by the coronation ritual of 973 was entirely new. It echoed the Carolingian view of the king as the Anointed of God, His Vicar on Earth, with all the power within his kingdom.[24] Edgar himself had already been called both Good Shepherd and Vicar of Christ (a title not yet reserved for the Pope). The coronation reinforced the secular powers Edgar already had, with what was possibly a renewed divine sanction. In a sense the interpretation put forward in the tenth century was that of *Rex et Sacerdos*, King and Priest.

The year 973 saw the 'high noon of the Anglo-Saxon empire'[25] as the united kingdoms of England now incorporated the people of Wessex and Mercia, the descendants of the Danish and Norse settlers of the ninth and tenth centuries and the English of the former Bernicia into one kingdom. So Edgar became, according to some historians, 'head of the Anglo-Saxon Empire'.[26]

The Frankish kings, descendants of Charlemagne (the Carolingians) regarded anointing as indispensable to the making of a king (or for that matter, of an emperor). The king was anointed to rule, and bishops, in anointing the king, augmented his power and the charisma of kingship.

One text of the English royal *Ordo* (now in Paris) had been used for Aethelstan, who was certainly consecrated King of the Anglo-Saxons and anointed with holy oil. (For the year 856, a century before Edgar's accession, it is reported that Humbert, Bishop of the East Angles, had anointed King Edmund (of East Anglia) with oil and consecrated him as king.) The English coronation rituals were most likely modelled on those originated by Hincmar, Archbishop of Rheims.[27] Aethelstan must also have been aware of the significance of some of the relics he was given, such as the Sword of Constantine and the Spear of Charlemagne. The English kings were adopting Frankish-style coronation rituals.

Anointing of kings in the tenth century was well on its way to being recognised as a sacrament of the Church alongside ordination of priests and bishops. It could be listed with baptism and confirmation as one of the sacraments, but theological opinion eventually decided against royal anointing as a full sacrament. It was left as a 'sacramental' rite, a solemn blessing. In the tenth century the matter had been seen in a very different light.

At a coronation, nobles were relegated to the role of witnesses and spectators, active only at the moment of acclamation and the enthronement of the new king 'in a clerically stage-managed liturgical drama'.[28] The magnates 'elected' the king (by acclamation) even if there *was* only one candidate, and a crown became a royal attribute, embodying the whole concept of kingship, which led naturally to the public ceremony of 'crown-wearings'.

Charlemagne's Holy Roman Empire was revived, significantly for English observers, in 962 (just after Dunstan's return from Rome) when Pope John XII offered Otto I the imperial crown and he accepted. The elevation of his uncle, Otto, to the rank of emperor cannot have escaped Edgar's notice.

It is accepted that the liturgy followed for Edgar in 973 is that described by Byrhtferth of Ramsey, whose account owes much to the *Ordo*, but is thought to be based on the report of an eye-witness, although borrowing its language from several sources. He describes how a *'princeps* elect' was transformed into a *'Rex'* by anointing, and, equally importantly, crowning.

Some argue that there was no fixed order of service in 973 but that the format used at Bath was derived from experimental drafts drawn up by Archbishop Dunstan.[29] Byrhtferth's account[30] emphasises the centrality of the anointing as the essence of the ceremony, setting the king apart from other men who had not received that anointing, just as a priest or bishop was set apart from other Christians. As a result, some historians conclude that the delay in Edgar's coronation should be attributed to a desire to postpone it until he had reached the age of thirty. But that cannot be a convincing argument. Edgar had been King of the English since the age of sixteen. His brother Eadwig had died young as had his uncle Eadred, and there would have been no guarantee in 959 that Edgar would reach such a mature age. His father had been murdered in a brawl; Edgar's second son, Edmund, died in childhood, and his first, Edward, was also to be murdered. It is almost preposterous to maintain in this way that Edgar would have risked delaying his coronation in this fashion.

Byrthferth's account has Edgar entering the Church wearing his crown. He then prostrated himself before the altar (as bishops-elect do) 'having first removed the crown from his head'. Various prayers were said and anthems sung, including the *Te Deum*. Edgar made the three promises of the *Promissio Regis*, was then anointed and given the rest of his regalia (ring, sword, sceptre and rod) and then crowned 'using the prayers written in the office'. Then Mass was said. This account clearly draws on the wording of the *Ordo*[31] or something very like it.[32] The king was said to have been 'decorated' with roses and lilies, meaning on his robes or regalia. Roses were for martyrdom and lilies for chastity. The crown might therefore have been the one shown on the frontispiece of the charter for New Minster, which has lily decoration.

The ceremony was followed by two separate banquets presided over, respectively, by the king and queen; Edgar with the magnates and the bishops and the queen with abbots and abbesses. She also had been anointed during the ceremonies.

Historians still differ over whether there had been one or two coronations. Those who accept that there was only the one have to acknowledge that this was done for some completely unknown reason. No convincing explanation for such an inordinate delay has ever been offered. The reasons advanced by eleventh- and twelfth-century writers can be discounted as unsubstantiated and even as downright ridiculous.

Those who accept the two coronation hypothesis suggest that the second coronation had an 'imperial' purpose.[33] They dismiss the use of the word 'aetheling' by the *Chronicle* as mere pedantry due to the fact that any candidate for coronation might be called 'aetheling'. From the eighth century onwards, any ruler who exercised the royal *potestas* or authority without the royal *nomen* and without a coronation was a mere *princeps*, or might be called the *electus* or chosen one. Edgar is never referred to in such terms, he is always 'the King'.

It is true that there was much 'imperial' iconography[34] and Christ was displayed in the tenth century as a king, even when on the cross, as in the Romsey Abbey crucifix. He was the imperial King of Kings. That theology had spread from Germany and underlines the suggestion that Edgar, either in 973 or later in the early eleventh century, was commonly understood by contemporaries to have ruled a 'British Empire', tenth-century-style.[35] It may be that there was something in this, in a very restricted sense, because Edgar was the head of an alliance of kings who accepted his leadership and did so because his fleet could deter the Vikings. (That makes him a sort of tenth-century 'Head of the Commonwealth'.)

The coronation of 973 can also be seen as a consummation, or celebration, of unity, inaugurating Edgar as King of all the nations in Britain.[36] Some argue that Anglo-Saxon England had become something akin to a nation state by 973, with an effective central authority, uniformly organised institutions, a national language and Church and a strong sense of national identity. The people called themselves English and their country England.

The suggestion is also made that there had been special instructions or recognition from Rome for some sort of rite similar to that of the imperial coronation of Otto I in 962. This is to argue that Edgar's repeated coronation, if that is accepted, was a papal privilege not granted to every king.[37]

Otto I, uncle by marriage to Edgar,[38] was in Rome in 972 for the anointing of his second, Greek, wife, Theophano, as Empress. She was to become Regent to Otto's young son, the second Otto, after the emperor died in 973. Oswald of Worcester was in Rome that year to obtain his pallium as Archbishop-Elect of York.

Earlier that same year, Oswald had also been sent, accompanied by another abbot and a king's thegn, on a mission to Otto I.[39] He visited the imperial court, returning with gifts better than those he had taken and, more importantly, a *Pactum Pacis* or Treaty of Peace and Amity between England and the Empire. Historians agree that this mission was a *negotium regni*, an official state mission, and that the aim was to secure papal approval for Edgar's coronation. If that is so, then it *must* have been a second coronation. Papal approval would not have been required or even asked for if it had been his first. Byrhtferth does not date the mission but it is logical to assume that it was 972, when Oswald was on the Continent and went to Rome. He is not known to have gone to Germany at any other time. (Byrhtferth had access to some lost annals from York and the *Abingdon Chronicle* B might have been at Ramsey around 1000.) Byrhtferth also knew Abbo of Fleury, who was at the coronation of 973, and could have supplied him with information.

There is a parallel here between Oswald and Earl Harold Godwinson. The latter went to Flanders to see Count Baldwin and there met the Emperor Henry IV in 1056. It is thought that he travelled with the Emperor to Regensburg and then with Pope Victor II to Rome.[40] Oswald might well have gone on to Rome with the Emperor and have attended the Empress's coronation. That would explain why Queen Aelfthryth was anointed in 973 and became the first English queen to be so consecrated.

Edgar had therefore received papal recognition as the sole monarch reigning, if not actually ruling, over all Britain. The *Vita Swithuni* of Aelfric the Homilist was to comment that 'all the kings who were in this island, Welsh and Scottish [*Cumera and Scotta*] came to Edgar whilst they were kings in those days and they all bowed [*bugon*] to Edgar's guidance [*wissunge*]'.[41] To bow to another (*bugon*) was to acknowledge his lordship. (The English, led by their earls and bishops, 'bowed' in surrender to the Conqueror in 1066.)

There was therefore a diplomatic and theological background to the coronation of 973, just as there had been to the events of 963–964. The privilege of Pope John XII[42] was probably granted in 960 (to judge by its indiction number which dates papal acts), which coincides with Dunstan's arrival in Rome for his pallium. It greets Edgar as 'most excellent king' and all his faithful people, and grants permission for the ejection of secular clerks in favour of monks from the Old Minster, Winchester. He compliments Edgar on his 'zeal for religion' and calls him *'Rex inclyte'* (renowned or illustrious King). It is only too likely that Dunstan, now Archbishop of Canterbury, proceeded shortly after his return to consecrate Edgar in 961, probably at Kingston. The Pope benefited from his decision to grant the privilege because shortly afterwards, Edgar's law code insisted on the payment of Peter's Pence or *Romescot*, at the same time as enforcing payment of tithes to clergy in England,[43] with quite swingeing penalties for non-payment.

The problem is that all writers reporting the coronation of 973 seem convinced that this was Edgar's only coronation. Even Aethelweard the Chronicler says Edgar was 'crowned to rule' and follows that with an account of the ceremony at Bath 'after he had reigned thirteen years'. But no charter written before 973 refers to a coronation; those produced after 973 do. The only possible exception, for Winchester, dates to between 963 and 975 and calls him *'rex gloriosus sancti spiritus carismate'* (glorious king by the grace of the Holy Spirit), which looks more like post-973. Another, to Malmesbury for 974, is dated 'the first [year] of royal consecration', as does a further one, though both are rejected by Whitelock as forged. The post-973 evidence, therefore, is not completely convincing.[44]

But observers at Bath in 973 were struck by the splendour of the ceremony, and what comes out in later accounts was not so much the anointing, which had been done before to other kings, but the adoption of a true crown. The point about Edgar not having been allowed to wear one might not, as later writers thought, have been the result of some mythical penance, but due to the possibility that English kings did not, before Edgar, actually wear a crown, only the kingly helmet. Pictorial evidence would have to be discounted as artistic licence. The *cynehelm* itself was very ornate and not an item of everyday wear. The helmets found at Sutton Hoo and at Coppergate in York give some idea of what a *cynehelm* could look like.

The implication of Byrhtferth's account is that Edgar was wearing a crown of some sort when he entered the church and discarded it before his prostration. Either he wore the *cynehelm* or, as has been put forward as more likely, some sort of wreath, perhaps laurels, which would be a reference to Roman practice. Then, after the anointing, he received the full royal regalia, including a crown. It was only after Edgar's time, possibly in the early eleventh century, that the ceremony of a crown-wearing was adopted, although the first recorded case applies to William the Conqueror.

What struck observers in 973, then, was the adoption of crown and full regalia, together with the impact of a tremendous ceremony performed, amidst the decaying grandeur of Roman Bath, by two archbishops, probably about ten diocesan bishops, an unknown number of abbots and abbesses, monks and priests, all the English ealdormen and Danish earls and possibly some or all of the eight kings who later attended Edgar's royal progress at Chester. The ruins at Bath would almost certainly have been in a less damaged state then than they are now and would have provided a magnificent stage for this show. The account in the *Vita Oswaldi* insists that there were princes from all over Britain present, summoned 'by an edict of the Emperor'. It further describes Edgar at his death as '*ducum et totius Albionis imperator*' (commander and emperor of the whole of Albion).[45] What is not so clear is what exactly the author meant by calling Edgar an 'emperor'.

This ceremony blotted out all memory of any routine 'hallowing' or raising to kingship performed at the beginning of the reign about ten years earlier. It is emphasised that the *Ordo* used at the coronation of 973 was 'a fully elaborated coronation service on the Frankish model'.[46] Stress was laid on the analogy between kingship and priesthood and it marked the height of the collaboration between Edgar and his three clerical advisers, Dunstan, Aethelwold and Oswald. All earlier accounts of coronations talk only of a hallowing or blessing, though Asser's tale about Edmund of East Anglia confirms the use of holy oil and an anointing.

Bath in 973 was therefore a tremendous occasion, and was to be further emphasised by the events at Chester shortly afterwards. The account of the ceremony, written some twenty-five years later, looked back beyond the renewed Danish invasions to Edgar's reign as a kind of golden age, as did the summaries of Edgar's achievements recorded in the *Chronicles*, which were also written up, and indeed amended and altered, in later decades. By then the exact significance of his coronation in 973 had plainly been forgotten and he was looked upon as an imperial figure. The language appears to be borrowed from charters, some of them attributed to Aethelstan, which may not be authentic in the form in which they have survived. But even suspicious or inauthentic charters, forged in the eleventh century or later, are evidence of the reputation of English kings at the time they were written.

Thus one charter, attributed to King Aethelstan[47] as a grant to the minster at Worcester, calls that king *'Basileus et Imperator regnum et nationum infra fines Brittanie'* (High King and Emperor of the kingdom and nation within the borders of Britain). It is a charter universally condemned as a forgery and is not contemporary evidence, but reflects what the forger thought of Aethelstan. A better example is a charter to the Bishop of Crediton, Devon,[48] in a late tenth-century hand. Aethelstan is *'Rex totius Britanniae'* or King of the whole of Britain. That is a claim to overlordship and much more acceptable.

Later writers also regarded Edgar as an emperor. A good example is Geoffrey Gaimar, who had access to a now-lost copy of the *Chronicle* and other earlier sources. He says that Edgar 'reigned alone over all the kings and over the Scots and the Welsh. Since Arthur died there had never been so powerful a king'.[49] He alleged that the three Welsh kings carried three swords before him (Edgar) at his royal festivals. That is poetic licence reflecting later practice. Similarly, Dunstan's *Vita* attributes to him a prediction, made at the time of Edgar's birth, that he would be the *Rex Pacificus* or 'Peacemaker King'. The claim was intended to emphasise and exaggerate the saint's prophetic gifts.

## THE SIGNIFICANCE OF THE CORONATION OF 973

More reliably, the *Vita* says that Edgar 'overcame kings and tyrants'.[50] The *Chronicle*[51] says that 'God helped him moreover to subdue kings and earls who submitted to his rule' and 'Kings honoured the son of Edmund far and wide over the gannet's bath [ocean] and did homage to that king as was his birthright'.[52] This again is a picture of an overlord or high king, like the *Ard Rí* in Ireland. He is a high king because, unlike the lesser kings who paid court to him and made alliances with him and accepted his leadership, he has not only been solemnly anointed but has been granted, possibly by papal privilege, the right to wear a crown and bear ring, sceptre, and rod and have a sword carried before him, like the Frankish and German kings.

Without actually being an emperor, Edgar manifested all the hallmarks of a sovereign independent ruler, responsible only to God, able to issue written law codes, so making 'a compelling demonstration of the neo-imperial mindset that underlay a commitment to Lex Scripta'.[53] Like other law-makers, Edgar was perhaps trying to reproduce 'the archetypal function of Roman Imperial sovereignty'. Tenth-century English kings who learned to put laws in writing, as emperors were accustomed to do, made law as the Romans had done. That act alone would have earned Edgar the appellation of 'emperor' from later writers.

The year 973 also witnessed a renewal of homage or commendation to Edgar on the part of the Celtic kings who attended his court. After his coronation, Edgar took his whole fleet, probably from Bristol, the nearest port to Bath, right around Wales to Chester. As the coronation had taken place at the time of Pentecost, Edgar had probably already carried out the Fleet manoeuvres described by Florence of Worcester and his combined Fleet had probably accompanied him to the Severn so that he could easily reach Bath.

At Chester, again according to Florence of Worcester, Edgar had himself ceremonially rowed on the River Dee by a number of Celtic princes, from his palace there to the Monastery of St John the Baptist. As the fleet was present, this looks remarkably like a review of the fleet, intended to overawe everybody with the sight of his naval power. He was rowed by either six or eight kings. The *Chronicle*[54] claims six and merely says they 'pledged that they would be his allies on sea and on land'. Six may be the number that did homage. Florence is more detailed and lists eight 'under-kings'. Edgar himself steered the boat, perhaps a sort of state barge, an action symbolic of his command over the other kings. He is reported to have said afterwards that any of his successors could also boast of being King of the English if they could 'have the pomp of such honours, with so many kings subservient' to them. Even the *Annales Cambriae* for 973 refer to 'a great gathering of ships at Chester by Edgar, king of the Saxons'.[55]

The kings are named as Kenneth, King of Scots, Malcolm (Malcoluim), King of the Cumbrians (and Kenneth's son), Maccus, King of many Islands, and 'Dufnal, Siferth, Hywel, Jacob and Juchil'.

Kenneth (Cinaed of Alba, 971–995) is the second of that name, and Maccus might have been the son of Harold of the Sudreys (Man and the Hebrides), a notorious pirate sea-king. Siferth might then be Sigeferth, under-king of (the Isle of) Man. Jacob could well be Iago ap Foel of Gwynedd (950–979), and Hywel probably Ap Ieual or Idwal (979–985), a nephew of Iago. 'Juchil' is unaccounted for but the name could be Cornish, as in the reference to 'Judhael of Totnes' in Domesday Book. 'Dufnal' is probably Dunmail of Strathclyde or, less probably, Domnall of Leinster.[56] Such a list, which comes from Florence of Worcester, could not have been simply invented by any Anglo-Norman writer. It is too specific to be the creation of literary licence.

This occasion is also reflected in the *Vita Swithuni*, which asserts that 'All the kings that were in this island, Welsh and Scots, came to Edgar whilst they were kings in those days and they all bowed to Edgar's guidance'.[57] Bowing (*bugon*) was the term used in Old English for accepting the authority of a lord in commendation. The significance is that such an act made Edgar more secure against attack by these men and they in turn were entitled to his assistance and protection, especially that of his fleet. It was a personal relationship and ended with the death of either party.

The 'bowing' can be related to Edmund's gesture in 'giving' Strathclyde to Malcolm, which was probably intended to secure an alliance by recognising his *de facto* rule there. It is similar to Edgar's own action early in his reign in ceding Lothian to Kenneth II.[58] On that occasion, Kenneth was brought to Edgar's court by Bishop Aelfsige of Chester-le-Street and Eadwulf, High Reeve of Bamburgh, where he did homage and received also some estates in England for his support whenever he came to court. That action had formidable consequences. The Firth of Forth ceased to be the northern frontier of England and it would have been an incalculable problem for later kings if it had not so ceased, as it lay open to attack from Strathclyde and Galloway. English kings owned no estates north of the River Tweed. The cession of Lothian made the Tweed the boundary on the eastern side of the Pennines.[59]

## THE END OF THE REIGN

Edgar's reign came to an unexpected end when he died without warning in 975 on 8 July at the age of thirty-two. He had ruled all England, including the Danelaw, for sixteen years. His authority, including that over the Danelaw, was immense. Even over the Danes, despite the degree of autonomy he granted them, he maintained his authority and made laws applicable as much to them as to the English. He could appoint earls and bishops through whom the Danelaw was governed and its leading magnates were his men. He possessed sufficient estates to support his authority there and to act as centres of administration and justice. He could punish breach of the peace more severely in the Danelaw even than in the rest of England.

Nonetheless, he was rarely seen north of the Thames, though visits to York and Chester are recorded and he certainly went to the great Fenland abbeys. The Danes were left a great deal of local autonomy, which goes a long way to explaining their acceptance of his rule. His readiness to accept their customs, along with his probable marriage *more danico*, would explain his reputation among churchmen for 'a liking for Danish ways'.

His reign was singularly devoid of recorded trouble or of any incidents other than those involving the establishment or re-foundation of monasteries. The magnificent display of pomp and circumstance in the quasi-imperial 973 coronation, not as merely King of the English, which he already was, but as *basileus* and monarch of the whole island of Britain, was an act seen by later writers as making him an emperor.

To Churchmen, the essential part of the ceremony had been the anointing with holy oil which set Edgar apart from other men and emphasised the parallel between kingship and priesthood, like Melchisedech who had been both king and priest. To the laymen present, what mattered was the assumption of a crown and regalia representing power and authority.

His power was then at its maximum extent. He had developed the legal institutions of shire, borough and hundred; there was a thorough and well-organised system for the raising and support of a truly royal fleet, the triple hundreds called ship sokes; and the fyrd had been put on a firmer basis under aspects of the same system and could put a fully trained and equipped warrior into the field, in most areas at least, from every five hides or, in the Danelaw, from every six carucates.

The system of weights and measures was uniformly enforced by royal decree, and one coinage had been established throughout England, complete with a system for *renovatio monetae*, with the periodic recall and re-issue of coins. It is quite likely that even the system of tax collection had been put on a proper basis with the establishment of the king's right to the periodic collection of a common or ordinary geld. This was to make the raising of the money to pay off the Danes at the end of the century a practical and efficient matter.

Edgar therefore left a reputation as a powerful and militant king, a firm supporter of the rights of the Church and especially of monasticism, and a stern law-giver. The royal navy in his day must have looked as if it was built to last, which, in a sense, it was. His reign has been called the high noon of the Anglo-Saxon State. Edgar was one of the most powerful kings of the early Middle Ages and his great power rested on foundations laid earlier in the century. England under his rule enjoyed seventeen years of unbroken prosperity, and he well deserves his traditional title of *Rex Pacificus*, the Peacemaker King.

# List of Illustrations

# Notes

## ABBREVIATIONS USED IN THE NOTES AND BIBLIOGRAPHY

ASE    Anglo-Saxon England.

DB    *Domesday Book: a Complete Translation*, ed. A. Williams & G.H. Martin (Penguin, 2002).

Encyc.    Lapidge, M., et al. (eds), *The Blackwell Encyclopaedia of Anglo-Saxon England* (Oxford, 2001).

HCY    Raine, J., *Historians of the Church of York* (Rolls Series, 1879–94).

NCMH    *New Cambridge Medieval History*, Vol. III: *c*. 900–1024, ed. T. Reuter (1999).

S    P.H. Sawyer, *Anglo-Saxon Charters: An Annotated List* (London, 1968).

TRHS    Transactions of the Royal Historical Society.

## INTRODUCTION

1    Dumville, D., *Wessex from Alfred to Edgar*.

2    Stevenson (trans.), Asser, *Annals of Alfred*, p. 464.

## I. THE FOUNDATION OF ENGLAND

1    Williams, A., *Kingship and Government*, ch. 7.

2    S 59.

3    Stenton, F.M., *Anglo-Saxon England* pp. 319ff.

4    For an account of the progress of the campaigns see Stenton op.cit. pp. 322–335; Jerrold, *Introduction to the History of England* pp. 310–316; or Oman, *England before the Norman Conquest*, ch. 24.

5    Williams op.cit., p. 82.

6    Jolliffe, p. 101; *Chronicle* MS Winchester A, 924.

7    S 360 and 374.

8    Sayles, G.O., *The Medieval Foundations of England*, ch. 8. Hunter Blair, *An Introduction to Anglo-Saxon England*, p. 82

9    Oman, C., *England before the Norman Conquest*, p. 510; also bk V, chs 24 & 25.

10    Williams op.cit., p. 84 and n. 19.

11   Dumville, D., *Wessex from Alfred the Great to Edgar*, p. 141.
12   *New Cambridge Medieval History*, Vol. II ch. 18 pp. 456–84.
13   Keynes, S., in N. Higham (ed.), *Edward the Elder*, p. 61.
14   Stenton op.cit., ch. 10; Hunter Blair, *An Introduction to Anglo-Saxon England*, ch. 2 sec. 5
15   Stenton op.cit., pp. 339–40.
16   Hunter Blair op.cit., pp. 83–86.
17   John, E., *Reassessing Anglo-Saxon England*, pp. 90–94.
18   Lloyd, J., *History of Wales*, Vol. I, p. 353. Durham Gospels MS A II 17 fol. 31v.
19   S 425 and 407.
20   Higham, N., *The Kingdom of Northumbria 350–1100*, pp. 192–3.
21   Crawford, S.J. (ed.), *Heptateuch*, p. 416.
22   S 416
23   Stenton op.cit., p. 356.
24   *HCY* II, p. 96
25   *Flores Historiarum* I, pp. 395–6
26   *English Historical Review* 38 (1926).
27   Stenton op. cit., p. 359, citing the *Annales Cambriae* and Roger of Wendover I, 398.
28   S 563.
29   John op.cit., pp. 95–6.
30   Higham op.cit., p. 211
31   Wendover I 402–3. C.S.883 (= S 1078)
32   *HCY* I, p. 197
33   S 1515
34   Sayles op. cit., pp. 105–7

## 2. THE KINGDOM OF THE ENGLISH

1    Dumville op.cit., p. 141.
2    Hindley, G., *A Brief History of the Anglo-Saxons*, p. 232.
3    *Chronicles* A and D, 911 (for 910).
4    Higham op.cit. p. 185.
5    Oman op.cit. p. 519; Previté-Orton, *Shorter Cambridge Medieval History* Vol. I, p. 519.
6    Compiled in Alfred's reign and updated in about 916.
7    John op.cit., pp. 85–6
8    Stenton op.cit., pp. 291.
9    *New Cambridge Medieval History* Vol. II ch. 18.
10   Stenton op.cit., pp. 345ff. Mynors, *Gesta Regum* I, p. 150.
11   Flodoard, *Annals* p. 36.
12   Oman op.cit., p. 429.
13   Idem., p. 179.
14   *New Cambridge Medieval History* Vol. III, ch. 6.
15   Mynors, *Gesta Regum* I, p. 149.
16   S 572; Fairweather, J., *Liber Eliensis*, p. 124.
17   Sayles, G.O., *The Medieval Foundations of England*, ch. 14.
18   Keynes, S., *The Diplomas of Aethelred the Unready*.
19   Idem., passim.
20   Higham op.cit., pp. 211–12.

21  Heriot: from *here-geatwu*, the military equipment of a vassal which on death reverted to his lord.
22  Dumville op.cit., pp. 173–82.
23  Dumville op.cit., pp. 166–7; Florence of Worcester.
24  *Liber de primo adventu Saxonum* from Durham; *Altitonantis Charter,* William of Malmesbury; *Gesta Pontificum,* bk 4 ch. 252.

## 3. EDGAR AND HIS CIRCLE RISE TO POWER

1   John op.cit., p. 99.
2   S 646 and 659.
3   *Worcester Chronicle* D, 958.
4   Grey Birch, W. de (ed.), *Liber Vitae Wintoniensis Ecclesia,* p. 57.
5   *Vita Dunstani* by 'B'; the author is unidentified.
6   Hart, C., in *ASE* 2 (1973).
7   Ormrod, W.M., *The Kings and Queens of England,* p. 43.
8   Worcester MS D, 955.
9   Abingdon MSS B and C.
10  Worcester MS D 1052 (for 1051).
11  *NCMH* III, p. 478.
12  S 677, 676 and 678
13  *ASE* 2 (1973). Hart, C., *Aethelstan Half King.*
14  Idem.
15  Whitelock, D., 'The Conversion of the Eastern Danelaw', *Saga Book of the Viking Society* 12.
16  Hart, C., *Early Charters of Northern England and the North Midlands.*
17  Gaimar, *L'Estorie des Engles* 3843–8.
18  See Chapter 5.
19  *Vita Oswaldi* 44.
20  Williams, A., '*Princeps Merciorum Gentis*', *ASE* 10 (1982).
21  *Liber Eliensis* II, 25.
22  Idem., II, 63; S 1486 (Aelflaed's will).
23  Nelson, J., in Sawyer & Hill (eds), *Early Germanic Kingship,* p. 69.
24  Stubbs, W., *Memorials of St. Dunstan,* p. lxxxix.
25  S 667, 674, 676, 677, 678 and 679.
26  DB fol. 175v.
27  Brooks, *Anglo-Saxon Myths.*
28  Stubbs, W., *Memorials,* p. xcv.
29  In S 675, but not 678, 676, 677 or 674.
30  A laudatory and high-flown passage in praise of a king or other prominent person.
31  Swanton, M., *The Anglo-Saxon Chronicles.*

## 4. ROYAL ADMINISTRATION

1   III Edgar cap. 8.
2   Chron. Maj. R.S. I p. 467.
3   Barlow. F., *Edward the Confessor,* pp. 181–2.

4    Williams, A., *Kingship and Government*, p. 232.
5    Hindley op.cit., p. 286.
6    Campbell, J., *Essays in Anglo-Saxon History* (1986); Hindley op. cit., pp. 296–7.
7    Jolliffe op.cit., p. 129; III Aethelred 2.1. & 3.1.
8    Matthew, D.J.A., *The Norman Conquest*, pp. 104–5.
9    John, E., *Land Tenure in England*, p. 120.
10   Robertson, A.J., *The Laws of the Kings of England*.
11   III Edmund cap. 2.
12   II Edward the Elder cap. 11.
13   Stubbs, *Select Charters*, p. 64.
14   Hunter Blair, P., *An Introduction to Anglo-Saxon England*, p. 232.
15   Written law rather than verbal.
16   Chron. Aethelweard p. 28; DB I, fol. 208.
17   Jolliffe, J.E.A., pp. 116–27.
18   Lantfred, *Translatio et Miracula S. Swithuni*.
19   III Edgar 7.3 & 4.
20   IV Edgar 9 & 11.
21   II Edmund 4.
22   Bk II, ll. 440–65.
23   II Cnut 30.
24   *Gesta Regum* I, p. 177.
25   But see Williams, *Aethelred the Unready* p. 24. Williams suggests he might have been Earl Oslac's son rather than Gunnar's.
26   S 834.
27   *Peterborough Chronicle* E, 966 & 969, Florence of Worcester, same date; Roger of Wendover I, p. 414–5.
28   Mutilation figures in II Cnut caps. 8 (1 & 2), 16, and 30 (4 & 5).
29   Wormald, P., *The Making of English Law*, Vol. I, pp. 127–31.
30   Barlow, F. (ed.), *Vita Edwardi I*, p. 13.
31   Kennedy, A., 'Law and Litigation', *ASE* 24 (1995).
32   VI Aethelstan cap. 4.
33   Hunter Blair op.cit. p. 232.
34   *Kingship and Government* p. 88.
35   'Judicia Civitatis Lundoniae' *ASE* 10, pp.161–2.
36   Stenton op.cit., pp. 354–5.
37   III Edgar 6 & 7.
38   John, *Land Tenure* p. 142.
39   Sayles op.cit., p. 142.
40   See IV Edgar.
41   IV Edgar 2a.2.
42   IV Edgar 2a.1.
43   IV Edgar 12.
44   IV Edgar 12.
45   IV Edgar 15 & 16.
46   S 710.
47   Hunter Blair op.cit., p. 232.
48   VI Aethelred II cap. 37.
49   *Blackwell's Encyclopaedia* p. 152.
50   Sayles op.cit., p. 109.

51   S 416; Stenton op.cit., p. 351.
52   Hunter Blair op.cit., pp. 232–4.
53   Sayles op.cit., p. 209; Jolliffe op.cit. p. 70.
54   Stenton op.cit., p. 495; S 659.
55   S 681.


# 5. SHIP SOKES AND SEA POWER

1    Oman op.cit., p. 543.
2    Florence of Worcester, 959.
3    Dumville op.cit., p. 117.
4    V Aethelred 27 and VI Aethelred 32.3 & 33.
5    II Cnut 79. See also II Cnut 10 (scipfyrðunga).
6    John, *Land Tenure*, p. 105; *Chronicle* E, 1008.
7    *Leges Henrici Primi* VI.1, in Stubbs, *Select Charters* pp. 104–5.
8    Dumville, D., *Wessex. from Alfred to Edgar*, p. 117.
9    Wormald op.cit., p. 150.
10   DB I fol. 172v.
11   Williams, *Kingship and Government* p. 116.
12   Charter S 786, seen by some as authentic but regarded with suspicion by others, may
     yet be accurate about the triple hundred. Williams, *Kingship and Government* p. 116.
13   DB fol. 172.
14   S 1488 & S 1492.
15   Harmer, *Writs*, p. 267A.
16   *Liber Eliensis*, bk II ch. 41.
17   Idem, bk II ch. 4.
18   Wills, S 1487.
19   DB fol. 64v.
20   Ibid. II, fol. 48.
21   Ibid., fols 26 & 238.
22   Ibid., fols 230 & 209.
23   Maitland, *Domesday Book and Beyond*, pp. 198 and 317–19. The original name was
     possibly 'Oslafe's lau', meaning 'Oslaf's hill', and was probably corrupted in the tenth
     century to Oswald's Low.
24   Charter S 731. Again some see this as interpolated and containing genuine material.
25   DB I fol. 172v. The Church of St Mary of Worcester has a hundred called
     Oswaldslow in which belong 300 hides.
26   S 1368 and Kemble CD 1287 (= S 1368).
27   S 1368.
28   *Archiductor* means 'chief leader'. Latham, *Word List*.
29   John, E., *Land Tenure in England*, pp. 82–8.
30   DB I fol. 173v: '*ductor exercitus ejusdem episcopi ad servitium Regis*'.
31   Shipful or ship soke.
32   Numbers 90 and 91 for Knightlow Hundred.
33   Hollister, *Anglo-Saxon Military Institutions on the Eve of the Conquest*, p. 110.
34   *Annales Cambriae* 19/20. See Jones, T., *Brut y Tywysogion*, 971: 'he collects a great fleet at
     Caerleon-on-Usk', an error for Chester as both places were 'the City of the Legion'.

35    Roger of Wendover I, 415–6.
36    Florence's text is sufficiently close to other texts of the *Chronicle* to make this idea feasible.
37    *Gesta Regum* II, p. 177–8.
38    Dumville op.cit., p. 142.

# 6. TENTH-CENTURY MILITARY INSTITUTIONS

1    Allen Brown, *Origins of English Feudalism*, p. 47.
2    *Blackwell's Encyclopaedia*, pp. 47–8.
3    DB fol. 142.
4    DB fol. 173v.
5    Grately Code, II Aethelstan 16.
6    John, *Reassessing Anglo-Saxon England*, p. 106
7    Stubbs, *Charters*, p. 65, cap. 2; Wormald op.cit. p. 391.
8    *Of People's Ranks and Laws* cap. 2 & cap. 3.
9    DB fol. 100.
10    Barnstaple, Lydford and Totnes gave the same service.
11    Fol. 56v.
12    Fol. 209.
13    Fol. 336.
14    Fols 107 & 48.
15    Fol. 375.
16    II Cnut Cap. 71. 'Heriot' is the obligation that a thegn's arms and armour were to be returned to his lord when the thegn died.
17    Brook, N., *Anglo-Saxon Myths*, p. 150.
18    See their wills, S 1484 & 1485.
19    *Gesta Pontificum Anglorum*, bk I ch. 18.
20    Domesday fol. 1; fol. 3 and fol. 10.
21    Chronicle D 1051 (for 1052) and E 1070 Hereward.
22    Aethelweard, *Chronicon*, 28
23    DB fol. 208.
24    Hides were notionally divided into four virgates of 120 acres, whereas carucates (from *caruca*, a plough) were divided into eight bovates of 15 acres each, in Scandinavian style.
25    Sulung: exclusive to Kent and equal to two hides.
26    Maitland, *Domesday Book and Beyond*, pp. 194–205 and 464.
27    Huscroft, *Ruling England*, pp. 32–3.

# 7. MEN, MONKS AND MONASTERIES

1    *NCMH* Vol. 3 p. 479.
2    Knowles, *The Monastic Order in England*, pp. 32ff.
3    Stevenson (trans.), Asser, para. 74.
4    John, *Reassessing Anglo-Saxon England*, p. 104.
5    Lapidge & Winterbottom (trans.), *Life of St. Aethelwold: Wulfstan of Winchester*.

6    Chambers, R.W., *England before the Norman Conquest*, p. 245.

7    Idem., pp. 114–15.

8    Jerrold op.cit., p. 320.

9    Idem. p. 320.

10   Lapidge & Winterbottom, *Life of St. Aethelwold*, xl.

11   *Blackwell's Encyclopaedia*, p. 348.

12   Winchester A, 964.

13   Hugh Candidus, ed. Sparke, p. 23.

14   Garmonsway, *The Anglo-Saxon Chronicle*, p. 115 note 1.

15   DB fol. 172v.

16   John, *Orbis Britanniae*, p. 249.

17   *HCY* I, p. 427.

18   Stevenson, Rev. J. (trans.), *Florence of Worcester*, p. 246.

19   John op. cit., p. 249.

20   *HCY* I p. 424.

21   Stevenson, *Florence of Worcester*, p. 246 (for 967).

22   Aelfric, *Vita Aethelwoldi*, p. 260.

23   *Liber Eliensis* ii 28, charters S 768, 796.

24   Kennedy, A., 'Law and Litigation in the *Libellus Aethelwoldi*', *ASE* 24 (1995).

25   *Vita Aethelwoldi* cited in Chambers, R.W., *England Before the Norman Conquest*, p. 243.

26   S 745 accepted as authentic by Finberg and by Wormald. London, British Library
     Cott. Vesp. A viii, fols 3–33v.

27   Hunter Blair op.cit., p. 177.

28   Brooks, *Anglo-Saxon Myths*, p. 200.

29   *Blackwell's Encyclopaedia*; Worcester; William of Malmesbury, *Gesta Pontificum* III, 115.

30   Brooks, N., & Cubitt, C., *St. Oswald of Worcester* p. 12.

31   Stafford, P., *Unification and Conquest*, p. 188; John, *Reassessing*, p. 122.

32   John, ibid., pp. 116–7.

33   *Liber Eliensis*, bk 1 caps 41–9.

34   *Liber Eliensis*, trans. Fairweather, pp. 148–9, bk 2 caps 52–4.

35   John op.cit., p. 118.

36   *Shorter Cambridge Medieval History*, Vol. I p. 394.

37   Knowles, *The Monastic Order in England*, p. 52

38   Whitelock, D., in *History, Law and Literature in the Tenth and Eleventh Centuries*, p. 242.

39   Letter published in Haddan & Stubbs, *Councils & Synods*, no. 29.

40   II Edgar 4.

41   VIII Aethelred 10.1 and I Cnut 9.1.

42   Sayles op.cit., ch. 9.

43   Knowles, *Monastic Order*, p. 41.

44   *Blackwell's Encyclopaedia*, p. 389.

45   *HCY* I, pp. 424–7.

46   John, *Orbis Britanniae*, p. 257–8.

47   Gretsch, M., 'Aethelwold's Translation', *ASE* 3 (1974).

48   Sayles op.cit., p. 115.

49   Jerrold op.cit., p. 320.

50   John, *Reassessing*, p. 118.

51   S 395 to his thegn Eadric.

52   S 786 and 876.

53   S 779.

54  John, *Reassessing*, pp. 127–9; Brook, *Anglo-Saxon Myths*, p. 207.
55  Brook op. cit., p. 208.
56  Brook, idem.
57  *Liber Eliensis* II, 8.
58  *Liber Eliensis* II, 10.
59  See also Stenton Later Charters of the Anglo-Saxon Period.
60  *Liber Eliensis* II, 11.
61  *Anglo-Saxon Chronicle* MSS D and E, 975.

## 8. ENGLAND IN THE REIGN OF EDGAR

1   *NCMH*, Vol. III, p. 22.
2   Blair op. cit., p. 186.
3   Beresford, G. Goltho, *The Development of an Early Medieval Manor c.850–1150.*
4   Robinson, *The Times of St. Dunstan* (1923), p. 122. Blair op. cit., p. 230.
5   IV Edgar 14; Robertson, *The Laws of the Kings of England*, p. 309.
6   Hindley op.cit., p. 283.
7   *NCMH* Vol. III, p. 71.
8   Ibid., p. 475.
9   Gesta Pontificum I, cap. 18.
10  IV Edgar I.5 and 2a. 1a.
11  Maitland op.cit., p. 35.
12  IV Edgar 2a cap. 2.
13  Whitelock, 'English Historical Documents I', no. 239.
14  Vita Dunstani c. 29; Whitelock, 'English Historical Documents I', no. 234.
15  Campbell, J., *The Anglo-Saxon State*, p. 158.
16  Williams, *Kingship and Government* p. 115.
17  DB I fol. 30.
18  DB I fol. 336v.
19  DB I fol. 132.
20  Book II cap. 11. The context of this section is undated but is concerned with transactions occurring at the end of Edgar's reign or just after his death.
21  Campbell op.cit., p. 163.
22  *Liber Eliensis* II, cap. 11.
23  Idem., p. 209.
24  Campbell, J., *The Anglo-Saxon State*, p.xii. Maitland op.cit., p. 536.
25  Maitland op. cit., pp. 524–39.
26  Campbell op.cit., pp. 13–14.
27  Sayles op.cit., p. 188.
28  Campbell op.cit., pp. 15–17.
29  Campbell, J., *The United Kingdom of England; the Anglo-Saxon Achievement,* p. 82.
30  Sayles op.cit., p. 109.
31  Stenton op.cit., p. 337.
32  Idem., p. 169.
33  IV Edgar cap. 12.
34  Idem. caps 2 and 2a sec. 2.
35  Stevenson (trans.), John of Wallingford p. 554; Simeon of Durham, *De Primo Adventu Saxonum* II, p. 382.

36  An independent Danish kingdom at York and English rule in Bernicia under the House of Bamburgh. See Higham op.cit., p. 183.
37  Sayles op.cit., p. 138. The Soke of Peterborough is a survivor of this system.
38  IV Edgar 12.
39  Idem., p. 141.
40  IV Edgar I cap. 6.
41  IV Edgar caps 2 and 2a para. 1.
42  IV Edgar caps 6 and 12 para. 1.
43  Blair op.cit., p. 259.
44  Sayles op.cit., p. 142.
45  See III Edgar caps 2, 3, 4 and 7, and IV Edgar cap. 2.
46  IV Edgar caps 4, 5 and 6.
47  Williams, *Kingship and Government*, p. 149.
48  S 751 to Brihtnoth, minister.
49  Jolliffe op.cit., pp. 91–2.
50  Geþyncðo cap 3.
51  S 1462.
52  Stenton op.cit., p 278.
53  John, *Reassessing*, p. 117.
54  *Liber Eliensis* bk II cap. 97.
55  Ibid., p. 63.
56  Fletcher op.cit., p. 125.
57  S 681.
58  Stenton op.cit., p 495.
59  S 659; Stenton ibid.
60  Stubbs, *Select Charters*, Glossary.
61  Robinson, *The Times of St. Dunstan*, p. 122; Blair op.cit., p. 230.
62  III Edgar 8; IV Edgar 3–11.

## 9. THE WITAN AND THE HOUSEHOLD

1  Old English, a decree or decision.
2  S 1447 & S 1211.
3  See Stenton, *Anglo-Saxon England*, p. 551; Sayles op.cit., p. 178; Jolliffe op. cit., p. 27.
4  Jolliffe op.cit., p. 101.
5  IV Edgar 2.2.
6  IV Edgar 4.13d.
7  Blair op.cit., p. 228.
8  Alexander, M. (trans.), *Beowulf and Grendel* (Penguin, 1973).
9  Blair op.cit., p. 211.
10  S 597.
11  Ibid., p. 212.
12  Ibid., p. 213.
13  Ibid., p. 214.
14  S 1515.
15  John, *Land Tenure*, p. 98.
16  Liber Eliensis II, 78.
17  A depository containing relics and valuables of all kinds, including documents.

18   S 853.
19   John, *Land Tenure*, p. 91.

# 10. QUEENSHIP, MARRIAGE AND MOTHERHOOD

1    Stafford, P., 'The King's Wife in Wessex 800–1066', *Past & Present* 91 (1981).
2    'Eadgyth', in Blackwell's Encyclopaedia.
3    *Anglo-Saxon Chronicles* MSS D, E and F, 959.
4    L'Estorie des Engles p. 771.
5    *Cwen* is a mere label; *Hlafdige* is equivalent to the male *Hlaford*, or 'Lord'.
6    *Past & Present* 91.
7    Stafford op.cit., p. 111.
8    Clayton, M., *The Cult of the Virgin Mary in Anglo-Saxon England* (Cambridge, 1990).
9    *Past & Present* 91; Stafford, P., 'Queens, Nunneries and reforming Churchmen: Gender, Religious Status and Reform in Tenth and Eleventh Century England', *Past & Present* 163 (1999).
10   Duggan, A.J., *Queens & Queenship*; Stafford op. cit., p. 323; Fell, C., *Women in Anglo-Saxon England* (London, 1984).
11   Foote & Wilson, *The Viking Achievement*, p. 112.
12   See Freeman, *Norman Conquest*, Vol. I pp. 612–14; Morris, C., *The Papal Monarchy* (Oxford, 1989), p. 329.
13   Foote & Wilson op.cit., p. 103.
14   Clunies Ross, M., 'Concubinage in Anglo-Saxon England', *Past and Present* 108 (1985).
15   Stafford, *Queens & Concubines*, p. 63; Clunies Ross op. cit.
16   Fletcher, *Blood Feud*, p. 127.
17   Stafford, Queens, Concubines and Dowagers, p. 74.
18   Ibid., p. 13; Nelson; *The Second English Ordo in Politics and Ritual in Early Medieval Europe* (London, 1986).
19   Liber Eliensis II, 56.
20   Henry Manning, Cardinal Archbishop of Westminster 1865–1892.
21   S 745 (for 966): 'legitimus praefati regis filius' and 'eodem rege clito procreatus'.
22   S 1485 (968x971).
23   S 739; Keynes, *Diplomas*, p. 164.
24   *Gesta Regum* II, 57.
25   Stafford, *Past and Present* 163.
26   Stubbs, *Memorials*, xcix and pp. 111–2, 114 and 120–4; Florence, 964.
27   See Williams, A., *Aethelred the Unready* ch. 1.
28   Liber Eliensis II, cap. 7; Libellus Aethelwoldi cap. 5.
29   See Williams op.cit., p. 4.
30   S 799.
31   *Passio S. Edwardi Martyris*, either by Goscelin or, more probably, an unknown nun from Shaftesbury. Williams, *Aethelred*, p. 160 n. 35.
32   Ibid., p. 6.
33   Blackwell's Encyclopaedia; Ampleforth Journal Vol. 8 No. 2 (1977); Revue Benedictine 87 (1927); *Past & Present* 91 (1981); Stafford, Medieval Queenship (1994).
34   HCY I, p. 449.
35   Stenton, *Anglo-Saxon England*, pp. 372–3.

## 11. THE CULT AND LOCATION OF RELICS

1   Dr Burton (ed.), *Epistle of the Church of Smyrna concerning the Martyrdom of Polycarp* (London: Ancient & Modern Library of Theological Literature), ch. 18.

2   Denzinger, H., *Enchiridion Symbolorum*, 13th ed. (London, 1921), p. 159.

3   Rollason, D.W., 'Relic Cults as an instrument of Royal power', *ASE* 15 (1986).

4   Campbell, J., *The Anglo-Saxon State*, p. 37.

5   Rollason, D. (ed. & trans.), Simeon of Durham, *Libellus de Exordio*.

6   Book ii, 10, p. 113.

7   NCMH, p. 112; Blackwell's Encyclopaedia.

8   Ibid., ii 17 p. 133.

9   Ibid., ii 18 p. 137.

10  *Historia Regum* ii 224 (for 934).

11  See ii 93–4; ii 126 & 143.

12  Liber Eliensis II, 53.

13  *Judicia Dei* I.2.1; VI. 1.II Aethelred 2.1.& 3.1

14  Robinson, J.A., *The Times of St. Dunstan* (Oxford, 1923), p. 72.

15  Liber Eliensis II, 78.

16  Crooke J., *ASE* 21 (1992).

17  Liber Eliensis II 79.

18  V Aethelred cap 16: 'The authorities have decided that St. Edward's festival shall be celebrated throughout England on 18 March'. I Cnut cap 17.1 adds Dunstan for 19 May.

19  Nelson, J., 'Royal saints and early medieval kingship', in *Politics and Ritual in Early Medieval Europe* (London, 1986).

20  S 765.

21  Ford, D.N., *The Abbey Church of St. Mary & St. Aethelflaed.*

22  Heywood, S., *The Site of the Anglo-Saxon Cathedral, North Elmham.*

23  Blair op.cit., p. 186.

24  Blair op.cit., p. 185.

25  Hare, M., *The Parish Church of St. Peter, Titchfield.*

## 12. KINGSHIP AND EMPIRE

1   See Pope, J., in Clemoes & Hughes pp. 96–7.

2   Memorials, p. 17; Peterborough Chronicle E, 959.

3   Loyn, H.R., 'The Imperial Style of the Tenth Century Anglo-Saxon Kings', *History* XL (1956). Sawyer, P., *Anglo-Saxon Charters: an annotated list.*

4   Wormald, P., *The Making of English Law*, Vol. I, p. 444.

5   Lifton is S 392 of the alliterative series ( S 548–50, 569, 572, 633).

6   IV Edgar 2.2.

7   S 751, 782, 795 and S 775, cited in text.

8   Fairweather, J., p. 100; S 779.

9   S 590, 598.

10  Dumville p. 174.

11  Ibid., p. 193.

12  Ibid., p 141, citing Aelfric, *On Judges.*

13   Ibid., p. 143; Asser, p. 467.
14   Corpus Christi, Cambridge MS 183 fol. 1v.
15   British Library MS Cott.Vesp.A VIII fol. 2v. Both the above pictures are in the
     Anglo-Saxon Chronicles, ed. & trans. Anne Savage.
16   Dumville, p. 166.
17   See Oman, p. 517; S 707 and 727; Loyn, History XL; S 796, 568, 605, 430, 806.
18   Williams, Kingship and Government, ch. 7.
19   Oman, p. 517.
20   IV Edgar 2, 2a.
21   S 761 (for 968) to Aelfwine, minister.
22   S 594 and S 587: an almost contemporary, certainly tenth-century copy.
23   Brook, Anglo-Saxon Myths, p. 192.
24   S 478; see also John, E., Orbis Britanniae, p. 448.
25   Orb. Brit., p. 49.
26   Larousse Encyclopaedia ch. 17.
27   Sayles op.cit., p. 87.
28   Orb. Brit., p 49; HCY p. 436.
29   HCY p. 448.
30   Bede, ch. 5.
31   MSS A 828 and E 828; Stenton, p. 34 n. 10.
32   S 89.
33   Oman, p. 527.
34   Wormald, Making of English Law, p. 446.
35   Anglo-Saxon Chronicle MS D, 926; Gesta Regum II, 148.2.
36   Wood, Dark Ages, p. 147, citing William of Malmesbury.
37   Ibid., p. 146.
38   Ibid., p. 155.

## 13. POMP AND CIRCUMSTANCE

1    MSS A to E, 973.
2    HCY I, pp. 436–8.
3    For example Oman op.cit., p. 544.
4    Florence, 959, p. 245. Oman op.cit., p. 548.
5    Robinson, Journal of Theological Studies 57, using MS Cott. Claud. A III and Vita
     Oswaldi, HCY I p. 355.
6    MSS B and C, 973.
7    Nicholas of Worcester, Epistle de Matre Sancti Edwardi Martyris, MS ccc 371, in
     Memorials of St. Dunstan p. 422.
8    Williams, Kingship and Government pp. 187–8.
9    S 781 (which is regarded as authentic), dated to 970. S 712 and 723 for 963; S 782 for
     971.
10   Liber Eliensis II, 39.
11   HCY I, p. 426–7; Chron. Abingdon ii, p. 260; Liber Vitae of Hyde Abbey, p. 7–8.
12   Hindley op. cit., p. 291; Wood, M., The Dark Ages, p. 198.
13   Nelson, J., 'Inauguration Rituals', in Sawyer & Wood (eds), Early Medieval Kingship,
     p. 63.
14   Ibid.

15  Robinson, Journal of Theological Studies 86.

16  Ibid., p. 71.

17  S 674 and many others.

18  S 673.

19  *Gesta Pontificum* ch. 292; S 796 (which might not be authentic).

20  *Gesta Regum* ii 148.2.

21  Text in *Memorials of St. Dunstan* and in Robertson, *Laws*.

22  *Cott. Cleopatra* B xiii fol. 56 (Old English); Vitellius A 7 (Latin). They are from Ramsay and the Pontifical of Egbert.

23  Making of English Law, Vol. I p. 447.

24  Loomis op. cit., p. 131.

25  Wood op. cit., p. 159.

26  Ibid., p. 193.

27  Wormald op. cit., p. 445.

28  Ibid., p. 107.

29  Stenton op. cit., p. 308, following Schramm, *The English Coronation* pp. 19–20.

30  In Vita Sancti Oswaldi, HCY I.

31  Cott. Claud. A iii.

32  Robinson, *Journal of Theological Studies* XIX no. 56 (1918).

33  Nelson, J., *ASE* 8 (1979).

34  Nelson, *Early Medieval Kingship*.

35  Wood, M. op. cit., p. 196.

36  Stubbs, *Memorials* CI, no doubt influenced by the fact that Victoria was an empress. The theme of unity is supported by Campbell, *The Anglo-Saxon State*.

37  Whitelock, D., *History, Law & Literature*, p. 175.

38  His first wife was sister to Eadred and Edmund.

39  Byrhtferth; *Vita Oswaldi* p. 15.

40  See Rex, P., *Harold II*, p. 128.

41  Pope, J., in Clemoes & Hughes (eds), *England before the Norman Conquest*, p. 103.

42  William of Malmesbury, *Gesta Regum* I, cap. 7.

43  II Edgar 1, 2 and 3.

44  S 827, 797 and 796.

45  *HCY* I, pp. 436 and 448.

46  Brooke, *Anglo-Saxon Myths*, p. 54.

47  S 406.

48  S 421.

49  Gaimar, p. 776.

50  *Memorials*, p. 17.

51  Peterborough E, 959.

52  Idem., 975.

53  Wormald op. cit., p. 55, on Frankish kings.

54  MS E 972 (for 973).

55  Also in *Brut y Tywysogion*: see Oman op. cit., p. 544 n. 4.

56  Stenton op. cit., p. 369; Williams, *Kingship & Government*, p. 116; Ormrod, *Kings and Queens*, p. 44

57  See Pope, J., in Clemoes & Hughes (eds), *England before the Norman Conquest*, p. 103.

58  Roger of Wendover, *Flores Historiarum* i. 416.

59  Jerrold op. cit., p. 316; Blair op. cit., p. 90.

# Bibliography

Allen Brown, R., *The Origins of English Feudalism* (London, 1973).

Alexander, M. (trans.), *Beowulf and Grendel* (London, 1973).

Armitage Robinson, J., *The Times of St. Dunstan* (Oxford, 1923).

—, 'The Coronation Order in the Tenth Century', *Journal of Theological Studies* XIX (1918).

Bede, The Venerable, *Ecclesiastical History of the English Nation* (London: Dent, 1954)

Beresford, G. Goltho, *The Development of an Early Medieval Manor c.850–1150* (London, 1987).

Brooke, C., *From Alfred to Henry III: 871–1272* (Edinburgh, 1961).

Brooks, N., *Anglo-Saxon Myths: State and Church 400–1066* (Hambledon, 2000).

Brooks, N., & C. Cubitt (eds), *St. Oswald of Worcester: Life and Influence* (Leicester, 1996).

Burton, Dr, *The Apostolic Fathers* (London, no date).

Campbell, J., *Essays on Anglo-Saxon History* (Hambledon, 1986).

—, *The Anglo-Saxon State* (London, 2000).

Chambers, R.W., *England Before The Norman Conquest* (London, 1928).

Chambers, W. & R., *The Pictorial History of England*, Vol. I (London, 1859).

Clayton, M., *The Cult of the Virgin Mary in Anglo-Saxon England* (Cambridge, 1990).

Clemoes, P., *The Anglo-Saxons* (London, 1959).

Clemoes, P., & R. Hughes (eds), *England before the Norman Conquest* (Cambridge, 1971).

Crooke, J., 'King Edgar's Reliquary of St. Swithun', *ASE* 21 (1992).

Denzinger, H., *Enchiridion Symbolorum*, 13th ed. (London, 1921).

Duggan, A.J., *Queens and Queenship in Europe* (Woodbridge, 1997).

Dumville, D.N., 'The Aetheling: A study in Anglo-Saxon constitutional history', *ASE* 8 (1979).

—, *Wessex and England from Alfred to Edgar* (Woodbridge, 1992).

Fairweather, J. (trans.), *Liber Eliensis: A History of the Isle of Ely* (Woodbridge, 2005).

Fleming, R., 'Monastic Lands and England's Defence in the Viking Age', *English Historical Review* 100 (1985).

—, *Kings and Lords in Conquest England* (Cambridge, 1991).

Fletcher, R., *Bloodfeud: Murder and Revenge in Anglo-Saxon England* (Penguin, 2003).

Foote, P.G., & D.M. Wilson, *The Viking Achievement* (London, 1974).

Ford, D.N., *The Abbey Church of St. Mary and St. Aethelflaed* (2006).

Ganshof, F.L., *Feudalism* (London, 1966).

Garmonsway, G.N. (trans.), *The Anglo-Saxon Chronicle* (London, 1953).

Gelling, M., & D. Johnson, 'A New Charter of King Edgar', *ASE* 13 (1984).

Greenway, D. (ed. & trans.), 'Henry of Huntingdon', *Historia Anglorum* (Oxford, 1996).

Gretsch, M., 'Aethelwold's Translation of the *Regula Sancti Benedicti*', *ASE* 3 (1974).

Haddan, A.W., & W. Stubbs, *Councils and Ecclesiastical Documents* (Oxford, 1871).

Hare, M., *The Parish Church of St. Peter, Titchfield, Hants* (Ramsgate, 1990).

Harmer, F.E., *Anglo-Saxon Writs* (Manchester, 1952).

Hart, C., 'Aethelstan 'Half King' and His Family', *ASE* 2 (1973).

Heywood, S., *The Site of the Anglo-Saxon Cathedral, North Elmham* (1998).

Higham, N.J., *The Kingdom of Northumbria AD 350–1100* (Stroud, 1993).

Higham, N.J., & D.H. Hill, *Edward the Elder, 899–924* (London, 2001).

Hindley, G., *A Brief History of the Anglo-Saxons* (London, 2006).

Hume, D., & W. Cooke-Stafford, *The History of England* Vol. I (London, 1867).

Hunter Blair, P., *An Introduction to Anglo-Saxon England* (Cambridge, 1956).

Jerrold, D., *An Introduction to the History of England* (London, 1949).

Jewell, H.M., *English Local Administration in the Middle Ages* (Newton Abbot, 1972).

John, E., *Land Tenure in England* (Leicester, 1964).

—, *Orbis Britanniae and other studies* (Leicester, 1966).

—, *Reassessing Anglo-Saxon England* (Manchester, 1996).

Jolliffe, J.E.A., *The Constitutional History of Medieval England*, 4th ed. (London, 1967).

Jones, T. (ed. and trans.), *Brut y Tywysogion* (Cardiff, 1955).

Kennedy, A., 'Law and Litigation in the *Libellus Aethelwoldi Episcopi*', *ASE* 24 (1995).

Keynes, S., *The Diplomas of King Aethelred 'the Unready', 978–1016* (Cambridge, 1980).

Knowles, Dom. D., *The Monastic Order in England* (Cambridge, 1956).

Lapidge, M., *et al.* (eds), *The Blackwell Encyclopaedia of Anglo-Saxon England* (Oxford, 2001).

Lapidge, M., & M. Winterbottom (eds), Wulfstan of Winchester, *Life of St. Aethelwold*
    (Oxford, 1991).

*Larousse Encyclopedia of Ancient and Medieval History* (London, 1965).

Latham, M.A., *Revised Medieval Latin Word-List* (Oxford, 2005).

Lloyd, J.E., *History of Wales*, 2 vols (London, 1911).

Loomis, D.P., *Regnum et Sacerdotium in the Early Eleventh Century*.

Loyn, H.R., 'The Imperial Style of the Tenth Century Anglo-Saxon Kings', *History* XL
    (1956).

Maitland, F.W., *Domesday Book and Beyond* (Fontana, 1965).

Mantello, F.A.C., & A.G. Rigg, *Medieval Latin* (Washington, 1996).

Morris, C., *The Papal Monarchy: The Western Church from 1050 to 1250* (Oxford, 1989).

Mynors, R.A.B. *et al.* (ed. & trans.), William of Malmesbury, *Gesta Regum: Deeds of the
    English Kings* (Oxford, 1998).

Nelson, J., 'A King Across the Sea: Alfred in a Continental perspective', *TRHS* 5th ser. 36.
    (1986).

—, *Politics and Ritual in Early Medieval Europe* (London, 1986).

Oman, Sir Charles, *England before the Norman Conquest*, 5th ed (London, 1921).

Ormrod, W.M., *The Kings and Queens of England* (Stroud, 2004).

Parsons, D. (ed.), *Tenth Century Studies: Essays in Commemoration of the Council of Winchester
    & Regularis Concordia* (Chichester, 1975).

Pelteret, D.A.E. (ed.), *Anglo-Saxon History: Basic Readings* (New York, 2000).

Platt, C., *The English Medieval Town* (London, 1986).

Pope, J.C. (ed.), *The Homilies of Aelfric* (London, 1967–68).

Preest, D. (trans.), William of Malmesbury, *Gesta Pontificum Anglorum* (Woodbridge, 2002).

Previté-Orton, C.W., *The Shorter Cambridge Medieval History*, Vol. I (Cambridge, 1952).

Raine, J., *Historians of the Church of York*, Vol. I: *Vita Oswaldi* (Rolls Series, 1879–94).

Ramsay, Sir J.H., *Foundations of England*, Vol. I (London, 1898).

Reuter, T. (ed.), *The New Cambridge Medieval History*, Vol. III (Cambridge, 1999).

Richards, J., *Blood of the Vikings* (London, 2001).

Richardson, H.G., & G.O. Sayles, *Law and Regulation* (Edinburgh, 1966).

Ridyard, S., *The Royal Saints of Anglo-Saxon England* (Cambridge, 1988).

Robertson, A.J., *The Laws of the Kings of England from Edmund to Henry I* (Cambridge, 1925).

Rollason, D.W., 'Relic Cults as an Instrument of Royal Policy, c.900–1050', *ASE* 15 (1986).

— (ed. & trans.), Simeon of Durham, *Libellus de Exordio*.

Savage, A. (ed. & trans.), *The Anglo-Saxon Chronicles* (Heinemann, 1982).

Sawyer, P.H., *Anglo-Saxon Charters: An Annotated List* (London, 1968).

—, 'The Wealth of England in the Tenth Century', *TRHS* 5th ser. 15 (1965).

Sawyer, P.H., & I.N. Wood (eds), *Early Medieval Kingship* (Leeds, 1977).

Sayles, G.O., *The Medieval Foundations of England* (London, 1948).

Stafford, P., 'Queens, Nunneries and Reforming Churchmen', *Past and Present* 163 (1981).

—, *Queens, Concubines and Dowagers: the King's Wife in the Early Middle Ages* (London, 1983).

—, *Queen Emma and Queen Edith* (Blackwell, 1997).

Stenton, F.M., *Anglo-Saxon England*, 3rd ed. (Oxford, 1971).

Stevenson, Rev. J., *Church Historians of England* (London, 1853 & 1854). Translations of: *The Anglo-Saxon Chronicle; The Chronicle of Florence of Worcester; The Chronicle of Fabius Aethelweard;* Asser, *Annals of King Alfred; The Book of Hyde;* Gaimar, *L'Estorie des Engles;* John of Wallingford.

Stevenson, J., *Chronicon Monasterii de Abingdon* (Rolls Series, 1858).

Stubbs, W., *Memorials of St. Dunstan* (Rolls Series, 1874).

—, *Select Charters* (Oxford, 1900).

Swanton, M. (ed. & trans.), *The Anglo-Saxon Chronicle* (London, 2000).

Taylor, P., 'The Endowment and Military Obligations of the See of London', *Anglo-Norman Studies* XIV (1992).

Tierney, B., & P. Linehan (eds), *Authority and Power* (Cambridge, 1980).

Warren Hollister, C., *Anglo-Saxon Military Institutions on the Eve of the Conquest* (Oxford, 1963).

Whitelock, D. (ed.), *English Historical Documents*, Vol. I: *c. 500–1042* (London, 1979).

—, *History, Law and Literature in Tenth and Eleventh Century England* (London, 1981).

Williams, A., '*Princeps Merciorum Gentis*: The family, career and connections of Aelfhere, Ealdorman of Mercia 956–83', *ASE* 10 (1982).

—, *Kingship and Government in Pre-Conquest England, c. 500–1066* (London, 1999).

—, *Aethelred the Unready: The Ill-Counselled King* (London, 2003).

Wood, M., *In Search of the Dark Ages* (London, 2005).

Wormald, P., *The Making of English Law: King Alfred to the Twelfth Century*, Vol. I: *Legislation and its Limits* (Oxford, 1999).

Wormald, P. et al., *Ideal and Reality in Frankish and Anglo-Saxon Society* (Oxford, 1983).

Yorke, B., *Kings and Kingdoms in Early Anglo-Saxon England* (London, 1990).

# Index

# TEMPUS – REVEALING HISTORY

## The Wars of the Roses
The Soldiers' Experience
ANTHONY GOODMAN
'Sheds light on the lot of the common soldier as never before' *Alison Weir*
£25
0 7524 1784 3

## The Vikings
MAGNUS MAGUNSSON
'Serious, engaging history'
***BBC History Magazine***
£9.99
0 7524 2699 0

## William the Conqueror
DAVID BATES
'As expertly woven as the Bayeux Tapestry'
***BBC History Magazine***
£12.99
0 7524 2960 4

## Agincourt: A New History
ANNE CURRY
'Overturns a host of assumptions about this most famous of English victories... *the* book on the battle' *Richard Holmes*
£25
0 7524 2828 4

## Hereward The Last Englishman
PETER REX
'An enthralling work of historical detection' ***Robert Lacey***
£17.99
0 7524 3318 0

## The English Resistance
The Underground War Against the Normans
PETER REX
'An invaluable rehabilitation of an ignored resistance movement' ***The Sunday Times***
£17.99
0 7524 2827 6

## Richard III
MICHAEL HICKS
'A most important book by the greatest living expert on Richard' ***Desmond Seward***
£9.99
0 7524 2589 7

## The Peasants' Revolt
England's Failed Revolution of 1381
ALASTAIR DUNN
'A stunningly good book... totally absorbing' ***Melvyn Bragg***
£9.99
0 7524 2965 5

If you are interested in purchasing other books published by Tempus, or in case you have difficulty finding any Tempus books in your local bookshop, you can also place orders directly through our website:
www.tempus-publishing.com

# TEMPUS — REVEALING HISTORY

 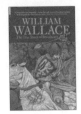  

## William II Rufus, the Red King
EMMA MASON
'A thoroughly new reappraisal of a much maligned king. The dramatic story of his life is told with great pace and insight'
**John Gillingham**
£25
0 7524 3528 0

## William Wallace The True Story of Braveheart
CHRIS BROWN
'A formidable new biography... sieves through masses of medieval records to distinguish the man from the myth' **Magnus Magnusson**
£17.99
0 7524 3432 2

## Elizabeth Wydeville
The Slandered Queen
ARLENE OKERLUND
'A penetrating, thorough and wholly convincing vindication of this unlucky queen'
**Sarah Gristwood**
£18.99
0 7524 3384 9

## The Battle of Hastings 1066
M.K. LAWSON
'Deeply considered and provocative' **BBC History Magazine, Books of the Year 2003**
£25
0 7524 2689 3

## The Welsh Wars of Independence
DAIVD MOORE
'Beautifully written, subtle and remarkably perceptive... a major re-examination of a thousand years of Welsh history' **John Davies**
£25
0 7524 3321 0

## Medieval England
From Hastings to Bosworth
EDMUND KING
'The best illustrated history of medieval England' **John Gillingham**
£12.99
0 7524 2827 5

## A Companion to Medieval England
NIGEL SAUL
'Wonderful... everything you could wish to know about life in medieval England'
**Heritage Today**
£19.99
0 7524 2969 8

## Edward V The Prince in the Tower
MICHAEL HICKS
'The first time in ages that a publisher has sent me a book that I actually want to read!'
**David Starkey**
£25
0 7524 1996 X

If you are interested in purchasing other books published by Tempus, or in case you have difficulty finding any Tempus books in your local bookshop, you can also place orders directly through our website:
www.tempus-publishing.com